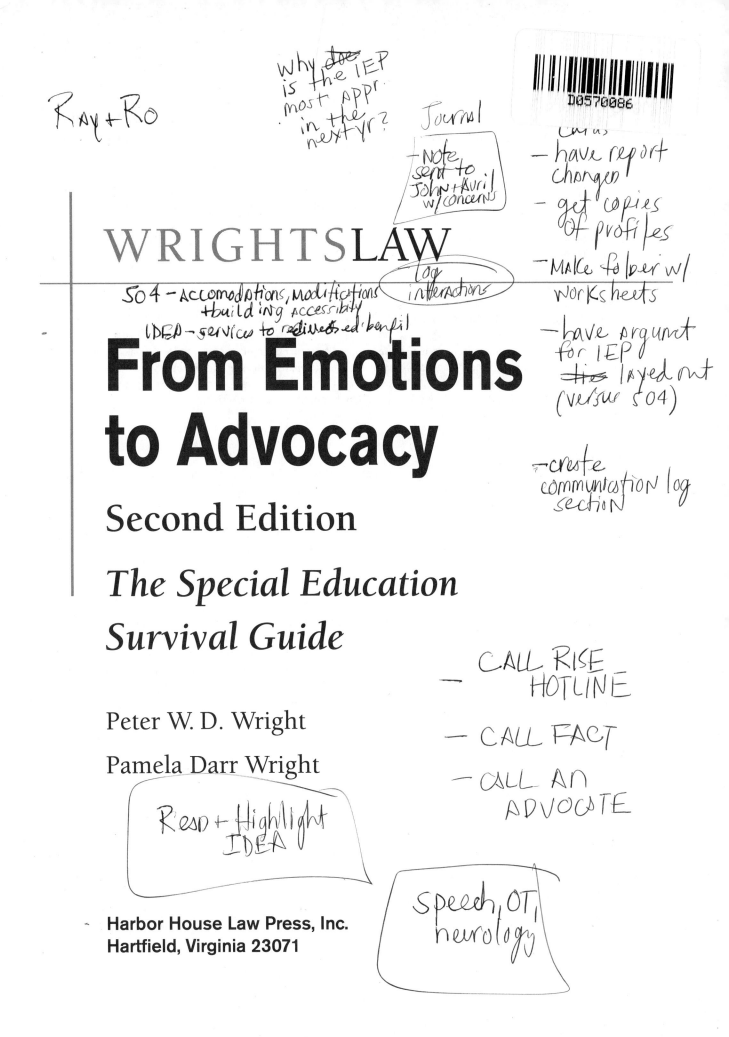

WRIGHTSLAW

From Emotions to Advocacy

Second Edition

The Special Education Survival Guide

Peter W. D. Wright

Pamela Darr Wright

Harbor House Law Press, Inc.
Hartfield, Virginia 23071

Wrightslaw: From Emotions to Advocacy - The Special Education Survival Guide, 2nd Edition
By Peter W. D. Wright and Pamela Darr Wright

Library of Congress Cataloging-in-Publication Data
Wright, Peter W. D. and Pamela Darr Wright
Wrightslaw: From Emotions to Advocacy – The Special Education Survival Guide /2nd. Ed.
p. cm.
Includes bibliographical references and index.
13 Digit ISBN: 978-1-892320-09-4
10 Digit ISBN: 1-892320-09-6
1. Education – parenting – United States.   I. Title
2. Special education – parent participation – United States.
Library of Congress Catalog Card Number: 2005933144

20   19   18   17   16   15

Printing History
Harbor House Law Press, Inc. issues new printings and new editions to keep our books current. New printings include technical corrections and minor changes. New editions include major revisions of text and/or changes.
First Edition: January 2002.
Second Edition   January 2006.
Thirteenth Printing: February 2011.
Fourteenth Printing: July 2011.
Fifthteenth Printing: March 2012

Disclaimer
The purpose of this book is to educate and inform. While every effort has been made to make this book as complete and accurate as possible, there may be mistakes, both typographical and in content. The authors and Harbor House Law Press, Inc. shall have neither liability nor responsibility to any person or entity with respect to any loss or damage caused, or alleged to be caused, directly or indirectly, by the information contained in this book. If you do not wish to be bound by the above, you may return the book to the publisher for a full refund. Every effort has been made to ensure that no copyrighted material has been used without permission. The authors regret any oversights that may have occurred and are happy to rectify them in future printings of this book.

When You Use a Self-Help Law Book
Law is always changing. The information contained in this book is general information and may or may not reflect current legal developments. This book is designed to provide general information in regard to the subject matter covered. It is sold with the understanding that the publisher and author are not engaged in rendering legal or other professional services. For legal advice about a specific set of facts, you should consult with an attorney.

Bulk Purchases
Harbor House Law Press books are available at half price discounts for bulk purchases, academic sales or textbook adoptions. For information, contact Harbor House Law Press, P. O. Box 480, Hartfield VA 23071. Please provide the title of the book, ISBN number, quantity, how the book will be used, and date needed.
Toll Free Phone Orders: (877) LAW IDEA or (877) 529-4332   Toll Free Fax Orders: (800) 863-5348

More Praise for
Wrightslaw: From Emotions to Advocacy – The Special Education Survival Guide

"A superb reference, *Wrightslaw: From Emotions To Advocacy* is very highly recommended reading for all parents of children who need special education services, and should be available in all community libraries . . . Filled with tips, tricks, and techniques and an immense wealth of resources, worksheets, forms, and sample letters to guide one's written communication." **– Midwest Book Review**

"*Wrightslaw: From Emotions to Advocacy* will serve as your guide, whether you are new to IEPs or a seasoned pro. Information is presented in a clear and concise format. You will not want to skip a single page . . . this is the book you will pull out before every meeting. Pete and Pam Wright give families a clear roadmap to effective advocacy for their child. We award their work the **Exceptional Parent Symbol of Excellence. – Exceptional Parent Magazine**

"*Wrightslaw: From Emotions to Advocacy* provides many practical suggestions to help parents who suspect a learning problem and those who have been thwarted or helped by public schools. Every parent who wants services for a child with special needs can benefit from having this book as a reference." **– Perspectives, International Dyslexia Association**

"This parent-friendly book is well-organized, easy to read, and easy to skim for that crucial piece of information. What a blessing to have this resource to call on for help. With *Wrightslaw: From Emotions to Advocacy*, parents have expert advice at their fingertips." **– Adoptive Families Magazine**

"Read the chapters about tests and measurements and the chapter about SMART IEPs in *Wrightlaw: From Emotions to Advocacy* - this information is essential for parents and professionals." **– Hands and Voices Communicator**

"In *Wrightslaw: From Emotions to Advocacy*, Pete and Pam Wright provide an abundance of well-organized and clearly presented information that teaches parents how to be effective advocates for children with disabilities." **– 2e: Twice-Exceptional Newsletter**

"Whether you are beginning to advocate or an experienced advocate who needs a good reference, *Wrightslaw: From Emotions to Advocacy* provides a clear roadmap to effective advocacy. You learn how to plan, prepare, organize, and get quality special education services. **– Developmental Disabilities Quarterly**

"An invaluable, user-friendly resource for parents of children with disabilities! This book is packed with critical information, and provides clear, practical professional guidance that will empower parents with the necessary skills, tools and knowledge for successfully advocating in their child's behalf." **– Sandra Rief, author of *How to Reach and Teach ADD/ADHD Children***

More Praise for
Wrightslaw: From Emotions to Advocacy – The Special Education Survival Guide

"If I were asked to choose just one book to help me learn advocacy skills, this is it!" – **Support for Families of Children with Disabilities Newsletter**

"Wrightslaw: From Emotions to Advocacy is one of the best special education advocacy books available because it gives parents an action plan to follow. It will prepare parents not just for this year's IEP, but for all the years ahead." – **First Signs, Inc.**

Wrightslaw: From Emotions to Advocacy is a wonderful resource that offers a wealth of insights on special education advocacy and will help parents - whether new or experienced advocates - in their quest to obtain better special education programs and services for their children. – **Mothers from Hell**

"Provides a roadmap for effective advocacy with hundreds of strategies, tips, references, warnings and resources to explore. Expect this book to be tabbed and dog-eared as it becomes an invaluable advocacy tool. – **Tourette Syndrome Association**

"Any lawyer seeking to expand his or her practice into special education law would be well-served by reading this work, and referring clients to it as well. The book offers a well-organized approach to a special education case, including learning about advocacy, creating a master plan, learning the rules, obstacles to success, resolving conflict, evaluations, tests and measurements, and developing a SMART IEP." – **NJ Lawyer**

"In reading this book, you will experience an array of emotions - fear, sadness, anger, excitement, relief and hope. This book will guide you step by step - how to organize, plan and use your emotions to become an effective advocate for your child." – **The Nashville News**

"Beautifully written, clear-cut . . ." – Linda Morrissey, parent and advocate

"*From Emotions to Advocacy* describes the steps for successful, effective advocacy. This book will help seasoned advocates and parents who are just beginning the advocacy journey." – Melanie Allen, advocate and parent of two special needs children

"This is the bible of special education advocacy . . . like having a trusted, knowledgeable friend to help you every step of the way. *From Emotions to Advocacy* shows you what to do so you do it right the first time!" – Darlene Trousdale, parent and advocate

"One of the most important how-to manuals ever written for navigating your way through special education and using the law to get a good education for your child . . . a goldmine of information! - Thom Hartmann, author, *Attention Deficit Disorder: A Different Perception – A Hunter in a Farmer's World*

Acknowledgments

We wish to acknowledge the contributions of several individuals who provided ideas for this book.

We thank Alaska attorney **Sonja Kerr**, Indiana advocate **Pat Howey, and** New Mexico advocate **Judy Bonnell** for their suggestions about how to use worksheets in IEP meetings.

We thank **Melissa Farrall** for her assistance in revising the chapters on testing. Thanks to Dr. Farrall, these chapters now include information about dozens of tests that are used in evaluating children.

We thank **Nissan Bar-Lev**, director of special education and pupil services of CESA-7 for information and practical examples of SMART IEPs.

We owe a special debt of gratitude to **Suzanne Heath.** From the beginning, Sue offered invaluable advice about the "ideal parent advocacy manual" and offered dozens of suggestions that are included in the second edition of *Wrightslaw: From Emotions to Advocacy–The Special Education Survival Guide*. Thanks to Sue, you have key information about the No Child Left Behind Act.

We thank **Lynn Trimble**, Phoenix writer, Assistant Editor of *Raising Arizona Kids Magazine*, and mother of three. Lynn edited the manuscript and offered many suggestions that we included in the book including advice about time management and taking care of oneself.

We want to acknowledge and thank several people who selflessly gave their time and energy to read and critique portions of the manuscript:

> **Loni Allen,** Family Resource Specialist at Parents Helping Parents in California and advocate for children in the juvenile justice system
> **Judy Bonnell,** parent advocate from New Mexico
> **Larry Goodwin,** parent from Ohio
> **Joe Jackson,** psychologist and advocate for people with disabilities in Virginia
> **Laurie Mix,** parent advocate for her child with ADHD in Washington
> **Linda and Kevin Morrissey,** parent advocates from Connecticut
> **Maureen Reyes,** parent and advocate for her child with multiple disabilities in Texas
> **Law Riskin,** special education teacher in California
> **Darlene Trousdale,** parent and full-time student in California
> **Maggie Wade,** parent advocate in Alaska
> **Catherine Worthington,** parent advocate for her child with multiple disabilities in Florida

We thank our copyeditor and proofreader, **Sara Murphy Wright.** Thanks to Sara, this book is clear, readable, organized, and grammatically correct.

We thank our talented graphic designer, **Mayapriya Long** of **Bookwrights.** Mayapriya designed the cover and layout for *Wrightslaw: From Emotions to Advocacy–The Special Education Survival Guide.*

Finally, we thank our families whose patience and support helped us to complete this book.

Dedication

We dedicate this book to you, the parents.

As you shared your struggles and successes, you invited us into your minds and hearts.

When you asked questions, you helped us to learn.

When you sent thank-you notes, we felt your support.

Thank you.

Contents

Section Two. Advocacy 101 21

Section Three. The Parent as Expert 59

Introduction

Many parents want to advocate for their child but hold back. If you want to advocate or need to advocate or believe you should advocate for your child but have excuses or reasons why you cannot, this book is for you. We will help you attack obstacles and learn the skills you need to be an effective advocate for your child.

From Emotions to Advocacy

As you read this book, you will experience an array of emotions – fear, sadness, and anger, to excitement, relief, and hope. You will make mental lists of things to do. Write your ideas down on a sheet of paper. Tuck your list into this book and use it as a bookmark. As you learn, your ideas and priorities will change.

You may be tempted to put this book aside and act on your ideas. Try to resist this urge. You have not yet learned what you need to know.

Our advocacy program teaches information and skills, step by step. When you know the information and skills you need to learn, you can make good use of your time. As you complete each step, you will acquire information and polish skills that you will use later.

Skim through the book. When you understand the program, you will know where to focus your energy. You will not allow urgent issues take precedence over important issues.

In the beginning, the process of advocating for your special needs child will feel overwhelming. This is normal. If you follow this program, you will learn how to organize, plan, and use your emotions to become an effective advocate for your child. You will not regret your journey from emotions to advocacy. Because of you, your child's life will change for the better.

Why Advocate?

As the parent of a special needs child, you represent your child's interests. When you negotiate with the school on your child's behalf, you increase the odds that your child will get an appropriate education. You cannot leave this job to others!

Most parents describe the process of negotiating with the school as a frustrating, exhausting ordeal. Some parents throw in the towel. Others prevail. What do effective parent advocates know? What are the secrets of their success?

Effective advocacy comes from research, planning and preparation. Successful advocates know what is important and what is not worth fighting about. When you finish this book, you will have acquired the knowledge and skills you need to be an effective advocate. You will avoid the mistakes that prevent many parents from successfully advocating for their children.

What You Will Learn

On your journey from emotions to advocacy, you will learn about the special education system and issues that make parent-school conflict inevitable. We describe how to learn about your child's disability, how the disability affects your child, and appropriate educational and remediation techniques. You will learn how to measure educational progress, and how to write annual goals and objectives for Individualized Education Programs (IEPs).

We teach you how to use tactics and strategies to prevent problems or resolve problems early. You will learn how to manage your emotions so you do not burn out or throw in the towel.

What This Book is Not About

Wrightslaw: From Emotions to Advocacy–The Special Education Survival Guide does not focus on the needs of children with specific disabilities, nor is the book an in-depth guide to writing Individualized Education Programs (IEPs).

Wrightslaw: Special Education Law, 2nd Edition was published by Harbor House Law Press, Inc. in January 2007, five months after the U. S. Department of Education published the final special education regulations. *Wrightslaw: Special Education Law, 2nd Edition* is available in two formats: as a print bound book and an electronic book. For more information about Wrightslaw products, please go to the Wrightslaw Publications page at www.wrightslaw.com/pubs.htm

In *Wrightslaw: No Child Left Behind* (ISBN: 1-892320-12-6), you learn to find answers to your questions about this controversial law. Learn what the law says about:

- Scientifically Based Reading Instruction
- Annual Proficiency Testing in Reading, Math, Science
- Tutoring, Summer School, After-School Programs
- Transfers from Failing Schools and School Choice
- Qualifications for Teachers and Paraprofessionals
- Bonus Pay, Stipends, for Teachers & Principals

Icons

The book includes icons that alert you to Tips, Warnings, Cross-references, and Internet Resources.

☑   Tip

     Warning – Be careful!

📖   Cross-reference

🖱   Internet Resource

How This Book is Organized

Section One is "Getting Started."

You will learn:

- Basic advocacy skills
- Supplies you need to get started
- How to develop a master plan for your child's education
- How to act as your child's special education project manager

Section Two is "Advocacy 101."

In this section, you will learn about:

- Schools as bureaucracies and the rules of the game
- Obstacles to success – school culture, myths, gatekeepers, and emotions
- Common causes of conflict
- Steps you can take to prevent or resolve problems
- Events that trigger parent-school crises

Section Three is "The Parent as Expert."

In this section, you will learn:

- Why you must become an expert about your child's disability and educational needs
- How to organize your child's file, step by step
- Commonly used tests of reading
- Commonly used intellectual, achievement, speech language, and behavior tests
- How to use information from tests to understand your child's disability
- How to use test scores to monitor and measure your child's progress
- How to write SMART IEP goals

Section Four is "Special Education Law."

In this section, you will learn about:

- The Individuals with Disabilities Education Act of 2004 (IDEA 2004)
- Findings and purposes of the IDEA
- Key definitions in IDEA 2004
- Extended school year (ESY), child find, least restrictive environment (LRE), private placements, and statewide assessments
- Evaluations, eligibility, parental consent, IEPs, and placement
- Prior written notice, procedural safeguards, mediation, due process hearings, appeals, discipline, and age of majority
- Section 504 of the Rehabilitation Act and the Americans with Disabilities Act (ADA)
- The No Child Left Behind Act (NCLB)

Section Five is "Tactics and Strategies."

In this section, you will learn about:

- The "Rules of Adverse Assumptions," proof and evidence, and image and presentation
- How to use logs, calendars, and journals to create paper trails
- How to write effective letters
- How to write a persuasive "Letter to the Stranger"
- How to use problem worksheets, parent agendas, visual aids, and graphs
- Roles of experts
- Pros and cons of tape recording meetings
- How to use problem resolution worksheets and post-meeting thank you letters

Appendices

The book includes these useful appendices:

- Glossary of Special Education Legal Terms
- Glossary of Assessment Terms

Companion Website

Visit the companion website for *Wrightslaw: From Emotions to Advocacy* at:

http://www.fetaweb.com/

Fetaweb.com includes articles, checklists, sample letters, charts, and free resources. We encourage you to submit letters, tips and favorite links.

Fetaweb.com will list changes that have occurred since the book was published. We appreciate your comments and suggestions about how we can improve the book.

A Note to Parents of Section 504 Children

If your child has a Section 504 plan and does not receive special education services under the Individuals with Disabilities Education Act, you should read Chapter 19 about Section 504 of the Rehabilitation Act. Next, read Chapters 10 and 11 to learn about your child's test scores. In many cases, Section 504 children are eligible for services under IDEA. Gatekeepers who limit access to special education services often make decisions about eligibility. If you understand your child's test data, you will be in a position to open the door to better services for your child.

A Note to Special Educators

Many parents bring Wrightslaw books to school meetings. If school personnel advise the parent that a request is against the law, the parent can use the law book to verify this statement.

If emotions are under control on both sides, you will find it easier to work with parents who learn the law. These parents want their children to learn. They expect you to teach their children. When parents organize the file, document events and agreements, and help their teams stay on task, they want to build strong working relationships with school personnel. Everyone wins, especially the children.

Are You Ready?

You cannot loiter in the introduction forever. It's time to learn about special education advocacy! Get a paper and pen so you can write down your ideas. If you are ready to learn, just turn this page.

Section One

Getting Started

Section One is "Getting Started." In Chapter 1, you learn that an advocate speaks, pleads, and argues on behalf of another person. We describe different kinds of advocates for children with disabilities and explain why parents are natural advocates for their children.

You learn that advocates gather information, learn the rules of the game, plan and prepare, keep written records, identify problems, and propose solutions. We provide you with a list of supplies you need to get started.

In Chapter 2, you learn that a master plan helps you stay focused, anticipate problems, and prepare for the future. We describe the components of a master plan, including a vision statement, mission statement, goals, strategies, and timelines.

You learn how to find and work with independent evaluators and educational consultants. If you are like most parents, you need information and support. We recommend that you join a parent group. Other parents will teach you the rules of the game, help you prepare for meetings, and provide emotional support.

Chapter 3 focuses on the parent as project manager. Project managers organize, plan, monitor progress, anticipate problems, and keep the team focused. Your childs special education is a long-term project. As the parent, you are the logical person to step into the role of special education project manager.

We describe the most common reasons why projects fail, and explain the need to make plans, define goals, organize information, and build relationships. You learn about the skills, information and attitude you need to act as your childs special education project manager.

1 | Learning About Advocacy

"If you think education is expensive, try ignorance." — Benjamin Franklin, inventor

In this chapter, you will meet children with disabilities. You will learn that there are different kinds of advocates for children with disabilities and why parents are natural advocates for their children. We provide a quick overview of advocacy skills. Finally, you will discover how advocacy helps parents use their emotions to become empowered.

Marie, a ten-year-old child from Maryland, had several strokes. She uses an electric wheelchair to get around and assistive technology to communicate. When Marie's parents asked their school district for support and services, the district refused, saying, "The Individuals with Disabilities Education Act doesn't apply to your child."

In Indiana, a blind child wanted to attend his neighborhood school. The school district refused and sent Joshua to a residential school for the blind, 25 miles away from home. Josh's parents objected, initiated a special education due process hearing, and prevailed.

Nancy is a bright child with dyslexia. Her New Jersey school district placed her in a special education resource room. Two years passed, but Nancy did not learn to read. Her parents wanted the district to train teachers in effective educational practices so children with dyslexia could be taught to read. The district refused. Nancy's parents advocated for her and prevailed.

In California, the parents of a seven-year-old child with mental retardation wanted their daughter to be educated in a regular classroom. When the school district refused, Rachel's parents spent five years fighting for her right to attend regular classes. After the court ordered the district to support Rachel, so she could attend school with her peers, the school district appealed – all the way to the U. S. Supreme Court. Rachel's parents were her advocates. Today, Rachel Holland is a high school student in regular education classes.

As a first grader in Washington, D.C. public schools, Saundra was misdiagnosed with mental retardation. After 12 years of special education, Saundra was functionally illiterate. Saundra did not have an advocate. "The school system has not given me what I needed," she says. "I feel as though no one really cares."

Why Advocate?

Good special education services are intensive and expensive. Resources are limited. If you have a child with special needs, you may wind up battling the school district for the services your child needs. To prevail, you need information, skills, and tools.

Who can be an advocate? Anyone can advocate for another person. Here is how the dictionary defines the term "advocate":

ad-vo-cate. Verb, transitive. To speak, plead or argue in favor of.

Synonym is support.

1. One that argues for a cause; a supporter or defender; an advocate of civil rights.

2. One that pleads in another's behalf; an intercessor; advocates for abused children and spouses.

3. A lawyer. (The American Heritage Dictionary of the English Language, Third Edition)

Special education advocates speak for children with disabilities and special needs who are unable to protect themselves. The advocate performs several functions:

- Supports, helps, assists, and aids
- Speaks and pleads on behalf of others
- Defends and argues for people or causes

Different Types of Advocates

Special education advocates work to improve the lives of children with disabilities and their families. You are likely to meet different types of advocates.

Lay Advocates

Lay advocates use their specialized knowledge and expertise to help parents resolve problems with schools. When lay advocates attend meetings, write letters, and negotiate for services, they are acting on the child's behalf. Most lay advocates are knowledgeable about legal rights and responsibilities. In some jurisdictions, lay advocates represent parents in special education due process hearings.

Educational Advocates

Educational advocates evaluate children with disabilities and make recommendations about educational services. When educational advocates go to eligibility and IEP meetings, they are acting on the child's behalf. Some educational advocates are skilled negotiators. Others are not knowledgeable about special education law or how to use tactics and strategies.

School Personnel

Teachers and special education providers often view themselves as advocates. Teachers, administrators, and school staff may provide support to children and their families. Because they are employed by school districts, it is unlikely that school personnel can advocate for children with disabilities without endangering their jobs.

Parents

Parents are natural advocates for their children.

Who is your child's first teacher? You are. Who is your child's most important role model? You are. Who is responsible for your child's welfare? You are. Who has your child's best interests at heart? You do.

You know your child better than anyone else. The school is involved with your child for a few years. You are involved with your child for life. You should play an active role in planning your child's education.

The law gives you the power to make educational decisions for your child. Do not be afraid to use your power. Use it wisely. A good education is the most important gift you can give to your child.

As the parent of a child with a disability, you have two goals:

- To ensure that the school provides your child with a "free appropriate public education" that includes "... special education and related services designed to meet [the child's] unique needs and prepare them for further education, employment and independent living ..." 20 U.S.C. 1400(d)
- To build a healthy working relationship with the school.

What Advocates Do

Advocacy is not a mysterious process. Here is a quick overview of advocacy skills.

Gather Information

Advocates gather facts and information. As they gather information and organize documents, they learn about the child's disability and educational history. Advocates use facts and independent documentation to resolve disagreements and disputes with the school.

Learn the Rules of the Game

Advocates take time to educate themselves about their local school district. They know how decisions are made and by whom.

Advocates know about legal rights. They know that a child with a disability is entitled to an "appropriate" education, not the "best" education, nor an education that "maximizes the child's potential." They understand that "best" is a four-letter word that cannot be used by parents or advocates. Advocates know the procedures that parents must follow to protect their rights and the child's rights.

Plan and Prepare

Advocates know that planning prevents problems. Advocates do not expect school personnel to tell them about rights and responsibilities. Advocates read special education laws, regulations, and cases to get answers to their questions.

Advocates learn how to use test scores to monitor a child's progress in special education. They prepare for meetings, create agendas, write objectives, and use meeting worksheets and follow-up letters to clarify problems and nail down agreements.

Keep Written Records

Because documents are often the keys to success, advocates keep written records. They know that if a statement is not written down, it was not said. They make requests in writing and write polite follow-up letters to document events, discussions, and meetings.

Ask Questions, Listen to Answers

Advocates are not afraid to ask questions. When they ask questions, they listen carefully to answers. Advocates know how to use "Who, What, Why, Where, When, How, and Explain Questions" (5 Ws + H + E) to discover the true reasons for positions.

Identify Problems

Advocates learn to define and describe problems from all angles. They use their knowledge of interests, fears, and positions to develop strategies. Advocates are problem solvers. They do not waste valuable time and energy looking for people to blame.

Propose Solutions

Advocates know that parents negotiate with schools for special education services. As negotiators, advocates discuss issues and make offers or proposals. They seek "win-win" solutions that will satisfy the interests of parents and schools.

The Parent's Journey From Emotions to Advocacy

On your journey from emotions to advocacy, you will learn about your child's disability, educational and remedial techniques, educational progress, Individualized Educational Programs (IEPs), and how to artfully advocate.

You will learn how to present your concerns and problems in writing, prepare for meetings, and search for win-win solutions. You will learn how to use your emotions as a source of energy and power, and how to focus on getting an appropriate education for your child.

Supplies

Are you ready to advocate? Here is a list of supplies that will help you get started:

• Two 3-ring notebooks (one for your child's file; one for information about your child's disability and educational information.

- 3-hole punch
- Highlighters
- Package of sticky notes
- #10 Envelopes
- Stamps
- Calendar
- Journal
- Contact log
- Small tape recorder

In Summation

In this chapter, you learned how parent advocates changed the lives of their children with disabilities. You learned about lay advocates and educational advocates, and that teachers and special education staff are limited in their ability to advocate. You learned that parents are natural advocates for their children.

You have an overview of advocacy skills and a list of supplies that will help you advocate. Now you will go one step further and learn about master plans.

Your Notes Here

2 | Creating Your Master Plan

"Failing to prepare is preparing to fail." —John Wooden, UCLA basketball coach

In this chapter, you will learn about planning. We explain how a master plan helps you focus, anticipate problems, and prepare for the future. We describe the five components of a master plan. We discuss how to find and use private sector evaluators and educational consultants. You will learn about the benefits of joining a parent support group or advocacy group.

— mistake: focus on long-term instead of using short-term

The Need to Plan

What do you want your child to achieve this year? What are your long-range goals for your child? What do you want your child to be able to do when he or she leaves the public school system? What steps do you need to take to help your child meet these goals?

What are your child's strengths and weaknesses? How does your child's disability affect his or her ability to learn? You need to plan for your child's future.

Can you imagine building a house without a blueprint? You do not know where to situate the house, what types of materials to use, or when to schedule work by subcontractors.

You do not know how large the house will be, how many rooms it will have, or what it will cost to build. You are not aware of obstacles you may encounter, legal requirements, contracts, or permits. Is it reasonable to think that you will figure this out as you go along?

Can you imagine starting a business without a business plan? You have not decided what products you will sell, how you will market your products, or how to fill orders. You do not know what services you should offer.

You have not done research into your market or your competition. You do not know what start-up expenses to anticipate, how much your business will earn, or when you can expect to break even. You do not know about obstacles, legal requirements, or contracts. Is it reasonable to think that you will figure this out as you go along?

Special Education Master Plans

Can you imagine educating a child with a disability without a master plan? You do not know about the child's disability, how the disability affects the child's learning, or how the child needs to be taught. You do not know what services and supports the child needs.

You do not know what steps you should take to ensure that your child receives appropriate services. You do not know if your child is making progress. You are not aware of obstacles you may encounter or how to resolve problems. Is it reasonable to think you will figure this out as you go along?

This year, millions of children with disabilities will spend hundreds of millions of hours in special education classes with no master plans. There is a better way to tackle the job of educating children with disabilities!

Have we sold you on the importance of a master plan? Great!

Planning for Efficiency

Raising a child is hard work. If you have a child who learns differently, has a disability, or has special needs, you work harder and longer. A master plan will help you work more efficiently.

When you have a child with a disability, you battle with insurance companies and schools, negotiate with employers and co-workers for time off, respond to the needs of family members, and deal with the unexpected. As these demands increase, your stress level increases too. It is easy to be sidetracked and forget what is important.

A master plan helps you stay focused, anticipate problems, and prepare for the future. Your master plan includes goals for your child in academic and non-academic areas – hobbies, interests, sports, play, and friendships. Master plans are clear, focused, concise, and flexible.

A master plan is different from an Individualized Educational Program or IEP. The IEP is not a long-term plan. The IEP includes annual goals and short-term objectives that address your child's needs that result from the disability. The IEP focuses on your child's needs now, in the present. The IEP document commits the school to provide agreed-upon services for a period of one year or less.

[Handwritten margin note: IEP is NOW present]

[Handwritten margin note: #1 she needs services AS well AS Accomodations]

Elements of a Master Plan

The master plan includes five elements:

- Vision statement
- Mission statement
- Goals
- Strategies
- Timelines

Vision Statement

Your vision statement is a visual picture that describes your child in the future. What does the future hold? Do you envision your child getting additional education and training? Do you see your child working at a job and raising a family? Will your child be a member of the community? What does you child need to be prepared for "further education, employment and independent living?" (20 U. S. C. §1400(d)).

Mission Statement

Your mission statement is a personal statement that describes the reasons you are advocating for your child. Your mission statement reflects your emotional commitment and passion.

☑ **Write your mission statement in positive terms:**

My mission is to obtain high quality special education services so my child will be prepared to lead a productive, independent life, to the maximum extent possible.

Make several copies of your mission statement. Put a copy in your child's file, another copy in your journal. You may want to post your mission statement around the house, in places where you will see it – on your refrigerator, by your computer, on the bathroom mirror. Tape your mission statement to the dashboard of your car!

Over the next few weeks, read your mission statement often. This will help you internalize the message. Save your mission statement. In a few months, this sheet of paper will be a reminder about how far you have come. It will be more than a mission statement. It will be your progress report.

Goals

Goals make you stretch, give you direction, and keep you focused when you lose perspective. When you write goals, think about what you need to do to accomplish these goals. Your master plan should include academic and non-academic goals for your child.

☑ **Write your goals as outcomes.**

Assume your child's reading skills are three years delayed. How much progress should your child make toward improving his reading skills this year? How much progress do you expect your child to make next year? When you write a goal, begin the goal with a statement like this: "My child will be able to _____."

What do you expect your child to learn this year? Next year? What do you expect your child to learn by the time he or she moves to the next academic level? What do you expect your child to know by the time he or she leaves the public education system?

Strategies

Strategies help you make decisions, solve problems, and overcome obstacles. Think of strategies as your roadmap.

Timelines

Timelines are statements about what actions need to be completed and when.

Planning for the Future

Imagine your child as a young adult. What do you want for your child? What should your child be able to do? Assume you want your child to have a job and be independent. Your child will need to learn how to be a good worker. How can you approach the goal of helping your child become a good worker?

Break this goal down into behaviors that you can observe: sharing, treating others with respect, listening, offering feedback, following directions, and so forth. For example:

- She shares ideas and information with other people;
- He honors written and verbal agreements;
- She doesn't talk behind other people's backs;
- He doesn't treat co-workers like subordinates;
- She doesn't belittle or talk down to other people;
- He listens to what others say;
- She listens without interrupting;
- He is not abrupt or short with others;
- She provides constructive feedback to others.

Beware of low goals!

How does planning work in real life? Laura and Steve describe planning for their son, Justin.

Laura and Steve: Planning

Laura and Steve have four children. Fifteen-year old Justin is their youngest child. Justin has autism. Laura and Steve have encountered obstacles in their son's education from the beginning. Today, Justin attends his local high school, takes general education courses, and earns "A's" in art and wood shop. Laura and Steve describe the importance of planning.

Do we have a clear view of what we want for our son? Yes.

We started out, as many parents do, with goals and aspirations for our son. With the diagnosis of autism, we had to modify what we saw as the path for his future.

We had to get through the grieving process before we could look forward to a future for our son. Forming a plan and thinking about possibilities for his future helped us to heal and to adjust our perspective in a positive way. We did not give up our vision; we modified it.

When you have a special needs child, you have to modify your expectations more often. Sometimes there are obstacles you do not see until it is too late.

What keeps me sane? Planning! I cannot emphasize this enough for parents. We make lists of expectations. We write out our goals. We post outcomes of what we want to see happen.

We have a plan for our son. We also have contingency plans. We realize that Justin may never be completely independent. We plan for that too.

Our main goal has always been for Justin to have the most fulfilling life possible. We broke this down into several areas. In the beginning, our goals were very basic – like communicating and cleaning his room. During our modification times, we add to them. Now, some of the goals are:

> *Life skills: cooking; cleaning; personal hygiene*
>
> *Social skills: answer phone; greet people*
>
> *Communication: express wants, needs, desires*
>
> *Job skills: develop talents and interests; identify fields of employment*

Plans are my emotional safety net. I know if things do not go as expected, we have ideas and plans to fall back on. We will make the best of the present situation or make temporary fixes until we can put changes into place.

Now we include the word "functional" in goals. When developing Justin's IEP, we bring a list of outcomes for his life that we developed. When the teachers list a goal, we look to see how it connects with these outcomes and if it is "functional." We also bring our list of educational expectations for the year. I have found that many teachers appreciate a list of ideas.

Writing Your Master Plan

Gathering Information

Begin by gathering information about your child, your child's disability, and how the disability affects your child's ability to learn.

In Chapter 9, you will learn how to request information about your child from all sources and how to organize your child's file.

Your master plan should include academic and non-academic goals. Begin by writing your goals in non-academic areas:

- Personal hobbies and interests
- Sports and fitness
- Friends and social life
- Family
- Community

As you think about your child's life in these areas, you may discover problems. Is your child inactive? Does your child spend too many hours on the computer or in front of the television? Does your child have friends? Does your child play with other children? Does your child have responsibilities at home? Special interests? Hobbies?

Working with an Independent Evaluator or Educational Consultant

Consult with a private-sector psychologist, educational diagnostician, or consultant to develop goals for your child. Your consultant will give you valuable information and help. Your consultant may:

- Teach you about your child's disability and educational needs
- Provide information about effective teaching and research-based educational practices
- Help you learn about tests, how tests measure educational progress, and how to interpret test results
- Help you design goals, objectives and timeframes
- Evaluate your child's progress toward IEP goals and objectives
- Make recommendations about your child's educational program

Qualities of a Consultant

Look for a consultant who is knowledgeable about your child's disability, child development, and special education. Ideally, your consultant will be available to work with you and your family for the long haul. In addition to making recommendations about your child's educational program, your consultant should attend school meetings to support these recommendations.

Depending on your child's disability and age, you may work with different specialists:

- Psychologists
- Speech-language pathologists
- Educational diagnosticians
- Occupational therapists
- Physical therapists
- Psychiatrists
- Pediatric neurologists
- Therapists and counselors

☑ To find a consultant, contact medical centers children's hospitals, mental health centers, and clinics. Ask other parents for recommendations.

Strategies: Finding a Consultant

Contact advocacy groups and organizations that represent individuals with your child's disability and ask them to recommend consultants. Contact private special education schools and ask for their recommended consultants. Before long, you will have a short list of recommendations from different groups and individuals. You will probably find your consultant in this list.

Strategies: Learning From Other Parents

Join a parent support group or advocacy group. How do you find a parent group? Do you know about parent groups in your child's school? Do you know about groups in your community?

The Yellow Pages for Kids site at www.yellowpagesforkids.com lists Parent Information Groups by state.

When you join a parent support group, you will meet other parents who have traveled down this road. Learn from them. In addition to emotional support, they will teach you the rules of the game.

Look for an active parent group that wants to meet the needs of their members. You may find groups that were established to meet the needs of children who have different disabilities than your child. Do not rule these groups out! Parents of children with disabilities share many common interests and concerns and want to get quality special education services for their children.

If your school district has a special education advisory board, contact a board member and ask about parent groups. If you contact a national or state organization for information, ask if there are local support groups in your community.

The Yellow Pages for Kids site at www.yellowpagesforkids.com lists disabilities organizations and information groups.

When you look for a parent or disability group, think about your interests and needs.

- Do you want emotional support?
- Do you want to meet other families who have a child with a disability?
- Do you want advocacy training?
- Do you want to learn more about your child's disability?
- Do you want to learn about special education issues?
- Do you want to get involved in school reform issues?

Your answers to these questions will help you decide what type of group to join.

Here is how a parent describes the support she receives from other parents:

As parents, we have experienced similar events and emotions. Our children have experienced acts of discrimination. Our hearts have been broken, our senses inflamed.

Each step along this path, we have been supported by other parents, people with disabilities, and advocates. Love for our children brought us together and keeps us to-gether. We have our stories, our experiences, our fears, and our hopes. We need each other.

In Summation

In this chapter, we discussed why plans and strategies are essential to successful advocacy. You learned about master plans and the need to develop goals for your child's future. You learned how to get help from a consultant and the importance of joining a support group.

Do you understand the need for long-term planning? Good! In the next chapter, you will learn about project managers.

3 | The Parent as Project Manager

"A good education is the next best thing to a pushy mother." —Charles Schulz, cartoonist

In the last chapter, you learned that your child's special education is a long-term project and that you need a master plan. In this chapter, you will learn about project managers who organize, plan, monitor progress, anticipate problems, and keep the team focused. As your child's parent and advocate, you are the logical candidate for this job. We describe the attitude, knowledge, and skills you need to act as your child's special education project manager.

Contractors and Project Managers

If you build a house, you may have a general contractor manage the project. Contractors manage schedules, deal with people, anticipate problems, and ensure that jobs are done. Contractors are project managers.

In the business world, project managers plan, organize, monitor progress, and ensure that projects are completed. Project managers remove obstacles and resolve conflicts between people. On long, complicated projects, project managers are invaluable.

The Special Education Project Manager

As the parent of a child with a disability, you have learned that you need to make long-range plans for your child. Schools do not make long-term plans for students. Although your child may have a case manager, this individual is not responsible for your child's education after your child leaves the public school system. If your child has an Individualized Educational Program (IEP), the IEP addresses your child's needs for one year or less.

You are the constant factor in your child's life. You represent your child's interests. If your child does not receive an appropriate education and master the skills necessary to be an independent, self-sufficient member of the community, you will deal with the outcome.

In the last chapter, Laura and Steve described how they planned for their son Justin. Here is how Laura and Steve describe their role:

As his parents, we are the bottom line. We must make decisions for Justin until he can decide for himself.

The educators, aides, psychologists, specialists, and doctors are resources to help him progress along the path of life. We look to them for expertise in their fields. We do not expect them to answer all the questions and deal with all the problems our son faces.

If you are like most parents, you do not have training in project management. Many parents learn about special education by jumping in. Sometimes, parents jump from the frying pan into the fire!

When you learn project management skills, you will be a more effective advocate. Set aside time to organize information about your child, make long-term plans, write goals with timelines, and build working relationships with school personnel. Here is the job description for a special education project manager.

Learns New Information

The special education project manager learns about the child's disability and how the disability affects the child's ability to learn. The manager does research about effective special education practices.

The special education project manager knows that the most common reasons why projects fail are:

- Lack of planning
- Fuzzy goals
- Team members who do not know what is expected of them
- Team members who do not get the training and support they need
- Team members who feel over-burdened and under-appreciated

The project manager knows that conflict is inevitable when people with different interests and perspectives work together, and that unresolved conflict causes good plans to fail. The project manager is aware of school obstacles and parent obstacles that can derail plans and cause small problems to erupt into major crises.

Masters New Skills

Your child's special education is a team project. A team makes decisions about your child's special education program and placement. At team meetings, the project manager identifies problems and offers solutions. The project manager uses facts and objective data to support requests, monitor progress, and persuade school officials to provide the services and supports the child needs.

The project manager gathers and organizes information in the child's file and keeps the file up to date. The manager maintains a contact log and writes follow-up letters after meetings, conversations, agreements, and events.

Builds Relationships

The project manager establishes good working relationships with people on the child's team. Acting as a coach, planner, and motivator, the project manager helps the team stay focused.

The project manager is organized, flexible, open to new ideas, and willing to learn. The manager understands the importance of keeping emotions under control and treating others with respect.

The manager tactfully educates teachers and other school personnel about the child's disability and how the child learns. The project manager knows that the child's teachers are usually not the problem and supports the teachers' need for training. When teachers receive better training, they can do a better job.

Takes Care of Self and Family

Raising a special needs child can be overwhelming. If you are not careful, special education can consume your life. Many parents drive themselves until they are exhausted and burned out.

Pace yourself. Listen to tapes about time management. Use a schedule to gain control of your life. Spend time with friends or family to re-charge your batteries and regain a healthy perspective. See Table 3-1 for more tips about taking care of yourself and your family.

Table 3-1	*Tips: Taking Care of Yourself*

▷ Set aside time with your partner. Use email or voicemail to stay in touch.

▷ Schedule one-on-one time with each child. Write the child's name by a date on the calendar. Let the child pick the place and activity.

▷ Master the art of the short escape. Visit a local attraction for an afternoon or a local resort for a weekend. Short escapes will help you unwind.

▷ Nurture friendships. Make time to go to the movies, have meals, exercise, or take walks with friends.

▷ Ask friends for help. Tell friends or family when you need help with child-care and errands.

▷ Find another parent whom you can contact when you are worried and need encouragement.

▷ Share child-care with another family. Pick times each week when you can help the family and when they can help you. You will each have someone to contact when you need a break.

Continued

In Summation

In this chapter, you learned about project managers. Your child needs a project manager who can plan, organize, and monitor progress. Project managers meet with people, anticipate problems, remove obstacles, and help the team focus. You learned about the attitude, knowledge, and skills required for the successful candidate for this job.

Are you willing to act as your child's special education project manager? Good! Let's move on to the next chapter where you will learn about the rules of the game.

Section Two

Advocacy 101

In the first section of *Wrightslaw: From Emotions to Advocacy–The Special Education Survival Guide,* you learned advocacy basics, the need to create master plan for your child's special education, and the role of the special education project manager. You are ready to move on to Advocacy 101.

Chapter 4 is "Learning the Rules of the Game." You will learn about gatekeepers, special education teams, and one-size-fits-all (OSFA) programs. When you learn the rules of the game, you will be a more effective advocate and negotiator for your child.

Chapter 5 will teach you about "Obstacles to Success." School obstacles include myths, rules, and school culture. Lack of information, isolation, and emotions are obstacles for parents. You will learn about personality styles and how to deal with difficult people. When you recognize obstacles, you can take steps to minimize or prevent problems.

Chapter 6 is "Creating and Resolving Parent-School Conflicts." When you understand the real reasons for conflict, you will understand why parent-school conflict is normal, predictable, and inevitable. We describe the most common reasons for conflict and recommend strategies you can use to resolve problems. When you use these strategies, you are more likely to resolve your problem without damaging your relationship with the school.

Chapter 7 is "Emergency, Crisis, Help!" If you are like many parents, emotions are your Achilles heel. In this chapter, you will learn how problems can erupt into crises. We explain common pitfalls and describe the steps parents should take in a crisis. If you use the short-term and long-term strategies in this chapter, you will improve your odds for a good outcome.

4 | Learning the Rules of the Game

"In the first place, God made idiots. That was for practice. Then he made school boards."
—Mark Twain, writer

As you begin to advocate for your child, you need to learn about school systems and how your district resolves problems and makes decisions. In this chapter, you will learn that your district is a bureaucracy with rules, customs and traditions and a chain of command. You will learn about Gatekeepers and One-Size-Fits-All (OSFA) special education programs.

When you learn the rules, you will be a more effective advocate and negotiator for your child. It's time to learn the rules of the game!

The Rules

"Those who play the game do not see it as clearly as those who watch."
— Chinese Proverb

Do you remember your first weeks on a new job? During those weeks, you felt insecure and uneasy. You did not know what to expect. You did not know how problems were handled and how decisions were made in this new environment. The fear of the unknown made you feel anxious.

In time, you found answers to your questions. When you learned what to expect, you felt comfortable. Your anxiety dropped.

When you begin to advocate, expect to feel anxious and insecure. As an outsider, you do not know how problems are solved and how decisions are made. As with new job jitters, your anxieties are caused by the fear of the unknown. During your first school meetings, expect to feel insecure and anxious. These jitters are normal reactions to your new role and the unfamiliar environment. As you gain experience, you will know what to expect and you will feel less anxious.

Understanding the School

What do you know about your child's school? What do you know about your school district? How are parents of children with disabilities perceived by the teachers at your child's school? How are parents of children with disabilities viewed in your school district? Who wields power in your school district? When you have answers to these questions, you will be able to advocate effectively for your child.

If you are like many parents, school meetings are confusing and frustrating. When you ask questions, you don't get answers.

Your child's team is a small part of a large system. School districts have a chain of command. If you have an unusual request, your child's school team may not have the authority to grant your request. An invisible administrator may be the person who answers your request.

School Bureaucracy Rules

Bureaucracies are created to fulfill missions. The mission of public schools is to provide a standardized education to all children. Public schools offer a standardized curriculum that children are expected to learn.

Schools are modeled after factories. The principal runs the school building, teachers provide the labor, and children are the raw material. Parents are outsiders. Power flows from the top. Teachers and parents do not have the authority to make decisions that involve a commitment of resources.

Special Education Rules

When you advocate for your child, you will learn about special education rules. You will learn about gatekeepers and one-size-fits-all (OSFA) programs. When you understand how the special education system operates and how decisions are made, you will be a more effective advocate.

Gatekeeper Rules

When you advocate, you are likely to meet gatekeepers. Gatekeepers limit the number of children who have access to special education services and limit the services children can receive. If you have health insurance through an HMO or managed care firm, you know about gatekeepers.

Gatekeepers may tell you that your child is not entitled to:

- An evaluation
- Any change in the IEP
- More services
- Different services

The Gatekeeper's job is to say "No!" One of your jobs is to persuade the gatekeeper that your child's situation is different and requires a different approach.

"We Can't Make Exceptions"

School districts have elaborate systems of rules that govern how decisions are made and by whom. When you try to develop an appropriate program for your child, you may run into the "We can't make exceptions" rule. "We can't make exceptions" is related to "We have never done that before." When you prepare and plan, you can defeat both arguments.

"One-Size-Fits All" (OSFA) Programs

Many school districts have standardized "One-Size-Fits-All" (OSFA) special education programs. If your district is creative, you may have two program options: OSFA #1 and OSFA #2. In a typical OSFA program, decisions about the child's program and placement are based on the child's disability category or label, not on the child's unique needs.

If you have a four-year-old child with autism, your child's program and placement may be the school's standardized OSFA preschool program for all children with autism. If your child has dyslexia, the child's program and placement is likely to be the district's standardized program for all children with learning disabilities.

What is wrong with this?

The school district is required to provide each child with an individualized special education program tailored to that child's unique needs. Standardized OSFA programs are not tailored to any child's unique needs. Schools design OSFA programs for the convenience of the adults in the system.

Individualized Programs

Individualized programs are labor-intensive and more difficult to administer. If you are trying to develop an individualized program for your child, expect to run into resistance. You are negotiating with a system that uses categories and labels to make decisions. If you plan and prepare, you can prevail.

When parents plan and prepare, they can design appropriate individualized programs. What is the secret to their success? They know what their child needs, and they know how the system operates--they know the rules of the game.

Learning About Your School District

What do you know about your school district? Who is in charge? What is the school's perception of parents of children with disabilities? To negotiate and advocate, you need to know the answers to these questions.

Learning About School Climate

Climate is a term that describes the learning environment created by teachers and administrators. What is the climate of your child's school?

If your child's school has a positive climate, you will be encouraged to play an active role in your child's education. Teachers and parents build healthy working relationships.

Learning About School Teams

If you are like many parents, you may not realize that your child's school team has invisible members whom you may never meet. These invisible members are school administrators who have the power to make decisions about special education programs.

If you request a special education program that is different from the district's standardized program, the team may not have the authority to grant your request. The team has to consult with invisible members who make these decisions. These invisible members may not know you or your child.

Who are your invisible team members? How will these people respond to your request?

Rules of the Game

To negotiate on your child's behalf, you need to be able to analyze your strengths and weaknesses and the school district's strengths and weaknesses. You need to learn the rules of the game. What are these rules?

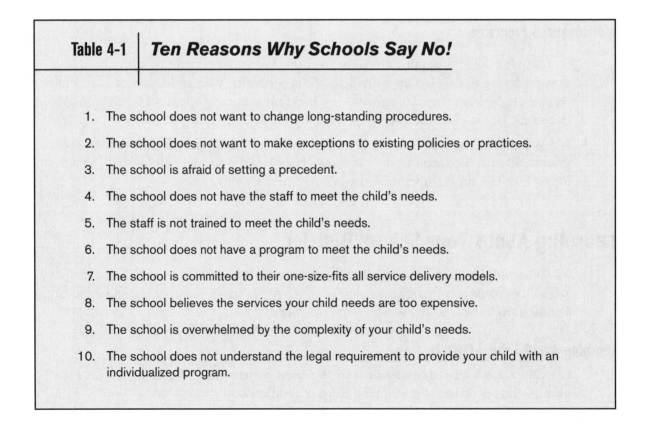

Table 4-1	*Ten Reasons Why Schools Say No!*

1. The school does not want to change long-standing procedures.

2. The school does not want to make exceptions to existing policies or practices.

3. The school is afraid of setting a precedent.

4. The school does not have the staff to meet the child's needs.

5. The staff is not trained to meet the child's needs.

6. The school does not have a program to meet the child's needs.

7. The school is committed to their one-size-fits all service delivery models.

8. The school believes the services your child needs are too expensive.

9. The school is overwhelmed by the complexity of your child's needs.

10. The school does not understand the legal requirement to provide your child with an individualized program.

If you know the rules of the game, you are on time for meetings. You prepare. You present your concerns and problems in writing. You work to develop "win-win" solutions to these problems. You keep your emotions under control and shake hands at the end of the meeting. You take steps to protect the parent-school relationship.

When parents do not know the rules of the game, they show up late for meetings. Some assume that school personnel always make good decisions about educating their children with disabilities. Others fight battles over issues they cannot win. Some lose their tempers, throw down the bat and go home.

When parents do not know the rules of the game, they do not understand the need to protect the parent-school relationship.

When you negotiate for your child, you will prevail on some issues. You will not always prevail. You need to identify your key issues and those issues that are less important. If the school refuses to negotiate on an important issue, you do not give up. You find other ways to tackle the problem and get your child the services he or she needs.

If you keep an open mind, you will learn from experience. After each school meeting, think about what you learned. When you have negative experiences, remember that you can learn from these bumps in the road.

As a parent, you represent your child's interests. If you do not represent your child's interests, no one else will. Special education is expensive. Resources are limited. School personnel act as gatekeepers, and limit access to expensive services.

These are the rules of the game.

In Summation

In this chapter, you learned about the rules of the game. You learned that schools are governed by rules and chains of command. You learned that invisible team members make important decisions. When you learn the rules, you will be a more effective advocate for your child.

In the next chapter, you will learn about obstacles to success. These obstacles include myths, emotions, and school culture. When you recognize these obstacles, you can prevent problems.

Your Notes Here

5 | Obstacles to Success

"Nothing in the world is more dangerous than sincere ignorance and conscientious stupidity."
—Martin Luther King, civil rights activist

In this chapter, we describe obstacles you may encounter as you advocate for your child. When you recognize obstacles, you can take steps to prevent problems. You will learn about school obstacles, including inaccurate information, myths, and school culture. We will describe common parent obstacles including isolation, lack of information, and emotions.

You will learn to recognize personality styles, from Pit Bulls to Wet Blankets, and strategies you can use to deal with difficult people. We describe emotional traps you need to avoid. This chapter ends with strategies to help you build a working relationship with school personnel.

Obstacles to Advocacy

When you advocate for your child, common obstacles include inaccurate information and myths about how children learn. You are likely to get conflicting answers to your questions.

Inaccurate Information

Never assume that legal advice or information you receive from school personnel is accurate. In most cases, school people who offer legal advice have not read the law. Their advice is based on information they received from sources within the school system.

Here are a few examples of inaccurate information and bad advice that parents and teachers receive.

From parents:

"I was told my child is not eligible for services because he is passing."

"My child is in fifth grade and can't read. The IEP team will not include a goal about teaching my child to read. They said IEP goals must relate to the curriculum."

"When I asked the district to evaluate my child, they said they don't have enough staff."

"The IEP team said they are not allowed to provide one-on-one speech therapy because this would violate the inclusion law."

Is this information accurate? No!

From teachers:

"Children who have ADHD are not eligible for special education. Maybe we can offer an accommodations plan."

"Some of my students need services in the summer. My supervisor says it is against the law to tell parents about extended school year services."

Is this information accurate? No!

Many people who offer legal advice have not read the law. Their advice is based on what they heard at a conference, read in an article, or overheard in the teacher's lounge.

Myths

Here are some common myths about how children learn:

"He has dyslexia. He will never learn to read." (Special education teacher)

"She is mentally retarded. She will be happier in a special class with other mentally retarded children." (Special education director)

"He has a disability. He will never be able to pass the state tests." (School psychologist)

Issues about who learns, who does not learn, and why children have trouble learning are not as simple as these statements lead you to believe.

If you have high expectations for your child, do not be surprised if the school views you as unrealistic and advises you to lower your expectations.

In 1953, educators told Pete Wright's parents: *"You need to lower your expectations for Peter. He is not college material. College is not a realistic goal for him."* Pete Wright is a successful attorney and co-author of this book.

Twenty-five years later, special educators told Pete Wright: *"You need to lower your expectations for Damon. He wants to go to law school. This is not a realistic goal for him."* Today, Damon is a successful trial lawyer.

If you have a child with a disability, teach your child to work hard and persevere. Because you are your child's role model, you must work hard and persevere too!

School Obstacles

Rich and Beth's four-year-old son has autism. If Alex receives intensive early intervention, he may be able to attend regular education classes in two or three years.

Rich and Beth are willing to sacrifice to ensure that Alex gets the help he needs. When they asked the school for help, they encountered resistance. The school placed Alex in a self-contained preschool class for a few hours a week. This is how Rich described the IEP meeting:

"They placed Alex in a self-contained class with disabled children because they think he will learn and imitate other children. Alex has autism! He does not notice other children. He will not learn by imitation. I thought we were partners in this process."

School Culture

School culture acts as an invisible wall that prevents parents and school staff from working together. When you advocate for your child, you need to understand the power of school culture.

When you recognize school culture, you will feel less frustrated. You will understand that school culture is not unique to you, your child, your school, your school district, your state, or region. As Pete says, *"The children's names and dates of birth change, but the facts and issues remain the same."*

Beliefs, Perceptions, & Attitudes

School culture includes beliefs, perceptions, and attitudes shared by people who work in schools–educators, school psychologists, administrators, and other personnel.

Beliefs affect the decisions we make and the actions we take. While beliefs may not be expressed openly, they have an enormous impact on relations between parents and school personnel, and influence how decisions are made for children with disabilities.

Still not sure you understand what "school culture" means? Try this exercise.

Think back to your childhood. Visualize the elementary school you attended. School culture is the unspoken feeling that "this is how things are done around here." You sensed it when you walked toward the school. You smelled it when you walked through the doors. You heard it when bells rang and lockers slammed. Schools are different. Nothing feels like "The School." Here are three examples of school culture.

5,000 Evaluations: Same Conclusion

Why do children have learning and behavior problems? To answer this question, a psychologist named Galen Alessi analyzed 5,000 evaluations by school psychologists to determine the importance of five factors: inappropriate curriculum, ineffective teaching, ineffective school management practices, inadequate family support, and child-based problems. He asked:

- Is the child misplaced in the curriculum, or does the curriculum include faulty teaching routines?
- Is the child's teacher not implementing effective teaching and/or behavioral management practices?

- Are the principal and school administrators not implementing effective school management practices?
- Are the parents not providing the home-based support necessary for effective learning?
- Does the child have physical and/or psychological problems that contribute to learning problems?

Dr. Alessi's findings will not surprise many parents of children with disabilities:

- Inappropriate curriculum was never mentioned as a factor.
- Ineffective teaching was never mentioned as a factor.
- Ineffective school management practices were never mentioned as factors.
- Parent and home factors were cited as problems in 10-20 percent of the evaluations.
- Child factors were cited in 100 percent of the evaluations.

When Dr. Alessi asked the school psychologists about their one-sided evaluations, they explained that they were not allowed to mention school related factors. Informal school policy or school culture required them to limit their findings to child and family factors.

How Principals View Children with Learning Problems

As school leaders, principals shape school culture. How do principals view children with learning problems? Researchers studied the attitudes of principals in elementary schools where large numbers of children were retained and referred to special education.

The principals did not have a positive view of young children with problems, nor did they believe schools were responsible for providing these children with help. The principals believed that children's learning problems were due to social and economic factors, including single parent homes and dysfunctional families. They believed that disadvantaged children were immature and slow learners.

Children who entered school with limited educational experiences were perceived as intellectually limited. Because the school did not provide enrichment or tutoring, many of these children failed. Eventually, the children were retained or referred to special education.

Belief: Parents are the Problem

This is how one insider describes the school's perspective of parents of children with disabilities:

"School personnel believe that on a subconscious level, parents of disabled children are disappointed or embarrassed by their children's disabilities. This disappointment or embarrassment is expressed by the parent demanding that the school take responsibility for fixing the problem."

Belief: We are the Experts

As you advocate for your child, you must understand that school personnel believe they are the experts about children and learning. Most believe they know what is best for your child. Although you have observed your child in hundreds of situations, many educators believe that because you are emotionally involved, you are incapable of knowing what your child needs.

What can you do to change these beliefs and attitudes? Nothing! You cannot change the beliefs of others.

Obstacles Within the System

As your child's advocate, you will negotiate with your school district. As you learned in the last chapter, school districts are bureaucracies. Let's take a closer look at schools.

In schools, rules govern how things are done. Because school bureaucracies depend on rules, it is difficult for school personnel to devise creative solutions to problems.

Schools have clear lines of authority. In most districts, power flows from the school board to the superintendent and administrative staff, then to principals and teachers. Teachers are at the bottom in power, pay, prestige, and autonomy.

Principals run the school building. Teachers educate the children. Because there are clear boundaries between positions, a teacher will not run the school while the principal is away.

Public schools are the education providers for all children. The mission of public schools is to provide students with a standardized education. Standardized educational programs are not individualized, nor are they designed to meet the unique needs of the child with a disability.

Parents are outsiders. School districts rarely solicit or accept advice from parents when they design special education programs. Most decisions are based on economics, tradition, and convenience.

Parent Obstacles

If you are like most parents, your obstacles include lack of information, isolation, and emotions. In the last chapter, we advised you to join a parent support group. When you take this step, you will begin to deal with the isolation and lack of information obstacles.

Emotions

As a parent, emotions may be your Achilles Heel. To be an effective advocate, you must control your emotions and use them as a source of energy.

How do you process the fact that your child has a disability? How do you deal with your fears that the disability may prevent your child from leading a productive, independent life?

If you are like many parents, when you learn that your child has a disability, you turn to school personnel and medical specialists for help. If your school district does not provide your child with appropriate services, you get frustrated and angry. If you believe your child was damaged, you are likely to feel angry and betrayed. Once broken, trust is hard to mend.

Anxiety and Intimidation

One father, a businessman who specializes in marketing and sales, describes his feelings about school meetings:

> *"There is something about this team business where you sit around a big table, and it's just you on one side, and six or seven school people on the other side. I always feel intimidated when I go to meetings."*

> *"I feel like I did when I was eight years old and had to go to the principal's office. I was in trouble then and it feels like I'm in trouble now!"*

Your school experiences will affect your feelings about schools, teachers, and school meetings. Many parents feel intimidated at school meetings. School teams often include several school representatives and one parent. Given these dynamics, anxiety is a normal reaction.

Pity and Over-protectiveness

As a parent, you may feel helpless as you watch your child struggle. Resist the urge to step in and take over. If you give in to this urge, you will do things for your child instead of teaching your child how to do things on his or her own. Your child may learn that helplessness is a useful tactic.

If you are tempted to lower your expectations, remember that your child will internalize your expectations and beliefs. If you feel sorry for your child, your child will sense this. Your child's self concept will change.

A vicious cycle will begin: low expectations lead to low achievement, which leads to lower expectations, which lead to even lower achievement. For many children with disabilities, negative beliefs are more disabling than their original problems.

Help your child to be strong and resilient.

Dealing with Difficult People

Personality conflicts crop up when people with different interests and personalities work together. These conflicts are draining, distracting, and can derail you from your goal. We will look at several personality styles, how to recognize them, and strategies you can use to work with them without getting angry, sidetracked, or throwing in the towel.

- Pit Bulls and Bullies
- Know-it-Alls and Experts
- Conflict Avoiders
- Wet Blankets
- Snipers
- Complainers

If you understand personality styles , you are less likely to take offense. As you learn about these personality styles, you will discover that they are familiar. You may even recognize yourself! If you discover your personality style, you will learn about the impact you have on others.

Behavior as Communication

One purpose of behavior is to communicate. People also use behavior to gain control of others. Most people are not aware of the impact their behavior has on others. If you have a personality clash with a school person, you need to:

- Control your emotions
- Minimize the negative impact of the conflict
- Work toward your mutual interests

Your goal is neither to passively take abuse, nor to change people. You need to:

- Recognize personality styles
- Understand the meaning of behavior
- Use this information to work more effectively with difficult people

When you analyze, plan, and prepare, you put your brain in charge of your emotions.

Pit Bulls and Bullies

Pit Bulls are aggressive, forceful people. If they cultivate a smooth image, they often rise to positions of power and authority. Pit Bulls have strong opinions about what people should do and strong needs to prove that their view of the world is right.

If you have a difference of opinion with a Pit Bull, expect him to take this personally. Pit Bulls are impatient people with quick tempers. They get angry when people do not do what they believe should be done.

Pit Bulls believe they are right. Because they believe they are right, they believe that their bad behavior is justified – you made them behave badly. Pit Bulls have little respect for people who lack confidence.

Strategies: Dealing with Pit Bulls and Bullies

When you deal with a Pit Bull, you may feel overwhelmed, confused, and afraid. Stand up for yourself. Do not back down or blow up.

When a Pit Bull explodes, give him time to run out of steam. Say, "Mr. Jones, you interrupted me." Do not worry about being polite.

Do not argue or attack. Do not demean the Pit Bull or his position. Express your views or perceptions about the issue. Maintain eye contact.

"In my opinion…"

"My experience has been different…"

Do not fight to win. Pit Bulls are expert fighters – they cannot back down or give in. If you win a battle, you are likely to lose the war. If the Pit Bull feels defeated, he will look for another battle to win.

If you let a Pit Bull push you around, he may become a Bully. The Bully will view you as worthless and believe you deserve to be squashed.

Stand up to the bully and he will be your friend. After you express your perspective, prepare to bury the hatchet. If the Pit Bull cannot overwhelm you, he may respect you. Pit Bulls want respect from people whom they view as strong. Make it clear that you do not intend to question their authority but you believe your perception has value.

"I know you are the principal. What you say goes. But I have some ideas that would make things work better."

Know-it-Alls and Experts Stephanie

When you attend meetings with school personnel, you will meet Know-it-Alls who will tell you what to do and how to solve your problems. Their unsolicited advice and patronizing attitudes may cause you to feel irritated and resentful.

Many Know-it-Alls *are* knowledgeable. They view themselves as experts and do not realize how they appear to others. Know-it-Alls are persistent people who will fight until they prevail.

Strategies: Dealing with Know-it-Alls

When you deal with a Know-it-All, try to get the person to consider alternative views. If you attack their expertise, they will view this as a personal attack. Do not confront them. When confronted, they will get defensive and will fight to prove they are right.

Use Facts and Information

Because Know-it-Alls *are* knowledgeable, facts and information are important to them. Use facts and information to support your requests. Review your information and check your facts for accuracy.

Ask 5 Ws + H + E Questions

Ask questions. Listen. Do not interrupt. Paraphrase their points. Show that you appreciate their knowledge.

"Let me make sure I understand. I think I heard you say . . ."

Use 5 W's + H + E questions to raise issues. When you ask questions, the Know-it-All may take another look at their assumptions. Use questions to move from abstract proposals to specific details.

- Specifically, how will this happen?
- How do you see this program working a year from now?
- What steps will the school take to implement the IEP?
- When?
- Who will take each step?
- What can we expect our child to learn within the next three or four months?

Acknowledge their competence. Defer to them as the Experts. Take a subordinate role.

If you take these steps deliberately and choose to deal with them in this manner, you will not feel diminished. You understand the rules of the game. You are in control. You will feel less helpless and angry.

Most school personnel cannot accept parents as experts about their children. If you try to assume an expert's role, you will be caught up in an endless "no-win" power struggle.

Conflict Avoiders SANDRA

When you deal with school personnel, you will meet Conflict Avoiders. Conflict Avoiders are pleasant, supportive people who want to help. Most are good listeners.

Conflict Avoiders dislike making decisions. After a meeting with a Conflict Avoider, you may believe that the person made a decision in your favor. Weeks pass and nothing changes. You request another meeting. Your Conflict Avoider listens, apologizes, and mentions unforeseen delays.

You have learned that your school district is a bureaucracy. In bureaucracies, people must make decisions about how to allocate scarce resources: money, labor, and time. When Conflict Avoiders have decision-making authority, they realize that any decision will disappoint or upset someone. Decision-making is painful for them so they procrastinate until the need to make a decision passes.

Conflict Avoiders are difficult to deal with because they cannot or will not tell you that they are procrastinating. You believe they agreed to your proposal. When nothing changes, you will feel let down.

Strategies: Dealing with Conflict Avoiders

Discover Reasons for Avoidance

Make it easy for the Conflict Avoider to tell you about conflicts or reservations that are preventing them from making a decision. Reassure them that you can take bad news. Pay attention to indirect words, hesitations, and omissions that signal resistance.

Help Solve Problems

After you clarify issues, help the person look at the facts, make a list of solutions, and prioritize the solutions. Help the Conflict Avoider solve the problem by making a decision.

Provide Support

Give Conflict Avoiders support after they make decisions. After making decisions, Conflict Avoiders often have buyer's remorse. Buyer's remorse describes the doubts and concerns that kick in after the person makes a decision. If you do not address these issues, you may discover that the Conflict Avoider revoked the decision!

📢 **If you see signs of anger or withdrawal, take your problem off the table until things cool off.**

Wet Blankets

> *"It won't work. They won't let us do that."*

When you deal with people who work in a bureaucracy, you will meet Wet Blankets. Wet Blankets respond negatively to any attempt to solve a problem. They see obstacles as impassable barriers. Wet Blankets feel disappointed, bitter, and hopeless. Their negativity is contagious.

Strategies: Dealing with Wet Blankets

When you deal with Wet Blankets, it is important to understand their sincere belief that nothing will change or improve. At some point, they were bitterly disappointed and concluded that people who have power do not care about them. They feel angry and defeated.

Don't Argue, Listen

If you get into a debate about issues, Wet Blankets dig in. They sincerely believe they are right. At some point, Wet Blankets were burned. They do not trust the system. If you listen to their complaints, you may learn about potential problems and pitfalls.

Ask Questions

Ask 5 W's + H + E questions. When you ask questions, you clarify your belief that you are dealing with problems that have solutions. You understand that there are obstacles but do not believe that the problem cannot be solved.

Snipers

Snipers are masters of the sneak attack, often delivered with a smile. If you have a run-in with a Sniper, you will feel pinned down by digs and sarcasm. Like Pit Bulls, Snipers have strong feelings about how other people should think and act. Their behavior is based on feelings of superiority and a desire to control.

Snipers get away with bad behavior because they understand that most people want to avoid scenes. The Sniper seeks revenge without responsibility. Deal with them as you do Pit Bulls.

Complainers

Complainers are irritating, exhausting and hard to ignore. They view themselves as blameless, innocent, and perfect and have strong views about how things should be. When reality does not fit their view, they believe this is someone's fault and blame others when things go wrong.

Complainers believe they are powerless. When they encounter obstacles, they believe powerful people must remove these obstacles. They complain so powerful people will pay attention, take action and solve problems.

"I've brought this to your attention. That is all I can do. Now, it is up to you."

Usually, complainers are placated, ignored or avoided. If you do not right their wrongs, Complainers feel angry and self-righteous. There is often a kernel of truth to their complaints. If you have a desire to help others, you may find yourself trapped by a Complainer.

Strategies: Dealing with Complainers

When you deal with Complainers, listen, acknowledge, and interrupt. Listen to their complaints. Acknowledge that you heard the complaints. Interrupt to set limits on their complaints. When you deal with Complainers:

- Interrupt to get control
- Sum up facts without comment or apology
- Do not agree
- Shift to problem solving
- Ask for their complaints in writing

Warning: Common Emotional Traps

When you advocate for your child, you need to be aware of common emotional traps and pitfalls:

- **Self pity.** If you find yourself asking, "Why does it have to be so hard?" or "Why can't things be different?" you are falling into the self-pity trap.
- **Resistance.** If you use passive-aggressive behavior to defeat them, you also defeat yourself.
- **Temper tantrum.** If you blow up, you prove that they were right about you!
- **Quitting.** OK, you quit. Now what?

Your Relationship with the School

Your goal is to develop a businesslike relationship with the staff at your child's school. To accomplish this goal, you need to recognize the power of school culture, myths, and misinformation.

Be careful about sharing information about your personal life or your feelings with school staff. If you share personal information, you may give ammunition to people who will blame you for your child's problems.

If you disagree with school staff, do not show your anger. If you lose your temper, you give ammunition to school personnel who look down on parents. Do not waste your time and energy getting mad or thinking about how you can get even. If you are feeling sorry for yourself or brooding about injustice, contact your support group or a special education friend.

Focus your energy in a positive direction—on solving problems. Use your emotions as a source of energy. Focus on what is important—getting an appropriate education for your child.

In Summation

In this chapter, you learned about obstacles you may encounter, including inaccurate information, myths and beliefs, and school culture. We described emotional obstacles for parents, including fear, anxiety and intimidation. You learned about the dangers of pity and helplessness.

You learned about personality styles and strategies you can use to deal with difficult people. We offered information about how to structure your relationship with the school.

In the next chapter, you will learn about conflict and why conflict between parents and schools is normal and inevitable. You will learn strategies to deal with common parent-school problems.

6 | Resolving Parent-School Conflict

"If you only have a hammer, you see every problem as a nail." —Abraham Maslow, psychologist

In this chapter, you will learn why conflict between parents and schools is normal and inevitable. We will discuss the impact that beliefs, perceptions, and interests have on conflict and identify six issues that increase parent-school conflict. You will learn about the high cost of conflict, including loss of trust, damaged relationships, and emotional and financial stress.

You will learn that your goal is to build a healthy working relationship with the school. If you build a working relationship with the school, it will be easier to negotiate for special education services and supports. This does not mean you will never have conflict!

The Nature of Parent-School Conflict

"I am so frustrated! The IEP team did not meet with us in good faith. The team members did not read the new private sector evaluations on our son. How can an IEP team make recommendations about a child's special education when they do not read the evaluations about the child?"

Conflict between parents and schools is not new. For 150 years, public schools decided who could attend school and who had to stay home. During these years, the schoolhouse doors were closed to many children with disabilities.

When Congress passed Public Law 94-142 in 1975, they knew about the tradition of excluding children with disabilities from school. For the special education law to work, this tradition had to end. Congress added procedural safeguards to the law. The purpose of procedural safeguards is to protect the rights of children and the interests of their parents.

📖 **You will learn about procedural safeguards in Section 4.**

When Congress reauthorized the Individuals with Disabilities Education Act of 2004, they focused on improving educational results and accountability. Congress found that over 30 years of research and experience demonstrated that special education would be more effective by:

"having high expectations for such children and ensuring their access to the general education curriculum in the regular classroom, to the maximum extent possible, in order to meet the developmental goals and . . . challenging expectations that have been established for all children; and be prepared to lead productive and independent adult lives, to the maximum extent possible." (Section 1400(c)(4)

The language about "access to general education curriculum in the regular classroom to meet the developmental goals and the challenging expectations that have been established for all children" is new in IDEA 2004.

Congress also expanded the purpose of the law. One purpose of IDEA 2004 is to prepare the child "for further education, employment and independent living." The words "further education" are new in IDEA 2004.

These changes clarify that the purpose of special education is to prepare children for life after school—including college and good jobs. Parents and school officials must jointly make decisions about the child's special education program. This shared responsibility makes conflict inevitable.

Beliefs, Perceptions and Interests

Conflict occurs when people have different beliefs, perceptions, and interests.

Beliefs are issues about which you feel strongly. Beliefs are based on emotions. Your beliefs affect your perceptions.

Perceptions are your thoughts about an issue or problem. When you disagree with your spouse about who is responsible for housework or how your earnings should be spent, you and your spouse have different perceptions and opinions about these issues.

Interests are your needs, desires, concerns, and fears. The strongest interests involve basic human needs—security, recognition, and control over one's life.

Conflict is not bad. Problems arise when people do not know how to handle conflict. Game-playing, vague communications, and hidden agendas happen because people are uncomfortable with conflict. Unresolved conflict carries a high price tag, from damaged relationships, betrayal, and mistrust, to financial and emotional stress.

When Interests Conflict

Assume you have a dispute with the school about your child's special education program. You ask for more help or different help. The school refuses because they believe they are providing enough help. You get angry because you believe the school is not doing enough for your child. The school personnel get angry because they believe you do not appreciate their efforts on your child's behalf.

Both sides believe they are right. These beliefs may drive you and the school to take positions based on the assumption that you are right. When you believe you are right, it is very hard to compromise.

You want the school to provide your child with a special education program that is individualized and effective. You want your child to benefit from special education. You believe the current program is damaging your child. You fear that if your child does not master basic skills, your child will not be an independent, productive adult.

What do you know about the school district's interests? What are their concerns and fears? What do they want? You know that your school district is a bureaucracy. Your school district fears change, loss of control, and loss of face.

Real Issues: Expense and Control

If you look closely at disputes between parents and schools, you will find that most disputes are actually about expense and control. Most special education disputes fall into four categories. (See Table 6-1)

Expense of Individualized Programs

Good special education services are intensive, individualized and expensive. Many parent-school disputes are actually about how to allocate scarce resources, not about the official "presenting problem."

Parents and schools have different objectives. As the parent of a child with a disability, you want your child to receive an individualized special education program that meets your child's unique needs. Individualized programs are labor-intensive and expensive.

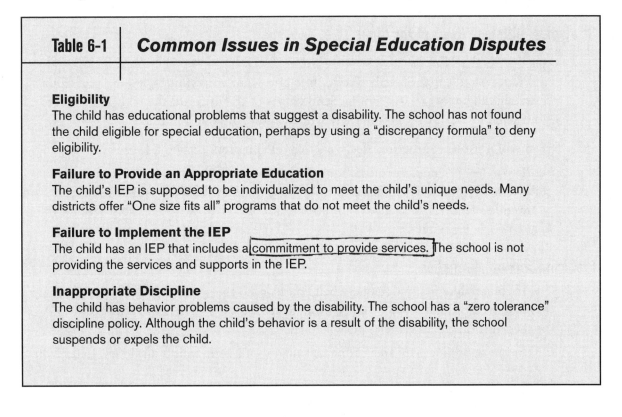

Table 6-1	*Common Issues in Special Education Disputes*

Eligibility
The child has educational problems that suggest a disability. The school has not found the child eligible for special education, perhaps by using a "discrepancy formula" to deny eligibility.

Failure to Provide an Appropriate Education
The child's IEP is supposed to be individualized to meet the child's unique needs. Many districts offer "One size fits all" programs that do not meet the child's needs.

Failure to Implement the IEP
The child has an IEP that includes a commitment to provide services. The school is not providing the services and supports in the IEP.

Inappropriate Discipline
The child has behavior problems caused by the disability. The school has a "zero tolerance" discipline policy. Although the child's behavior is a result of the disability, the school suspends or expels the child.

Loss of Control

Teachers and special education service providers are the designated education experts. When you actively advocate on your child's behalf, your assertiveness may cause some school personnel to feel threatened. When the school views a parent as a threat, school personnel often try to limit that parent's ability to advocate.

Common Parent-School Problems

Here are six common parent-school problems and strategies you can use to resolve these problems.

Problem: Different Views of the Child

"When I go to meetings, they never say anything good about my daughter."

If you are like many parents, you feel sad about the school's perception of your child. You view your child as an individual with unique qualities and abilities. When you offer information about your child's skills and interests, the school ignores, discounts, or rejects your information. If the school does not observe a skill or behavior, it does not count.

What do you appreciate about them so far?

You may believe the school must see your child as an individual before there can be agreement on the services your child needs. The school may believe you are a single-minded emotional parent who is incapable of making rational decisions about your child's educational program.

Strategies: Different Views of the Child

If you and the school have different views of your child, try to narrow the gap.

Write a letter that describes your child and what you want for your child. Your letter should be factual and polite. Send copies of this letter to the regular members of your child's team. Ask that your letter be included in your child's file.

You will learn how to write effective letters in Chapters 23 and 24.

If you feel offended by disparaging comments about your child, mention this in your letter. Explain that these comments focus on your child's weaknesses only, not on your child's abilities, strengths, aspirations, and needs. Stick to the facts. Do not try to make people feel guilty.

Problem: Lack of Information

If you are like many parents, when you learned that your child had a disability, you felt lost. You did not know what to do or where to turn. When you entered the world of special education, you felt overwhelmed.

In the beginning, you spent time learning about your child's disability. Later, you learned how the disability affects your child's learning and how your child needs to be taught. As you learned, you had more questions. You may have questions about your child's progress, special education program and placement, or the instructional methods used to educate your child.

What happens if the school cannot or will not answer your questions? What happens if your child's teacher says, "*I really shouldn't tell you this but...*" or "*You can't tell anyone I told you this but...*"

You begin to listen for evasions. You spend more time talking with the teacher who said, "*I really shouldn't tell you this but . . .*"

As you become aware of the imbalance of knowledge and information, you feel anxious and frustrated. "*They know the rules. We do not. We are at a disadvantage. How can we advocate for our children?*"

If you do not get straight answers, you will turn to people outside the system for answers. You will use the Internet, participate in online chats, and join listservs. When you get answers to your questions from outside sources, you will feel differently about the school.

After conversations with the teacher, you may realize that invisible strangers are making decisions about your child's special education program. Your perspective will change.

Strategies: Lack of Information

If you have a problem getting the school team to hear you, write a parent agenda for the next meeting. Your parent agenda should include your perceptions, your concerns and problems, and your proposed solutions. Keep your agenda short — one or two pages are usually best.

In Chapter 25, you will learn how to write and use a parent agenda.

A few days before the meeting, send your parent agenda to the team members. Assume that no one will read the agenda before the meeting. Some people will lose it; others will forget about it. Do not take offense. Bring extra copies of your parent agenda to the meeting.

When you present a written document to the school team, you make it more difficult for the team to ignore your concerns or overlook your comments. Your agenda will become part of your child's educational file. If you continue to have problems with the school, your agenda is evidence of your attempts to resolve problems.

Ask for it to go in the file

Problem: Lack of Options

If you have questions about your child's progress, placement, program, or instructional methods that the school cannot answer, you may view this as proof that something is wrong. Despite the requirement to provide your child with a program tailored to his or her unique needs, most schools do not offer many program options.

You may view this lack of options as evidence that the school does not understand your child's needs. New thoughts crowd into your mind, *"Something is wrong with the services my child is receiving."* You try to push these unwanted thoughts away.

Although school districts should involve parents in program planning, few do so. Districts that involve parents learn that parents offer fresh ideas and creative solutions. When parents are involved in planning, they are more committed to making the solutions a success.

If you express concerns about your child's program or placement, the smart school district will ask, *"What do you want for your child?"* Smart districts do not say, *"We don't do that."*

Strategies: Lack of Options

If you have a problem with limited program options, write a letter to the school team. Explain that you understand the district is supposed to provide a program that meets your child's needs. You are requesting information about all program options that are available. Advise that you need this information before you can make an informed decision about an appropriate program for your child. You appreciate their help. The tone of your letter should be polite.

Never use the word "best" or the terms "maximum potential" or "most appropriate."

Eliminate these words from your vocabulary. Ask your consultant or private sector expert not to use these terms in reports or evaluations.

By law, your child is **not entitled to the "best" program**, nor to a program that maximizes the child's potential. If you ask for the "best" program, your words will come back to haunt you. Your child is entitled to an appropriate program, no more, no less.

You will learn about the words "best" and "appropriate" in Chapters 15 and 16.

Problem: Hidden Issues

"I should not be made to feel guilty because my child needs services, or that my child's services are expensive."

The school is required to provide your child with a special education program that is tailored to your child's unique needs. By law, these services must be free – "at no cost to child's parents."

Schools act as gatekeepers. When schools provide special education services that are tailored to the unique needs of the child, the school must commit personnel and financial resources.

Assume you request an unusual or expensive program at the next IEP meeting. At the end of the meeting, you realize the team did not respond to your request. Perhaps someone changed the subject. What happened? The IEP team could not admit that they did not have the authority to approve your request.

According to the IDEA, the IEP team that includes the child's parents makes all decisions about the child's special education program and placement. In fact, if you request an unusual or expensive program, the decision is likely to be made by an administrator who does not know you or your child and did not attend the meeting.

No one will tell you this! The IEP team may pretend that you did not make a request. The team leader may suddenly cancel the meeting. The school may claim that the IEP meeting was not really an IEP meeting.

Strategies: Hidden Issues

Hidden issues cause tremendous confusion and mistrust. The simplest strategy is to put your request in writing. When you write your post-meeting thank you letter, explain that you made a request about your child's program that the team did not address. Ask for a response to your request. (To see how one parent handled this, read Jim Manners' letter in Chapter 24 about Writing Letters to the Stranger.)

Problem: Feeling Devalued

"My child's school doesn't value children with disabilities enough to help them prepare for life. Prepare them for placement in a sheltered workshop—that's enough."

Several factors make conflict between you and the school more likely:

- When you are lied to
- When important information is withheld from you
- When you are patronized
- When you sense hidden issues or agendas
- When you feel devalued

School personnel also feel devalued. Several factors make conflict with parents more likely:

- When you do not share your concerns with the school
- When you request a due process hearing without trying to work things out
- When school personnel sense that you have hidden agendas or issues
- When they feel devalued

Strategies: Feeling Devalued

You must learn how to disagree without devaluing the other side. If you feel devalued, do not react. Include a factual description of what happened in a letter or post-meeting thank you note. Express your hope that this will not happen again. *Do not discuss your feelings.* The tone of your letter should be polite.

Problem: Poor Communication and Intimidation

"The IEP team leader was rude and condescending. She monopolized the meeting, interrupted us when we tried to talk, and misstated our position."

Common parent-school communications problems include:

- Lack of follow-up
- Misunderstandings
- Intentional vagueness
- Intimidation

When schools bring large numbers of school personnel to meetings, they are usually trying to intimidate parents or prepare their witnesses for a due process hearing. When parents request a service or program and the school responds by scheduling another meeting without responding to the parents' original request, the school is trying to wear the parents out.

Strategies: Poor Communication and Intimidation

When conflict reaches this degree of intensity, the parent-school relationship is polarized. Both sides feel angry and betrayed. If your district uses bullying tactics, this ensures that you will feel betrayed and lose trust. Bullying makes conflict inevitable. There are no simple solutions to these problems.

If the school is unwilling to resolve problems, you are at a crossroads. To secure the services your child needs, you may have to engage in litigation. Litigation has significant risks. If you prevail and force the school to accept your solution, as occurred in civil rights litigation in our country, you may win a victory that takes years to implement. (Example: Massive resistance after the U. S. Supreme Court decision in *Brown v. Board of Education.*)

You are left with the option of extending an olive branch, while protecting yourself and your child and preparing for litigation. Throughout this book, you will learn how to use tactics and strategies to build healthy working relationships with school personnel. If you use these strategies, you can often cause a positive shift in your relationship with the school.

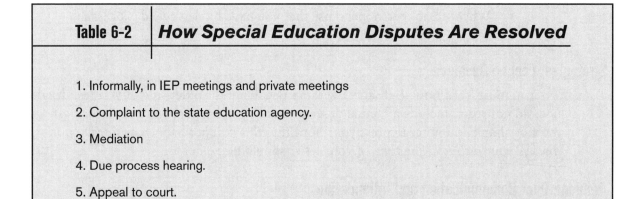

Table 6-2	*How Special Education Disputes Are Resolved*

1. Informally, in IEP meetings and private meetings

2. Complaint to the state education agency.

3. Mediation

4. Due process hearing.

5. Appeal to court.

Problem: Loss of Trust

"We know that our child was damaged by the school. We do not know how severe or enduring the damage will be. Often, our feelings of betrayal are so strong and bitter that we will never trust again."

If you lose trust, your belief that the school knows how to help your child changes to a belief that the school does not know how to help your child or does not want to help your child.

When you lose trust, you feel insecure and anxious. You may believe that your child has been damaged. Is the damage permanent? From your perspective, the people you trusted violated your trust. If you feel betrayed, or you view the school relationship as worthless, you are in crisis. In the next chapter, we will help you deal with a school crisis.

If conflict is inevitable, what can you do? Hide? Duck? Fight?

Strategies: Loss of Trust

If you discover that your spouse committed adultery, you will suffer loss of trust. You will feel betrayed. Special education disputes involve similar emotions, including loss of trust and betrayal.

In marital conflict, some relationships heal and become stronger. Other relationships terminate. The child's life may improve because the parents reconcile or because the parents divorce. The child's life may worsen after the parents reconcile because of continuing discord. The child's life may improve because the parents' relationship is healthier. How conflict affects the child depends on how adults handle the conflict.

When communication breaks down, this may lead to litigation or to improved relationships. To improve relations, the parent will have to take the first step and extend the olive branch. Yet, the parent must also anticipate that litigation may be necessary to resolve ongoing problems.

Tips to Resolve Problems

How do you resolve work schedule problems with your co-workers? You negotiate. How do you resolve financial problems with your partner? You negotiate. How do you resolve problems with your school? You negotiate.

Negotiate to Resolve Problems

When you negotiate, you put yourself in the shoes of the other side and answer questions like these:

- Perceptions: How do they see the problem?
- Interests: What do they want?

- Fears: What are they afraid will happen if they give me what I want?
- Positions: What is their bottom line?

If you have a dispute with the school, you have two goals: to resolve the issue and to protect the parent-school relationship. In parent-school disputes, emotions run high on both sides. Your emotions and the emotions of school personnel merge with the issue, leading to anger, mistrust, and bitterness. When this happens, relationships are polarized and a good outcome is less likely.

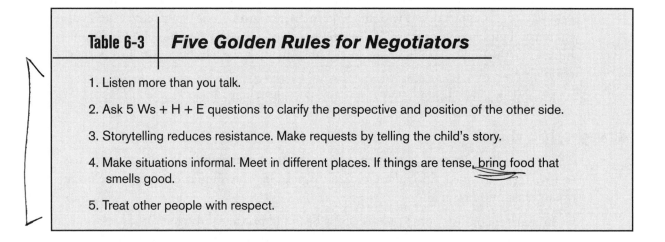

Table 6-3	*Five Golden Rules for Negotiators*

1. Listen more than you talk.

2. Ask 5 Ws + H + E questions to clarify the perspective and position of the other side.

3. Storytelling reduces resistance. Make requests by telling the child's story.

4. Make situations informal. Meet in different places. If things are tense, bring food that smells good.

5. Treat other people with respect.

If you have a problem with school personnel, remind yourself that you are dealing with people. People are emotional. When people feel emotional, it is difficult for them to think about new solutions to problems.

Never Underestimate the Importance of "Face"

Some parents initiate litigation because they want the school to admit their failures. Do not do this!

You have learned that your school district is a bureaucracy. Bureaucracies cannot admit that they did not or cannot fulfill their mission. If you confront the school with evidence that they failed, they will attempt to save face by claiming that:

- The child is really making progress. (We did not fail.)
- The child is choosing not to learn. (The child failed.)
- The child's problems are due to poor parenting. (You failed.)

Many disputes boil down to positions taken to save face. If you seek a "win-lose" solution to your dispute with you as the winner, you do not understand the importance of face. You risk losing the issue *and* destroying your relationship with the school.

☑ Try to resolve disagreements and problems early.

Table 6-4	*Four Deadly Sins for Negotiators*
1. Blaming and shaming	
2. Criticizing and finding fault	
3. Sarcasm, scorn and ridicule	
4. Judging, patronizing and bullying	

In Summation

In this chapter, you learned that parent-school conflict is normal and inevitable. We described the impact of beliefs, perceptions, and interests on conflict. We identified issues that cause conflict and provided simple strategies that you can use to resolve conflict before things get out of hand.

Your Notes Here

7 | Emergency, Crisis, Help!

"In Chinese, the word crisis is composed of two characters. One represents danger and the other represents opportunity."   —John F. Kennedy, President

In the last chapter, you learned that parent-school conflict is normal, predictable and inevitable. In this chapter, you will learn how to manage a crisis. We will describe typical parent-school crises that cause parents to seek outside help. You will learn that the crisis has two sides: danger and opportunity. We will describe how to avoid common pitfalls and will provide strategies you can use to weather a crisis.

Help! Events That Trigger Crises

Here are common events that trigger crises and requests for help from parents. The school:

- Placed the child in a less desirable program, despite objections by the parents;
- Refused to change the child's program and placement, despite recommendations from a private sector professional that the program is not appropriate;
- Refused to consider or include private sector test results and recommendations in the child's IEP;
- Refused to provide accommodations and modifications so the child failed high-stakes tests;
- Decided the child is not learning disabled but is emotionally disturbed or mentally retarded, and unilaterally changed the child's label and placement;
- Decided the child is not emotionally disturbed, but has a conduct disorder and is not eligible for special education services;
- Decided the child is not mentally retarded, but is a slow learner and is not eligible for special education services;
- Caused the child to be arrested at school and suspended or expelled the child for behavior that is related to the child's disability;
- Sent the child home because they do not have an appropriate program and do not want the child in school;

- Insisted that inclusion means all special education services must be delivered in the classroom;
- Terminated the child from special education because the child did not benefit from the only program they offer;
- Terminated the child from special education after the child's IQ scores dropped because there is no longer a severe discrepancy between the child's ability and achievement scores;
- Refused to provide necessary services because these services are expensive or would establish a precedent.

Three factors increase the chances of a crisis:

- The school makes a unilateral decision;
- The school ignores information from others, including professionals and parents;
- The decision or action may harm the child.

In a crisis, you will feel frightened, confused, guilty, angry, and helpless. Your common sense and good judgment vanish. What should you do? During a crisis, your first response is likely to be a big mistake!

Crisis Management, Step-by-Step

"It's not whether you get knocked down. It's whether you get up again."
—*Vince Lombardi, football coach*

A crisis hits! What should you do?

For the first few days, do nothing. You are feeling helpless and emotionally overwhelmed. If you believe you must do something, resist this urge!

Do you start a fight when you have no ammunition? No! Do you start a fight before you know where the high ground is? No! You do not start a fight until you have a good chance of prevailing.

Short-Term Solutions

Think. Regroup. Analyze the issues. Gather information. Locate the high ground. Think about how to solve the problem. Plan a strategy so you can take the hill and prevail, without firing a shot.

Use your energy to prepare. Focus on short-term solutions and long-range planning. In a crisis, you need to:

- Control your emotions.
- Remove your child from the middle.
- Make long-range plans.

Control Your Emotions

Keep your emotions under control! Do not obsess about unfairness. If you allow yourself to obsess about unfairness or revenge, you will make mistakes.

Be careful about revealing your feelings to school personnel. If you share your feelings, the school will perceive you as emotional and vulnerable. If you discuss your personal problems, you are likely to appear to be more problem-ridden than you are.

Spend your time and energy thinking, planning, and preparing. When you prepare, it is more difficult to make mistakes. Put your emotions in your backpack. Use your emotions as a source of energy to keep you moving, step-by-step, to high ground.

Remove Your Child from the Middle

Children who are embroiled in battles between their parents and their school are similar to children in custody battles. As they travel back and forth between the two sides, they are in the middle.

Many children assume that parent-school problems are their fault. You may explain the situation to your child but you should not allow or encourage the child to take sides.

Long-Term Planning

A crisis is an opportunity. The crisis forces you to face reality. You realize that you must take steps to change your child's educational situation. You need to do long-term planning.

Begin a Program of Self-Study

You need to learn about the law, your child's disability, how your child learns, and how your child should be taught. Where do you begin? Join one or two special education organizations for one year. Immerse yourself in information about disabilities, educational remediation techniques, legal rights and responsibilities, and tactics and strategies.

For information and resources about education of children with disabilities, visit NICHCY at www.nichcy.org/

For websites for disabilities organizations and information groups, visit the Yellow Pages for Kids site at www.yellowpagesforkids.com/

Join a Support Group

Get help from other parents. Look for a support group or advocacy group in your community. Members of the group will provide information, recommend experts, offer support, and alleviate the sinking feeling that you are fighting this battle alone.

For advice about how to find a support group, read Chapter 2.

Learn About Legal Rights and Responsibilities

You need to learn about your legal rights and responsibilities. Read and re-read the Individuals with Disabilities Education Act (IDEA). Use a highlighter. Attach sticky notes on those pages that relate to your child's situation.

There are dozens of good legal research sites on the Internet.

FindLaw is an encyclopedic law site. http://www.findlaw.com/

Versuslaw offers full-text access to appellate state and federal decisions, including decisions from the U. S. Supreme Court. http://www.versuslaw.com/

Wrightslaw at www.wrightslaw.com has a wealth of information about special education law and advocacy.

Learn About Special Education

You need accurate information about your child's disability and appropriate educational techniques. When you use the Internet, you can find answers to many of your questions.

Visit wrightslaw.com, fetaweb.com, nichcy.org, ncd.gov, and ldonline.org for information.

Get Advocacy Information From Your State

Contact the Special Education Division of your **State Department of Education**. Ask for a copy of your state special education laws, regulations, and guidelines. Request all material about special education, IEPs, and Section 504 programs. Visit the site maintained by your state department of education.

For contact information for your state Department of Education, check your state page at the Yellow Pages for Kids with Disabilities at www.yellowpagesforkids.com

Your state has an independently operated and funded **Protection and Advocacy Office**. Protection and Advocacy Offices are not associated or affiliated with state Departments of Education. Request the publications about special education, IEPs, and parent rights and responsibilities from your state P & A office.

The National Protection and Advocay site is at www.napas.org

Contact your state **Parent Information and Training Center**.

For a list of your state Parent Information and Training Centers with contact information, go to the Yellow Pages for Kids at www.yellowpagesforkids.com

Request Your Child's Records

Request a complete copy of your child's cumulative and confidential files from your child's school and from the administrative office where the special education department is located. Request a copy of your child's records from all agencies and individuals that may have information about your child.

For a list of state Parent Information and Training Centers with contact information, visit the Yellow Pages for Kids with Disabilities site at www.yellowpagesforkids.com

Get a Comprehensive Evaluation

Get a comprehensive evaluation of your child from an independent expert in the private sector. The purpose of this evaluation is to identify your child's problems and develop a plan to address these problems. Before you can make wise decisions about your child's special education program, you need accurate diagnostic information about the child's disability, strengths, weaknesses, and needs.

At this point, many parents say . . .

"But the school is supposed to test my child . . ."

"I want an independent evaluation and I want them to pay for it!"

If the school arranges and pays for an independent evaluation, you should expect this evaluation to support the school's position. You need accurate diagnostic information about your child's problems from an evaluator who is independent of the school district. With this information, you will be able to develop solutions to problems.

You are likely to have to pay for this evaluation. View the evaluation as an investment in your child's future. A comprehensive evaluation will give you a roadmap for the future.

☑ **Many universities have child development clinics and education and psychology departments that will evaluate your child at low or no cost.**

Examine Your Beliefs

Examine your beliefs about your child and your child's disability. Do you feel sorry for your child? Do you feel guilty about your child's problems? When you tried to protect your child from painful experiences, did you become over-protective? Will pity, guilt, and over-protectiveness help your child grow up into an emotionally healthy adult?

If your child has a disability, your child learns differently. Your child must be taught differently. When your child is taught correctly, your child can and will learn. Conditions that are disabilities in large classroom environments often have powerful, corresponding strengths. When the child learns to channel these qualities, they can be assets.

In Summation

In this chapter, you learned how to manage a crisis with the school. We described events that trigger school crises. You learned crisis management techniques, including the need to control your emotions, remove your child from the middle, and begin a program of self-study. You learned about the steps you should take in long-term planning.

Section 3 is "The Parent as Expert." In this Section, you will learn about tests and evaluations, how to organize your child's file, what test data means, how to measure educational progress, and SMART IEPs.

Your Notes Here

Section Three

The Parent as Expert

As a parent, you negotiate with the school on your child's behalf. To be an effective negotiator, you need to be an expert about your child. You need to know about:

- Your child's disability
- Your child's educational needs
- Your child's educational progress

In Chapter 8, "Evaluations and Your Child's Disability," you will learn about comprehensive evaluations. We explain the limitations of testing by the school. We provide strategies you can use to learn about your child's disability and effective educational practices.

Chapter 9 is "The File: Do It Right!" In this chapter, you will learn how to organize your child's file. The process of organizing your child's file will help you understand your child's disability and educational history. When your child's file is organized, you will be prepared for the next school meeting.

In Chapter 10, "Understanding Tests and Measurements 101," you will learn how to use the bell curve to measure educational progress. In this chapter, you will learn about percentile ranks and standard scores, composite scores, and subtest scatter. You will learn that tests do not always measure what they appear to measure, and not all tests measure reading, writing, and math skills comprehensively.

Chapter 11, "Understanding Tests and Measurements 102," will teach you how to use pre- and post-tests to measure your child's progress. You will learn about norm referenced and criterion referenced tests, standard deviations, and standard scores. You will learn how to convert standard scores into percentile ranks, and percentile ranks into standard scores.

You will learn about the Wechsler Intelligence Scale for Children (WISC-IV) and many other tests that are used with children, how to chart your child's test scores, and how to create progress graphs.

Chapter 12 teaches you about SMART IEPs that are specific, measurable, use action words, are realistic, and time-limited.

You will learn about significant changes in IDEA 2004 that require IEPs to include a statement of the child's present levels of academic achievement and functional performance, including how the child's disability affects the child's involvement and progress in the general education curriculum, and a statement of measurable annual goals, including academic and functional goals.

You will learn how to use present levels of performance to write measurable goals and objectives about what your child will learn and be able to do.

8 Evaluations and Your Child's Disability

"Parents have become so convinced that educators know what is best for children that they forget that they are the experts." —Marian Wright Edelman, educator

In this chapter, you will learn about the comprehensive evaluation and how to use information from the evaluation to design an appropriate educational program. You will learn how to do research about your child's disability, educational needs, and your legal rights and responsibilities.

Help! My son has dyslexia. He can barely read and write. The school will not put anything in his IEP about teaching him how to read and write. What can I do?

Help! My daughter has a cochlear implant. She can listen and speak. The school placed her in a class with deaf children where they are teaching her sign language and lip reading. What can I do?

Help! The school took my son out of special education. He is failing. When I asked them to put him back in special education, they said he does not qualify. What can I do?

Many parents feel powerless in their dealings with their school. Although you may feel powerless, *you are not powerless*. The best antidote to helplessness is information. Knowledge is power!

Get a Comprehensive Evaluation

Until you know where you are and where you need to go, you cannot develop a master plan. A useful master plan for your child's special education uses information about your child's present levels of functioning. When you have accurate information, you can develop realistic goals and objectives.

Base your master plan on a comprehensive evaluation of your child by an expert or experts who are independent of your school district. You cannot always rely on the school district to do a quality evaluation of your child.

Finding Evaluators

You want to find an evaluator who is knowledgeable about your child's disability. Evaluators work in the private sector, in university medical centers, children's hospitals, and child development centers. To find an evaluator, contact advocacy groups organizations and private special education schools. Ask other parents for recommendations.

📖 **For information about finding and working with consultants or evaluators, review Chapter 2.**

You want to establish a good working relationship with the evaluator or consultant. If possible, interview two or three individuals. When you schedule an appointment to meet with an evaluator, explain that you are looking for an independent professional who can evaluate your child, help you design an appropriate educational program for your child, and monitor your child's progress in the program. If possible, look for an evaluator who can work with you and your child for several years.

Understanding Test Results

If you are like many parents, when you read an evaluation, you feel confused. Ask the evaluator to give you all scores as standard scores, percentile ranks, grade equivalents and age equivalents. Schedule a follow-up appointment in a week or two.

Make two or three extra copies of the evaluation. File the original report in your child's Master File. Use a copy as you study. Read the evaluation several times. Make margin notes. Use a highlighter on your copy. Do not write on or mark the original document. As you read and re-read the evaluation, make a list of questions you have about the test results and what the test scores mean.

When you return for the follow-up session, bring this list of questions. Ask the evaluator to explain the test data and help you understand the educational implications of the data. For example:

Does the data explain your child's difficulties in the classroom?

Does the data explain your child's difficulty learning new skills?

What does the data tell you about educational approach that should be used to teach your child?

If you are like many parents, school personnel may have told you that you cannot expect your child to make progress because your child has a disability. In most cases, this is simply not true. If a special needs child receives intensive, individualized instruction, the child may make more than one year of progress in an academic year. When this happens, the child is "closing the gap."

what wouldthegoalbe?

next yr

what is the issue identified?

how is it impacting her learning?

what is the appropriate remediation strategy?
- accom
- mod.
- services
→ eqt

next week

private speech eval!

attentional issue
sensory issue
social issue

Speech + OT evals

Your child may need intensive, individualized instruction to acquire skills. Think about Helen Keller. Helen Keller was blind and deaf. What happens to children with multiple handicaps who are enrolled in special education programs? Helen Keller was fortunate. Her teacher was Anne Sullivan. Anne Sullivan used intensive, individualized direct instruction techniques to teach Helen Keller the skills she needed to be an independent, self-sufficient adult.

Ask the evaluator to help you design a plan for your child's special education. Where should you start? Of the problems identified in the evaluation, what problems are most important? What needs should be addressed first? Does the child have communication problems that are affecting the child's ability to acquire other skills? Should the child's communication problems be addressed first?

Does the child have deficiencies in social skills? Is the child's inability to relate to others a primary deficit? Does the child have psychological problems that are causing social problems? Does the child have psychological problems because her educational skills are not being remediated?

What skills should be addressed now? What skills can wait? What skills may improve after the child receives remediation in basic reading, writing, arithmetic and spelling skills? The only way to answer these questions is by a comprehensive evaluation.

How do you translate test results into a master educational plan? What is your child's most important educational need? What specific educational services does the child need now? How often should the child receive these services?

Assume your eight year-old-son has autism. The evaluator identifies speech and language problems as your child's most important need. What services does he need now? How frequently? In what setting? Does he need a 20-minute group speech session once a week? Does he need 30 minutes of one-on-one speech therapy three times a week? Does the evaluator recommend a particular technique?

Assume your daughter is in sixth grade. Her reading skills are at the second grade level. The evaluator identifies her most important need as the acquisition of reading skills. What type of remediation program does she need to bring her reading skills up to the level of her peers?

Assume the evaluator recommends this as an appropriate goal for your daughter:

In one academic year, the child's reading skills will increase by two years, from the second grade level to the fourth grade level, with progress measured twice a year on an individual standardized test.

To meet this goal, the child requires one-on-one remediation 60 minutes a day from a teacher who is specially trained in the remediation of children who have severe reading disabilities.

If your child meets this goal, you will use new data to update your child's performance levels. You will revise the goal so the child's skills continue to improve as measured by test data.

Limitations of School Evaluations

Assume your child was evaluated by the school district. You cannot rely on school testing to design your master plan.

According to a report from The Council of Exceptional Children, teachers say that school evaluations do not provide the information they need to design instruction, including information about children's achievement, learning styles and learning patterns. (Check the Bibliography for the citation of this report)

In some cases, school assessments were too narrow to provide an accurate picture of the child's abilities. In other cases, teachers received computer score sheets of composite intelligence and achievement test scores that were useless in designing instruction.

Your independent evaluator should conduct a comprehensive evaluation, including intelligence and educational achievement testing. The evaluator should observe your child's responses and do additional testing to identify specific areas of weakness. If possible, the independent evaluator should observe the child in the classroom. The child should be evaluated in all areas that affect learning (i.e., hearing, physical therapy, speech-language therapy, occupational therapy, academic skills remediation).

After the comprehensive evaluation is completed, you may need help to translate the test results and data into an appropriate educational program for your child. Many parents work with an educational consultant who is trained to design special education programs.

See Chapter 2 for information about educational consultants.

Learn About the Disability

If you followed the suggestions at the end of Chapter 1, you purchased two large 3-ring notebooks. Use one notebook for your child's Master File. Use the other notebook for information about your child's disability, educational techniques, and advocacy information.

Learn from Organizations

As you gather information, begin with organizations that deal with your child's disability. Appendix F is a comprehensive list of organizations, associations and clearinghouses.

For links to organizations, visit the Yellow Pages for Kids with Disabilities at www.yellowpagesforkids.com

Learn from the Treatment Team

Get information about your child's disability from your child's doctor, psychologist, and other members of the treatment team. Ask for patient information pamphlets and recommended reading. Members of your child's treatment team should be able to answer questions about your child and can be an excellent resource.

Learn from School Personnel

You may learn about your child's needs from school personnel. Although some school personnel may not be willing to help, most knowledgeable educators will help you understand your child's educational needs.

When you take these steps—join a special education organization, do research, get information from your child's treatment team and special educators, you will soon be knowledgeable about your child's disability and needs.

Although the Internet can be a great resource, some web sites and listserv posts contain inaccurate information and bad advice that encourages acrimony between parents and schools.

Learn About Effective Educational Practices

To gather information about how your child learns, read books and articles, get information from special education associations, your child's doctor and treatment team, and special education professionals. Use the Internet to find answers to questions.

In Summation

Lack of accurate information is a big obstacle for most parents. When you follow the steps in this chapter, you will learn about your child's disability and effective special education practices. You are becoming an expert.

As you gather and organize the information about your child into a master file, you may be surprised at what you learn. We guarantee that organizing your child's file will give you a new perspective about your child's disability and educational history. In the next chapter, you will learn how to organize your child's file the right way!

Your Notes Here

9 | The File: Do It Right!

"Do the hard jobs first. The easy jobs will take care of themselves."
— Dale Carnegie, motivational speaker

As the parent of a child with a disability, you know the special education system generates mountains of paper. Some information is important so you are afraid to throw anything away. The mountain of paper grows higher every year. What do you do with it? How do you organize this information?

You need a simple, foolproof document management system. In this chapter, you will learn how to organize your child's file. After you organize the information about your child into a file, you will have a clearer understanding of your child's disability and educational needs.

Document Management System

Think about the last school meeting. Did the IEP team members have a complete copy of your child's file? Did you have a complete copy of your child's file? How can the IEP team make decisions about your child's special education program if they do not have complete, accurate information about your child?

Schools keep records in different places. Information and reports are misplaced. When you organize your child's file, you will have all the information about your child in one place. With our document management system, you can track your child's educational history. When you use this parent-tested system, you can quickly locate any document in your child's file.

When you take your organized file to the next school meeting, you will understand the power of getting organized. You will gain a sense of control.

Gather Information About Your Child

Follow these steps to get information about your child.

Make a Master Provider List

Make a list of all individuals and agencies that may have information or records about your child. Your list should include the names and titles of all professionals who have provided medical or mental health treatment services, including doctors, therapists, and other health care providers. Include their addresses, telephone and fax numbers, and email addresses. Maintain your list by category of service rendered, e.g., medical, educational, psychological evaluations.

Request Your Child's Records

Send a letter to the individuals and agencies on your list and request a copy of your child's records. Explain that your request relates to a school issue and the need to secure an appropriate education for your child. Ask if you should expect to pay a photocopying fee and what this fee will be. Your letters should be neat and convey a professional image.

See Chapter 23 for sample letters to request information and records.

If you do not receive a response within ten days, send a short letter explaining that you requested information ten days ago and have not received a response. Attach a copy of your original letter to the second request letter. Ask if you can do anything to expedite the request. Offer to visit the office to help copy the information. Be polite. Appendix I includes a sample second request for information letter.

☑ **Make photocopies of all letters for your file.**

Request Your Child's Educational Records

Write a letter to the school and request a complete copy of your child's entire cumulative file and confidential file, omitting nothing. You want copies of all evaluations, records, correspondence, and other documents the school has about your child. Use a word processor for your letter. Expect to pay a reasonable photocopying fee.

See the sample letters at the end of Chapters 23 and 24.

Send one letter to the principal of your child's school and one letter to the director of special education. If you do not know the director's name and address, call the main office of the school district and request this information. If your child does not attend a public school, send the letter to the principal of the last public school your child attended.

Before you mail these letters, sign them and make copies of the signed letters for your Master File. Log the letters into your contact log.

Organize the Master File

You will organize and file all information about your child in three-ring notebooks. Gather all documents that relate to your child. Bring all paper in boxes, file folders, and bags together in one place. Begin by organizing the documents by year.

request copies of report + progress cards since Kindergarten

☑ Do not skip this section, even if you have organized your child's file.

Step 1: Date All Documents

With a pencil, lightly write the date of each document in the lower right corner of the first page (Example: 11/09/05).

☑ **Use a soft lead pencil when you date the documents. You may need to erase your notations later.**

Before long, mail will roll in from your requests. Using a pencil, lightly date each document in the lower right hand corner. Date everything - evaluations, reports, correspondence, report cards, and medical reports.

When you find duplicate documents, compare the duplicates, decide which document has the best photocopy quality, and use this as your master. Put the duplicates in a box. You will not need them for your notebook. Do not throw them away. You may need to provide copies to other people later.

☑ **Do not write on original documents. You may need copies of these documents later.**

Work samples provide useful information about your child's skills. Include a few samples of your child's schoolwork.

Many parents say that when they organize documents, they begin to read and are sidetracked. Force yourself to stick with this job until you finish. Do not stop to read the documents. Just date and organize! Lightly pencil the date on the bottom right corner of the first page.

Step 2: File All Documents in a Three-Ring Notebook

Hole-punch, then file all dated documents in a large three-ring notebook. When you hole-punch, be careful that you do not destroy important signatures or dates. When documents are formatted horizontally, hole-punch on the top edge.

File all documents in chronological order, oldest document on top and newest document at the end. Some parents use the child's birth certificate as the first document in the file. The last document is the most recent piece of information. This may be a report card, IEP, or letter from the school.

☑ **Do not put documents in clear plastic envelopes. If you are in a meeting and need to find a document in the file, removing documents from plastic envelopes takes too long.**

Do not file documents by category (i.e., IEPs, psychological evaluations, correspondence, etc.). If you file documents by category, your system will fail. Assume you have a comprehensive letter written by a child psychologist three years ago. The Eligibility Committee and the IEP team used the psychologist's letter. Is this document a letter? A report? An evaluation?

Trying to figure out categories is confusing and time-consuming. If your system is confusing and difficult, it will fail. Use our parent-tested system. You have better things to do with your time!

Step 3: Read the Master File for the "Big Picture"

After you complete Step 2, read your child's Master File from beginning to end. When you read the information chronologically, you will see the big picture.

At the beginning of this chapter, we mentioned the mountains of paper generated by the special education system. After reports are written, they are filed away. Few people will read or review this information again. Because there is no master plan, no one looks at the big picture.

Instead of looking at the forest, parents and school staff focus on the bark of the trees. When you organize your child's file, you will see the forest, perhaps for the first time. You will understand. Many parents say that making a neat, organized, chronological Master File is a powerful educational experience.

Table 9-1	*Four Rules for Organizing the File*

1. Do not write on your original documents.

2. Do not use a marker or highlighter on your original documents.

3. Do not release your original documents to anyone.

4. Keep your notebook current.

Create Your List of Documents

You have dated the documents and filed them in chronological order, oldest document on top, most recent on the bottom. Now you need to create your Master Document List. When you organize documents chronologically and generate your Master Document List, you can compress your child's history into a few pages. You can locate any document in seconds.

☑ **If you want to make a note on a document in your Master File, write on a sticky note that you attach to the document.**

To create your Master Document List, make a table with four columns. If you are using a word processing program, insert a four-column table. If you are not using a computer, draw a table with four columns on several sheets of paper. Label the columns: Date, Author, Type, and Significance. (Table 9-2 shows you how to format your list)

Enter each document by date, author, and type. Leave the Significance column blank. Attach sticky notes to all pages in your Master File that have test scores (i.e., the Wechsler Intelligence Test or the Woodcock Johnson Tests.)

Table 9-2	Format for Master Document List		
Date	**Author**	**Type**	**Significance**

☑ **If you use a word processing program, the program can sort the list by date, author, or type of document.**

When you use a word processing program, you can change the font to highlight test data and other important information. You make it easier to find important information. To see how a Master Document List looks, look at Table 9-3.

☞ Download a Master Document List from the Fetaweb site: www.fetaweb.com/

When you organize your child's file, you will learn about your child's disability and educational history. This is an important step in becoming an expert. When you finish this job, you will have a clearer understanding of your child's educational needs.

You do not need to complete the "Significance" column yet. When you learn more about evaluations and test scores, you will recognize what information is important in documents and records.

Table 9-3	Sample Master Document List		
Date	Author	Type	Significance
7/16/05	Cannon	Psychological Evaluation	School evaluation. **WISC-IV IQ** above avg. **WJ-R**: Reading, writing skills 3 years delayed.
8/23/05	Center Elementary School	IEP	Placed in resource program. Progress will be 80% on teacher made tests and observations.
5/14/06	Collins	Educational Evaluation	School evaluation with **WJ-R, TOWL, K-ABC**. No gain in reading and writing skills. Percentile ranks dropped.
6/6/06	Center Elementary School	Report Card	B's in Reading and Writing. Promoted to next grade.
9/10/06	Stein	Psychiatric Evaluation	**Severely depressed**. Anti-depressant meds increased. MD recommends psychiatric hospitalizaton.
10/14/06	Barton	Educational Eval	Private sector evaluation. **WRMT-R & GORT-4**. Child illiterate; requires 1:1 direct instruction.
11/5/06	Stein	Discharge Summary	Severe depression from school failure, poor academic skills; needs 1:1 remediation.

In Summation

In this chapter, you learned how to organize your child's file. The process of organizing this information helps you understand your child's disability, history, and educational needs. You created a Master Document List that will enable you to find a specific document quickly and easily.

To be an expert, you need to learn how to identify your child's needs and how to measure your child's educational progress. This information is in your child's test scores. It is time to learn about tests and measurements.

10 | Tests and Measurements 101

> "If something exists, it exists in some amount. If it exists in some amount, it is capable of being measured."   — Descartes, philosopher

To be a successful advocate, you must learn about tests and measurements—statistics. Statistics allow you to measure your child's progress or lack of progress (regression) using numbers.

In this chapter, you will learn how to use statistics to measure change. You will learn about the bell curve and how to use the bell curve to measure educational progress. You will learn about percentile ranks and standard scores, composite scores, and subtest scatter.

Mike

Assume you have an eleven-year-old child who is in the sixth grade. In third grade, Mike was found eligible for special education services as a child with a specific learning disability. He has not made much progress in reading, spelling, or writing since he entered special education three years ago. Mike is angry and depressed and says, "I hate school."

You are afraid. What if Mike never masters the basic academic skills? What kind of future will he have?

At the next IEP meeting, you share your concerns about Mike's lack of progress. You want the school to provide a different program. The IEP team disagrees. One member says Mike is getting all the help he needs. Another member says your expectations are too high. The psychologist says if you do not accept Mike's limitations, you will damage him.

The IEP team offers accommodations and modifications for his special education program. They want to reduce his assignments and give him "talking books." They do not propose to teach Mike to read, write, spell, and do math. You know what is happening. The IEP team is lowering the bar.

What can you do? How can you get the IEP team to listen? How can you persuade the IEP team to develop a different educational program for Mike? You need to learn what Mike's test scores mean and how to chart these scores.

Before you can develop an appropriate special education program, you must understand your child's strengths and weaknesses. When you understand your child's test scores, you can use a computer or graph paper to create progress or regression graphs.

The principles of tests and measurements are not difficult to learn. You use statistics in many areas of life. When you read these two chapters, you will discover that you already know many of these concepts.

Pollsters use statistics to measure attitudes and preferences. Reporters use statistics to measure change or lack of change. If you read articles about economic and social changes, politics, or the weather, you are reading about statistics.

Plan to read these two chapters about tests and measurements several times. When you study, make notes. You will encounter some terms and concepts that are new to you — standard deviations, standard scores, grade equivalents, and age equivalents. You are likely to be familiar with other terms like percentiles and averages.

When you master this information, you will understand your child's test scores. You will be able to use information from objective tests to make decisions about your child's special education program. You may find that your expertise exceeds that of many special education team members. You will have the tools you need to change your child's life. When you go to the next school meeting, you will be glad you did your homework!

You will be able to answer questions like these:

• How is your child functioning, compared with other children the same age?

• How is your child functioning, compared with others in the same grade?

• How much educational progress has your child made since the child was last tested?

• If your child receives special education, has your child progressed or regressed in the special education program?

• If your child's age and grade equivalent test scores have increased, has your child made progress when compared to the peer group?

When you learn about tests and measurements, you will be able to compare test results and measure your child's progress.

Measuring Growth: Rulers, Yardsticks, and Other Tools

How do you measure your child's physical growth? You measure growth with a measuring tape and scales. You measure how much the child's height increases in inches, and how much the child's weight increases in pounds over a period of months and years.

You use simple tools to monitor your child's physical growth. Even if we present this information in millimeters and kilograms, you know that when your child's height and weight increase, your child is growing. With a table or formula, you can easily convert this information into inches and pounds.

Assume that one year ago, your child was five feet, three inches tall. One year later, your child is five feet, six inches tall. There are several ways you can report this information. You can say that your child was sixty-three inches tall one year ago, and is now sixty-six inches tall. You can say that your child was 5.25 feet tall and is now 5.5 feet tall. You can say that one year ago, your child was 160 centimeters tall and is now 168 centimeters tall. You can even say that one year ago, your child was 1.75 yards tall, and is now 1.83 yards tall!

If you measure your child at regular intervals, you can create a chart or graph that tracks changes in your child's height and weight. You can use growth charts at the doctor's office to compare your child's growth with the growth of the average child.

Measuring Educational Change: Test Scores

Your child's educational growth can be measured and charted in a similar fashion. Although the tools you use to measure educational growth are different, the principles are the same. How do you measure educational growth and change? Instead of a tape measure and a set of scales, you use psychological and educational achievement test scores.

You can begin with the standardized educational achievement tests that school districts administer to students. Although standardized educational achievement tests are general measures, they provide useful information. Standardized educational tests are similar to medical screening tests. Standardized tests may suggest that the child has a problem, and that additional individual testing should be completed to diagnose the child's problem and develop a treatment plan.

The process of identifying a child's disability unfolds in a similar manner. Schools are required to use a variety of individually administered tests to determine if the child has a disability and if the disability adversely affects educational performance. The child is usually evaluated by two or more individuals (e.g., a school psychologist, educational diagnostician, speech-language evaluator, occupational therapist, etc.).

Learning About Evaluations

As a parent, you need answers to questions about your child's disability and educational needs. How does your child's disability affect learning? What specific areas are affected? How serious are your child's problems? What are your child's strengths and weaknesses?

Does your child need special education? What academic skills need to be remediated? How will you know if your child is making progress? How much progress is sufficient? You will find answers to these questions in the tests and evaluations administered to your child.

Overcoming Fears

"I'm just a parent. I did not finish college. The people who tested my kid went to school for years. I can't understand this stuff!"

Some parents believe they cannot understand test results. If you believe you cannot understand tests, it is time to change your beliefs.

Perhaps you are reading this book because your child is performing poorly in school or has been identified with learning problems. Perhaps your child believes that he or she cannot learn to read, write, spell, or do arithmetic. Your child needs to overcome these beliefs. So do you!

Learning What Tests Measure

There are two important realities in testing. Tests do not always measure what they appear to measure, and not all tests measure reading, writing, and math skills comprehensively.

Reading comprehension, for example, is a complex entity. Although we may think of it as a single skill or a single subtest score, students with poor reading comprehension may struggle with a variety of deficits. Some children may not understand as well when they read silently as when they read aloud. Some children may have difficulty understanding what they have read because they work too hard at word recognition. Other students may have gaps in their phonics skills and may not recognize words with accuracy. It is important to understand exactly what the child's weaknesses are before designing an effective remedial program.

Learning About Reading Tests

There is no one reading test that measures reading skills comprehensively. Different reading tests measure different types of reading skills. Some tests that measure different skills in reading are briefly described below.

The *Woodcock Reading Mastery Test – Revised (WRMT-R)* is a commonly used educational achievement test. The WRMT-R has two forms and includes several subtests.

Letter Identification. Children are required to name a random selection of upper and lower case letters that are written in a variety of fonts.

Word Identification. Children are required to read words in a list format aloud. They have five seconds to identify each word before they are prompted to move on to the next word.

Nonsense Words. Children are required to read words that are not real. Nonsense words allow the evaluator to determine how the child recognizes words without using compensatory strategies (i.e., looking at pictures, guessing based upon context, or reading words by sight). Children have five seconds to respond before they are prompted for a response, and then moved on to the next word.

Word Comprehension. This subtest has three sections: antonyms (word opposites), synonyms (words with the same meaning), and analogies (up is to down as slow is to fast). Children have fifteen seconds before they are prompted for a response, and then moved on to the next item. Children who have weaknesses in word finding or word retrieval may have difficulty with this task.

Passage Comprehension. Children are required to read passages to themselves, then fill in the blanks to demonstrate their understanding. This type of reading comprehension test can be challenging for children with expressive language disorders. The fill-in-the-blank format requires a precise understanding of sentence structure and grammar, and the ability to retrieve the exact word needed. Children have approximately thirty seconds after reading the passage to respond.

The *Gray Oral Reading Tests, Fourth Edition (GORT-4)* measures oral reading rate, accuracy, and comprehension. Information about rate and accuracy is important because children who read slowly take longer to complete assignments and understand and remember less of what they have read.

On the GORT-4, after the child reads a series of passages aloud, the child's oral reading is scored for rate and accuracy. After reading each passage, the child is asked to answer multiple choice questions that are read by the examiner.

Children may do poorly or well for a variety of reasons. For children with expressive language challenges, multiple choice questions may permit them to express what they know more easily. Children who have weak memories may have difficulty holding the choices (A,B,C, or D) in memory for consideration. Some children can answer questions correctly by relying on their verbal thinking skills, not on what they actually understood by reading.

The *Kaufman Test of Educational Achievement, Second Edition (KTEA-2)* is another achievement battery that measures some, but not all, of the important skills in reading. The reading subtests include the following:

Letter & Word Recognition. Children are required to identify letters and words in list format. There is no time limit.

Nonsense Word Decoding. Children are required to identify nonsense words. There is no time limit.

Reading Comprehension. Children read passages aloud or silently, then answer multiple choice questions and open ended questions that they must read for themselves. Open ended questions are scored on the basis of content, not on form, sentence structure, or grammar. There are no time limits.

Decoding Fluency. Children are asked to read nonsense words while being timed.

Word Recognition Fluency. Children are asked to read real words while being timed.

You can see from these three tests that there is considerable variation from one reading test to another. You need to know what tests measure and how tests are administered. You also need to know that the testing has addressed all related concerns and weaknesses.

Learning About Comprehensive Evaluations

Reading

Comprehensive evaluations in reading should include measures of phonological awareness and rapid naming, word recognition, nonsense words, fluency, silent reading comprehension, and oral reading comprehension. The evaluator often examines the child's receptive language skills, such as vocabulary, and listening comprehension. The same weaknesses in oral language will also affect language in print.

Writing

Comprehensive evaluations in writing should include measures of handwriting and/or keyboarding, spelling, the ability to formulate sentences, writing fluency, paragraph writing, and the ability to plan and organize a story or an essay. Evaluators may also examine oral language skills. The same deficits that compromise expressive language will also affect the ability to express thoughts in writing.

Mathematics

Comprehensive evaluations in math should include an inventory of all pertinent computational skills, number formation for younger students, math related vocabulary, computational fluency, and math reasoning.

Statistics 101

When you learn a new subject, you must also learn new words and concepts. At first, these terms and concepts may be confusing. Be patient. These terms will soon be familiar to you.

You Use Statistics to Measure and Describe Relationships

You use statistics to measure things and describe relationships between things, using numbers. Let's look at a simple topic that is familiar to many people – your car's gas consumption.

When you describe your car's gas mileage, you can make any of the following statements:

- My gas tank is half full
- My gas tank is half empty
- My tank is at the fifty percent mark
- I have used eight gallons
- I have eight gallons left in my tank
- My odometer shows that I will need to fill the tank in 150 miles
- My odometer shows that I've traveled 150 miles since I last filled the tank

Each of these statements accurately describes your car's gas consumption.

You Use Statistics to Make Decisions

When should you fill your gas tank? You know your gas tank holds sixteen gallons of gas. Your gas gauge shows that the tank is less than half full. You have been driving in the city. You will be driving on the highway for the rest of the day. You have used an exact amount of gas. An exact amount of gas remains in your tank.

There are several ways to describe this—gallons used, gallons remaining, miles driven, miles to go, percentage left, and so forth. With this information, you calculate that your car averages between seventeen and twenty-three miles to a gallon of gas, depending on driving conditions.

You Use Statistics to Measure Change

Using this data, you can also measure change. If you compare your car's present mileage to the mileage you obtained before a tune-up, you can measure miles per gallon before and after the tune-up. You can measure the impact of the tune-up on your car's gas consumption.

Let's look at another way that we use tests and measurements. Assume you went to the doctor a few months ago because you were feeling weak and tired. Your doctor asked questions about your symptoms and ordered some lab tests. After reviewing your test results, the doctor explained that your blood glucose level was moderately elevated. To reduce your blood glucose level, the doctor developed a treatment plan that included changes in your diet and a daily program of exercise.

After one month, you returned for a follow-up visit. The doctor ordered another round of lab tests. If your blood glucose level had returned to normal, you probably did not require additional treatment. If your blood glucose level remained elevated, you may need treatment that is more intensive. When you use objective tests to measure change after an intervention, you and your doctor can make rational decisions about your health.

You can use statistics to compute your car's gas consumption, make medical decisions, and measure your child's growth. You can also use statistics to measure educational progress. When you measure educational growth or progress, as when you measure gas consumption or glucose levels, you can report the same information in different ways.

Because educational test results are reported in different formats and compared in different ways, you need to understand all the different scoring methods that are used to measure and evaluate progress, including:

- Age equivalent scores (AE)
- Grade equivalent scores (GE)
- Standard scores (SS) and standard deviations (SD)
- Percentile ranks (PR)

When you learn to use statistics, you will be able to measure your child's progress or lack of progress in an educational program. Regression is the term for lack of progress. You need to recognize educational regression, a common problem in special education.

You Use Statistics to Compare

You can use statistics to evaluate how one child performs, when compared to other children who are the same age or in the same grade.

Let's look at one component of physical fitness in a group of elementary school students. Our group or sample consists of 100 fifth grade students. The children are enrolled in a physical fitness class to prepare them for the President's Physical Fitness Challenge. We will assume that the average chronological age (CA) of this group is exactly ten years, zero months (CA=10-0). The children are tested in September, at the beginning of the school year.

To qualify as physically fit, each child must meet several goals. Push-ups are used to measure upper body strength. Each child must complete as many push-ups as possible within a specified time. The child's raw score is the number of push-ups the child completes. Raw score is a term for the number of items correctly answered or performed.

After all the students complete the push-up test, we list their scores. Here are the results:

- Half of the children completed 10 push-ups or more.
- Half of the children completed 10 push-ups or fewer.
- The average child completed 10 push-ups.
- The average or mean number of push-ups completed by this group of fifth graders is 10.
- Half of the children scored above the mean or average score of 10.
- Half of the children scored below the mean or average score of 10.
- Fifty percent of the children scored 10 or above.
- Fifty percent of the children scored 10 or below.

When we analyze the children's scores, we see patterns:

- One-third of the group completed between 7 and 10 push-ups.
- One-third of the group completed between 10 and 13 push-ups.
- Two-thirds of the group scored between 7 to 13 push-ups.
- Half of the group (50 percent) completed between 8 and 12 push-ups.
- The lowest scoring child completed one push-up.
- The highest scoring child completed 19 push-ups.
- The remaining one-third completed fewer than seven or more than 13 push-ups.
- Nearly all the children—96 out of 100—completed between 4 and 16 push-ups.

This information is presented in Table 10-1.

Table 10-1 | ***Push-Up Scores and Percentile Ranks***

Push-ups	Percentile Rank
19	99
18	99
17	99
16	99
15	98
14	91
13	84
12	75
11	63
10	50
9	37
8	25
7	16
6	9
5	5
4	2
3	1
2	1
1	1

These test results provide us with a sample of data. We can use this data to compare the performance of an individual child to the entire group. In making these comparisons, the data will allow us to identify an individual child's strengths or weaknesses when compared to the peer group of fifth graders.

If we use the same push-up test for children in other grades, we can compare our original group of fifth graders to other groups – older children, younger children, children who attend different schools. If we gather enough information or data, we can compare our original group of fifth graders – or an individual child within that group – to a national population of children whose upper body strength was tested by their ability to do push-ups.

The Bell Curve: A Powerful Tool

In nature, characteristics are distributed along theoretical curves. For our purposes, the most important curve is the normal distribution or bell curve. Because the percentages along the bell curve are well known and researched, the bell curve is our frame of reference.

Why is the bell curve such a powerful tool? When you use the bell curve, you can compare scores, measure progress, and measure effectiveness. You can compare one child to others and you can compare groups.

You Can Make Comparisons

Using the bell curve, you can draw a visual map or graph that provides additional information. You can use the bell curve to see where a single child scores when compared to the peer group. You can compare one child's score on an arithmetic test in terms of the number of correct answers to the average number of correct answers by children of the same age.

When you compare the push-up scores of children who attend different schools, you can learn whether the physical fitness of children, as measured by their ability to do push-ups, varies between schools, neighborhoods, states, or countries.

You Can Measure Effectiveness

When you use the bell curve, you can measure the effectiveness of a class or program. Assume you want to know if the physical fitness class is effective for the group of fifth graders. You ask, "Did the children's fitness levels improve?" How will you answer this question?

To measure the effectiveness of the fitness class, you measure the children's fitness before they begin the class and after they complete the class. If the fitness class has been effective in improving physical fitness, you will see individual and group improvement. If the program is effective, the children's ability to perform fitness skills will improve measurably over time.

You Can Measure Progress

The bell curve allows you to measure progress. Before you can use the bell curve, you need to know how the bell curve is designed.

On the bell curve, the bottom or horizontal line is called the X-axis. In our sample of fifth graders, the X-axis represents number of push-ups. An up-and-down or vertical line would be the Y-axis. In this sample, the Y-axis represents the number of children who earned a specific score. The highest point is ten. Most of the children completed ten push-ups.

As you see in Figure 10-1, the midway point on the X-axis equals a score of 10 push-ups.

Figure 10-1 | *Bell Curve: Number of Push-Ups*

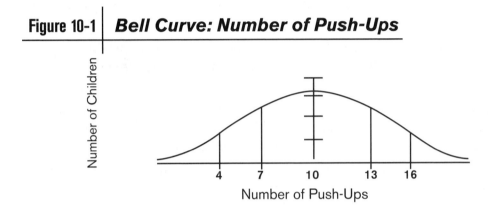

Number of Push-Ups

Because more children completed 10 push-ups than any other number, the highest point on the bell curve represents a score of 10. The second most frequent scores were 9 and 11, followed by 8 and 12. This pattern continues to the far ends of the bell curve. In the sample, the ends occurred at 1 and 19 push-ups.

You Can Compare Scores

You can use the bell curve to compare one child's score to the scores achieved by other members of the child's peer group. Figure 10-2 is a bell curve with the push-up scores of our fifth graders.

Figure 10-2 | *Bell Curve with Push-Up Scores and Percentages*

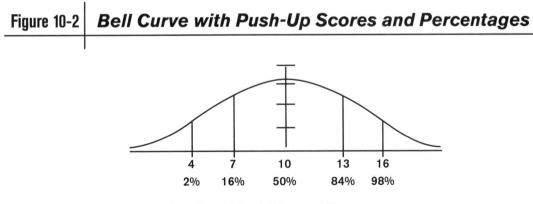

Number of Push-Ups and Percentages

Amy completed 10 push-ups. Her raw score is 10. You know that the raw score describes the number of items correctly answered or performed. Amy performed 10 push-ups. Her raw score of 10 places her in the middle of the class. Half of the children in Amy's class did 10 push-ups or more. Half of the children did 10 push-ups or less. Amy's score places her at the 50th percentile. The term for an individual's percent level is percentile rank (PR). Amy's percentile rank is 50 (PR=50).

Erik did 13 push-ups. When you look at the bell curve in Figure 10-2, you see that Erik's score of 13 places him at the 84th percent level. Erik's percentile rank is 84 (PR=84). Erik's ability to do push-ups places him in the 84th position out of the 100 fifth graders tested on the measure of upper body strength.

Sam completed seven push-ups. His raw score of 7 places him at the (bottom) 16 percent. Sam's percentile rank is 16 (PR=16). In the sample of 100 fifth grade children, 84 children earned higher scores than Sam.

Larry completed six push-ups. You convert his raw score of 6 to a percentile rank of 9 (PR=9). You know that 91 children scored higher and eight children scored lower than Larry in upper body strength, as measured by the ability to do push-ups.

Oscar completed two push-ups. His raw score of 2 places him in the bottom 1 percent of our group of fifth graders (PR=1).

Nancy's raw score of 17 places her in the top 99 percent. You know that Nancy scored at the 99th percentile rank (PR=99).

You can see the relationship between the number of push-ups completed and the child's percentile rank (PR) in Table 10-2.

Table 10-2 | *Push-Up Scores of Fifth Grade Students*

Child's Name	Raw Score	Percentile Rank
Oscar	3	1
Larry	6	9
Sam	7	16
Amy	10	50
Erik	13	84
Frank	15	95
Nancy	17	99

You Can Compare One Child to Many

When you use the bell curve, you can compare one child's score to those of a group of children. You can compare a single child's progress or regression to the progress of others in the child's peer group. The bell curve allows you to compare one child's score to the scores earned by older children, younger children, children in different grades, or children who attend different schools.

Let's see how this works. You will measure the children's upper body strength, as measured by the number of push-ups they can perform. You decide to expand your study to include all children in the elementary grades, from Kindergarten through fifth grade. You will assume that the average chronological age of elementary school children is eight years, zero months (CA=8-0 years).

You Can Compare Groups

After you test the third graders and analyze the data, you find that the average or mean score of the third graders is six push-ups. The average third grade child (who is 8 years old) can do six push-ups.

You ask, "How can we compare children in different groups?" Look at Larry, a member of the original group of fifth grade students. Although the average fifth grader performed 10 push-ups, Larry completed only six push-ups. You convert Larry's raw score of six to a percentile rank of 9 (PR=9).

When you compare Larry's performance to that of all elementary school students, you see that Larry is functioning at the level of the average third grader who is eight years old. This means that Larry's age equivalent score is 8 years, zero months (AE=8-0) and his grade equivalent score is third grade, zero months or beginning third grade (GE=3-0).

Find Amy in Table 10-2. When Amy was tested, she was a 10-year-old fifth grade student. Amy scored 10 push-ups, which is the mean for her peers. Amy's grade equivalent score is fifth grade (GE=5-0). Her age equivalent score is 10.0 years (AE=10-0).

Find Frank in Table 10-2. You see that Frank has a raw score of 15 push-ups. His raw score of 15 converts to a percentile rank of 95 (PR=95). Frank's score looks great, until you learn that Frank was "held back" three times! Although Frank is in the fifth grade, he is 13 years old.

You need this information about Frank's age to analyze his performance. Frank's raw score is 15. The average raw score for eighth graders (who are 13 years old) is 15. Frank has a grade equivalent score of 8th grade (GE = 8.0). His age equivalent score is 13 years (AE = 13-0).

At age 13, Frank was included in the sample of fifth graders whose average age was 10. When compared to other fifth graders, Frank scored at the 95th percentile rank (PR) level. When you compare Frank to other children in his expected grade, he scored at the 50th percentile rank. His achievement is in the average range. If you compare Frank's performance to children who are three years younger, does this provide an accurate picture of his physical fitness? No.

Frank helps you understand two important issues. First, you see that Frank performs at a superior level when compared with other children in his grade. Second, you see that Frank performs at an average level when compared with children who are the same age.

Many children with disabilities are held back or retained between kindergarten and first grade. This practice is based on the mistaken belief that early school problems are due to immaturity and will resolve if the child has an extra year to mature. In some districts, school personnel describe this practice of holding children back as "readiness." In fact, the child is retained. If your child received a year of "readiness," make sure your child's achievement levels are described as age equivalent scores, not grade equivalent scores.

Learning How Test Scores Are Reported

To understand what test data means, you need to know how scores are reported. Test scores are reported as:

- Percentile ranks
- Age equivalents
- Grade equivalents
- Raw scores
- Scale scores
- Subtest scores
- Standard scores

The Glossary of Assessment Terms is in Appendix B.

Although Frank's performance is superior for his grade, it is average for his age. If you did not know Frank's grade and age, you could easily have misinterpreted Frank's achievement.

Learning About Raw Scores

The child's raw score is the number of push-ups completed. Assume you want to get an overall fitness score for a child. To get an overall or composite score, you measure three skills: sit-ups, push-ups, and a timed 50-yard dash. The overall fitness score includes the child's scores on these three skills.

Learning About Scale Scores

Next, develop a weighting system to convert each child's raw score to a scale score. After you convert the raw scores to scale scores, you can compare each of the three scores to each other (push-ups, sit-ups, 50-yard dash). How can you convert raw scores into scale scores?

One way to convert scores is to use a rank order system. In a rank order scoring system, the child who scores highest in an event (most push-ups, most sit-ups, fastest run) receives a scale score of 100. The lowest scorer receives a scale score of 1. The remaining 98 children receive their respective "rank" as their scale score.

After the children's raw scores are converted into scale scores, it is easy to compare an individual child's performance to the group, or to all children who are of the same age or in the same grade. You can easily compare one child's performance at different times, i.e., before and after the fitness class.

☑ **Scores on standardized norm-referenced tests are reported as standard scores, percentile ranks, age equivalent scores, and grade equivalent scores.**

Learning About Composite Scores

After you develop a composite score, the child's raw scores on the different fitness subtests have less significance. This is what happens in educational and psychological tests.

Most educational and psychological tests are composed of several subtests. The scores on these subtests are combined to develop composite scores. When you rely solely on composite scores for information, you can run into problems.

Learning About Subtest Scatter

Subtest scatter is the difference between the highest and lowest subtest scores. If you find a significant amount of subtest scatter on a test, this suggests that the child has areas of strength and weakness that need to be explored. How do you know if there is significant subtest scatter?

Most subtests have a mean or average score of 10. Most children score + 3 to - 3 points from the mean of 10, so most children will score between 7 and 13.

Assume Ann was evaluated on a test that includes 10 subtests. On three subtests, she earned a score of nine. On four subtests, she earned a score of ten. On three subtests, she earned a score of eleven.

On the 10 subtests, Ann scored between 9 and 11. Subtest scatter is the difference between the highest and lowest scores. Ann's subtest scatter is 2 (11 – 9 = 2). Ann's subtest scatter is minimal. Her overall composite score is 10.

Assume that Brandon is evaluated on the same test. On four subtests, Brandon scored 10; on three subtests, he scored 16; on three subtests, he scored 4. Brandon's composite score is 10. He performed average on four subtests, very well on three subtests, and very poorly on three subtests. When you compute the difference between his highest and lowest subtest scores, you find that Brandon's subtest scatter is 12 (16 - 4 = 12).

Brandon's composite score of 10 is average. Is Brandon an average child? Because Brandon's subtest scores demonstrated significant subtest scatter, you need to know more about his weak and strong areas.

You need to understand your child's disability and how the disability affects your child's learning. You need to know what skills need to be strengthened and what strengths can be harnessed to help remediate the child's weaknesses. Tests and measurements will give you answers to these important questions.

In Summation

In this chapter, you learned about the bell curve, percentile ranks and standard scores, composite scores, and subtest scatter. You should re-read this chapter from time to time.

In the next chapter, you will learn how to use pre- and post-tests to measure progress. We describe norm-referenced and criterion-referenced tests, standard deviations, and standard scores. You will learn about the Wechsler Intelligence Scale for Children (WISC-IV) and other tests that are used with children.

You will also learn how to chart your child's scores and how to create progress graphs.

11 | Tests and Measurements 102

"Underlying all assessments are a respect for children and their families, and a desire to help children. A thorough assessment should allow us to learn something about the child that we could not learn from simply talking to others about the child, observing the child, or reviewing the child's records."   —Jerome Sattler

In this chapter, you will learn about composite scores and how to use pre- and post-tests to measure progress. You will learn about norm-referenced and criterion-referenced tests, standard deviations, and standard scores. You will learn how to convert standard scores into percentile ranks, and how to convert percentile ranks into standard scores.

You will learn about the Index and subtest scores of the Wechsler Intelligence Scale for Children, Fourth Edition (WISC-IV) and other measures of intellectual functioning. You will also learn about screening tests, single-subject tests, comprehensive educational achievement tests, personality tests, behavior rating scales, speech and language tests, vocabulary tests, and neuropsychological tests. You will learn how to chart test scores, how to use computer software programs to create progress and regression graphs, and how to incorporate objective scores in your child's IEP.

Katie

Katie is a fourteen-year old ninth grader who is failing several subjects. Katie is angry and sullen, and wants to quit school. Katie's desperate parents take her to a child psychologist. Before the psychologist diagnoses Katie's problems and develops a treatment plan, she administers a complete comprehensive psychological and educational test battery to Katie.

When the psychologist meets with Katie and her parents to discuss the evaluation results, she explains that Katie scored two standard deviations above the mean on the Similarities subtest of the Intelligence Scale for Children, Fourth Edition (WISC-IV). She says Katie scored two and a half standard deviations below the mean on the spontaneous writing sample of the Test of Written Language, Third Edition (TOWL-3).

What do these test scores mean? Do they explain Katie's academic problems? Do they account for her moodiness and dislike of school?

You will learn more about Katie in this chapter. When you finish reading this chapter, you will understand why Katie's test scores were significant and you will know why Katie's self-esteem plummeted.

Learning About Composite Scores

School evaluators often use composite or cluster scores as the sole basis to determine eligibility and educational progress. Using composite scores as the sole basis to determine eligibility and progress is inappropriate and leads to poor decisions.

The Wechsler Intelligence Scale for Children, Fourth Edition (WISC-IV), is the most commonly administered test of ability. Psychologists typically provide a Full Scale IQ (FSIQ) and four Index scores. The Full Scale IQ is a composite score that includes ten of the fifteen WISC-IV subtests. The Index scores are composite scores that describe verbal reasoning skill, visual perceptual thinking, working memory, and processing speed. IQ and Index scores that fall between 90 and 110 are within the average range, that is, between the 25th and 75th percentiles.

The Woodcock-Johnson III (WJ III ACH) is the most commonly administered individual achievement test. The Woodcock-Johnson Psycho-Educational Battery - Revised (WJ-R) may have been used previously to evaluate your child. However, this test is no longer current. The Woodcock-Johnson III ACH includes a wide selection of subtests that are scored by computer. These subtests are combined into composite or cluster scores.

What do you know about the composite scores and subtest scores in your child's evaluations? If you rely on composite or cluster scores and do not examine your child's subtest scores, you may overlook significant strengths and serious weaknesses.

Katie is the 14-year-old you met at the beginning of this chapter. On the WISC-IV, Katie earned a Full Scale IQ of 101. You know that IQ scores between 90 and 110 are "average." If the only information you had was Katie's Full Scale IQ score, you would assume that Katie's IQ of 101 placed her in the "average range" of intellectual functioning. Is Katie an "average" child?

You also learned that Katie's Verbal Comprehension Index (VCI) is 124 and her Perceptual Reasoning Index (PRI) is 88. If you subtract the Perceptual Reasoning Index from the Verbal Comprehension Index, you find a 36-point difference between these scores.

If you did not have these two Index scores, you might view Katie as an "average" child – and you would be mistaken. In fact, many psychologists would not report Katie's Full Scale IQ score because her test scores had an unusual amount of scatter. Because of the wide scatter, the Full Scale IQ is not a valid indicator of Katie's intellectual abilities.

Katie's Verbal Comprehension Index of 124 translates into a percentile rank of 95 (PR=95). Her Perceptual Reasoning Index of 88 converts to a percentile rank of 21

(PR = 21). When you look at Katie's scores as percentile ranks, you see a difference of 74 points (95 − 21 = 74) between her verbal and visual perceptual abilities. We will look more closely at Katie's test scores shortly.

When Apparent Progress Means Actual Regression

If you are like many parents, you do not know if your child's special education program is appropriate or if your child is making acceptable progress. Health care professionals use data from objective tests to diagnose health problems and measure the success of medical interventions. In the last chapter, you saw how to use pre- and post- tests to make decisions about continuing, terminating, or changing a medical treatment plan.

You should apply these principles to special education planning and decision-making. The Individuals with Disabilities Education Act of 2004 (IDEA 2004) requires schools to use a variety tests and assessments to gather functional, developmental, and academic information about the child.

Use information from these objective tests to identify the child's present levels of academic achievement and functional performance and determine the child's educational needs. The IEP team, which includes the child's parents and school staff, should develop an IEP that includes measurable goals, including academic and functional goals designed to meet the child's unique needs. After a specified time, the child's progress is measured with objective tests. When you compare test results, you will know if your child is learning and making progress, or regressing.

Using Pre- and Post-Testing to Measure Progress

Pre- and post-testing allows us to measure educational benefit or regression. Using scores from pre- and post-testing, we can create graphs to visually demonstrate a child's progress or regression.

To see how pre- and post-testing work, we will revisit our fifth grade fitness class. On the first test, Erik's score of 13 push-ups placed him in the top 84 percent of the group. At the end of the fitness class, the children were re-tested. Erik completed 14 push-ups on the post-test. Did Erik make progress? Yes and no.

The average performance of the fifth graders improved by two push-ups, from a raw score of 10 to a raw score of 12 push-ups. Erik's raw score improved by 1, from 13 to 14 push-ups. Erik's age equivalent and grade equivalent scores increased slightly over the first testing but his position in the group dropped from the 84th to the 75th percentile level. Although Erik is still ahead of his peers, he regressed slightly when compared to his prior rating within the peer group.

What about Sam? In Chapter 10, you learned that Sam completed seven push-ups. On the post-test, Sam's performance improved from a raw score of 7 to a raw score of

8. Sam's age equivalent and grade equivalent scores increased slightly but his position in the peer group dropped from the 16th to the 9th percentile rank. Sam continues to fall further behind his peers.

Assume we test Sam again when he returns to school in the fall. We will have three sets of data (beginning 5th grade, end 5th grade, beginning 6th grade). If Sam's percentile rank continues to drop, he is regressing. How long will it take Sam to recoup the skills he lost during the summer? Regression and recoupment are key issues in determining the child's legal right to extended school year services (ESY).

Norm-Referenced and Criterion-Referenced Tests

Most educational achievement tests are norm-referenced or criterion-referenced. When we use a norm-referenced test, we analyze progress or regression by measuring changes in the child's position within the group, i.e., the norm.

When we evaluated our original group of fifth graders, we compared each child's performance to the norm group of fifth graders. Erik (raw score of 13, percentile rank of 84) and Sam (raw score of 7, percentile rank of 16) were referenced or compared to the norm group of fifth graders. Using percentile ranks, we computed each child's change in position, i.e., progress or regression.

We also referenced the criteria of number of push-ups completed. A criterion-referenced test determines whether a specific criterion is met, without reference to a norm group. Assume that the criterion for success is eight push-ups. When Sam was tested at the beginning of the year, he completed seven push-ups. Sam failed to reach the criterion for success of eight push-ups. Assume that Sam received a year of physical fitness remediation. At the end of the year, Sam completed the eight push-ups. Did Sam meet the criterion for success? It depends.

The answer to this question depends on whether the criterion for success changes when a child is one year older.

If you rely on criterion-referenced measures, you can be misled about whether your child is making progress or falling behind the peer group. When you use a criterion-referenced test, you need to know the criterion for success.

Learning About Standard Deviations

To understand test scores, you need to know the mean and standard deviation of the test. On most educational and psychological tests, the mean is 100 and the standard deviation is 15 (Mean = 100, SD = 15). On the smaller subtests within these educational and psychological tests, the mean is 10 and the standard deviation is 3 (Mean = 10, SD = 3).

See Appendix B for a Glossary of Assessment Terms.

Average scores do not deviate far from the mean. As scores fall above or below the mean, they are a certain value or distance from the mean – for example, 1 or 2 standard deviations from the mean.

The mean is 0 (zero) standard deviations from the mean. The next markers on the bell curve from left to right are -1 and +1 standard deviations from the mean, followed by -2 and + 2 standard deviations from the mean. Figure 11-1 shows standard deviations and the relationship to percentile ranks and standard scores.

Figure 11-1 | ***Bell Curve: Standard Deviations and their Relationship to Percentile Ranks and Standard Scores***

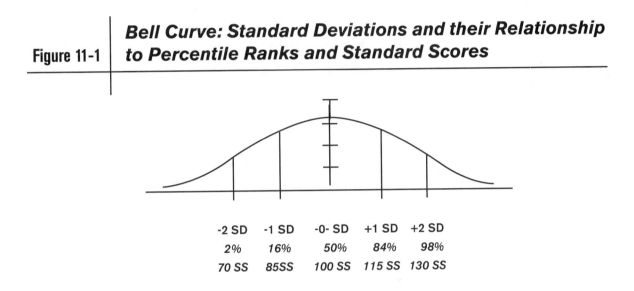

-2 SD	-1 SD	-0- SD	+1 SD	+2 SD
2%	16%	50%	84%	98%
70 SS	85SS	100 SS	115 SS	130 SS

In our original push-up test, the mean was 10 push-ups and the standard deviation (SD) was three push-ups. The push-up example in Chapter 10 uses scores that are the same as subtest scores on most educational and psychological tests.

On subtests, one standard deviation above the mean is 13 (10 + 3 = 13). One standard deviation below the mean is 7 (10 - 3 = 7). (See Figure 11-1)

One standard deviation above the mean is **always** at the 84th percent level (PR = 84). If a child scores 13 on a subtest, this score is at the 84th percentile. Zero standard deviations from the mean is **always** at the 50th percentile. One standard deviation below the mean is **always** at the 16 percent level (PR = 16). If a child scores 7 on a subtest, this score is at the 16th percentile. (See Figure 11-1)

Two standard deviations above the mean are **always** at the 98th percent level (PR = 98). Two standard deviations below the mean are **always** at the 2nd percent level (PR = 2). (See Figure 11-1)

When you look at your child's test scores, you may find that the child scored one standard deviation below the mean on a test or subtest. If the score is one standard deviation below the mean, your child's percentile rank is 16.

Review the **Wrightslaw Quick Rules of Tests** in Table 11-1.

Table 11-1	*Wrightslaw Quick Rules of Tests*

All educational and psychological tests based on the bell curve report their scores as standard scores and percentile ranks. To interpret test results, you need to know the mean and the standard deviation of the test. Most tests use a mean of 100 and a standard deviation of 15.

When educational and psychological tests use standard scores (SS) with a mean of 100 and a standard deviation of 15, a standard score of 100 is at the 50th percentile rank (PR). A standard score of 85 is at the 16th percentile rank. A standard score of 115 is at the 84th percentile rank.

When educational and psychological tests use subtest scores with a mean of 10 and a standard deviation of 3, a subtest score of 10 is at the 50th percentile rank.

A subtest score of 7 is at the 16th percentile rank; a subtest score of 13 is at the 84th percentile rank.

A standard score of 100 is at the 50th percentile rank. One-half of children will fall above and one-half will fall below the mean at the 50th percentile, which is represented as a standard score of 100.

Two-thirds of children will score between + 1 and - 1 standard deviations from the mean.

Two-thirds (68 percent) of children will score between the 84th and 16th percentile ranks. (84 minus 16 = 68)

Half of 68 percent is 34 percent. When you subtract 34 percent from the mean of 50 percent, you have 16 percent. When you add 34 percent to the mean of 50 percent, you have 84 percent.

A standard deviation of -1 is at the 16th percentile. A standard deviation of 0 is at the 50th percentile. A standard deviation of +1 is at the 84th percentile.

A standard score of 85 is at the 16th percentile. A standard score of 100 is at the 50th percentile. A standard score of 115 is at the 84th percentile.

A standard deviation of -2 is at the 2nd percentile. A standard deviation of +2 is at the 98th percentile.

A standard score of 70 is at the 2nd percentile. A standard score of 130 is at the 98th percentile.

A standard score of 90 is at the 25th percentile. A standard score of 110 is at the 75th percentile.

One-half (50 percent) of children will score between the 75th and 25th percentiles (75 minus 25 = 50).

One-half of children will have standard scores between 90 and 110, which is within the "average range."

Learning About Standard Scores

Assume that at an IEP meeting, the school psychologist said your child had a standard score of 85 in reading and a standard score of 70 in written language. If you are like many parents, you may feel relieved. You assume these scores mean your child is "passing." Many parents believe standard scores are like grades, with 100 as the highest score and 0 as the lowest. Standard scores are not like grades!

In standard scores, the average or mean score is 100 with a standard deviation of 15. An "average child" will earn a standard score of 100. If the child scores 1 standard deviation above the mean, the child's standard score is 115 (100 + 15 = 115). If the child scores 1 standard deviation below the mean, the child's standard score is 85 (100 - 15 = 85).

Because a standard score of 115 is 1 standard deviation above the mean, it is always at the 84 percent level. Because a standard score of 85 is 1 standard deviation below the mean, it is always at the 16 percent level. A standard score of 130 (+2 SD) is always at the 98 percent level. A standard score of 70 (-2 SD) is always at the 2 percent level.

If your child has a standard score of 85 in reading, your child is functioning at the 16th percentile. If your child's standard score is 70 in written language, your child is functioning at the 2nd percentile. This information is summarized in Wrightslaw's Quick Rules of Tests. (Table 11-1)

Do you remember Katie? On the Wechsler Intelligence Scale for Children (WISC-IV), Katie earned a Full Scale IQ of 101. You realized that Katie's "average" Full Scale IQ of 101 was misleading after you learned that her Verbal Comprehension Index was 124 and her Perceptual Reasoning Index was 88.

Katie's psychologist also found that she scored 2 standard deviations above the mean on the Similarities subtest of the WISC-IV. What does this mean?

If a subtest score is 2 standard deviations above the mean, the subtest score is 16, which is at the 98th percentile. The WISC-IV Similarities subtest measures verbal reasoning ability. If Katie scored 2 standard deviations above the mean on the Similarities subtest, her reasoning ability is at the 98th percentile.

The psychologist also found that Katie had a standard score of 68, more than 2 standard deviations below the mean, on the spontaneous writing sample of the Test of Written Language, Third Edition (TOWL-3). A score that is more than 2 standard deviations below the mean is lower than the 2nd percentile. Katie's standard score is 68 means her ability to spontaneously produce a writing sample is at the 1st percentile.

When we introduced Katie to you, we asked two questions:

- Do Katie's test scores explain the academic problems Katie is having?
- Do Katie's test scores help us understand her moodiness and dislike of school?

Table 11-2 | *Conversion Table: Standard Scores and Percentile Ranks*

Standard Score	Subtest Score	Percentile Rank
145	19	>99
140	18	>99
135	17	99
130	16	98
125	15	95
120	14	91
115	13	84
110	12	75
109	–	73
108	–	70
107	–	68
106	–	66
105	11	63
104	–	61
103	–	58
102	–	55
101	–	53
100	10	50
99	–	47
98	–	45
97	–	42
96	–	39
95	9	37
94	–	34
93	–	32
92	–	30
91	–	27
90	8	25
89	–	23
88	–	21
87	–	19
86	–	18
85	7	16
80	6	9
75	5	5
70	4	2
65	3	1
60	2	<1
55	1	<1

Katie's verbal reasoning ability is at the 98th percentile. Her ability to convey her thoughts in writing is in the 1st percentile. If Katie is very bright but cannot convey her ideas or knowledge on written assignments and tests, would you expect her to feel frustrated and stupid? Do you understand why Katie is angry, depressed, and wants to quit school?

The results of most educational and psychological tests are reported in standard scores. You need to learn how to convert standard scores into percentile ranks. You can use Table 11-2 to convert standard scores into percentile ranks and percentile ranks into standard scores.

Learning About Index and Subtest Scores

On the Wechsler Intelligence Scale for Children, Fourth Edition (WISC-IV), the Index scores are composites or averages of different subtests, with each subtest measuring different abilities.

When we presented Katie's test results, you learned that variation among the subtest scores (subtest scatter) is a valuable source of information. Look at Katie's WISC-IV Index and subtest scores in Table 11-3.

Table 11-3 | *Katie's Subtest Scores on the Wechsler Intelligence Scale, 4th Edition (WISC-IV)*

	Standard Score or Scaled Score		Standard Score or Scaled Score
WISC-IV Full Scale IQ	101		
Verbal Comprehension Index	124	**Perceptual Reasoning Index**	88
Similarities	16	Block Design	11
Vocabulary	14	Picture Concepts	7
Comprehension	12	Matrix Reasoning	6
Information	(13)	Picture Completion	(8)
Word Reasoning	(12)		
Working Memory Index	110	**Processing Speed Index**	75
Digit Span	14	Coding	4
Letter-Number Sequencing	10	Symbol Search	7
Arithmetic	(8)	Cancellation	(8)

Note: Scores in Brackets ( ) are supplementary subtests. They are not included in the Full Scale IQ or the Index Scores.

On the WISC-IV, subtest scores range from a low score of 1 to a high score of 19. WISC-IV subtest scores have a mean of 10 and a standard deviation of 3. A subtest score of 7 is one standard deviation below the mean (-1 SD). By using the Conversion Table (Table 11-2), you can convert the subtest score of 7 to a percentile rank of 16 (PR = 16).

When you look at Katie's subtest scores, you see that she has significant subtest scatter, from a high score of 16 on the Similarities subtest (98th percentile) to a low score of 4 on the Coding subtest (2nd percentile). You know that subtest scatter is the difference between the highest and lowest subtest scores. Subtract the lowest score of 4 (Coding) from her highest score of 16 (Similarities). Katie's subtest scatter is 12 (16 – 4 = 12). The WISC-IV manual tells us that scatter this great is unusual.

You need to know what the different subtests measure. When we discussed Katie's subtest scores earlier, you learned that the Similarities subtest is correlated with abstract reasoning ability. The Coding subtest measures visual-perceptual mechanics. Assessment experts Jerome Sattler[a] and Ron Dumont[b] describe the Coding subtest as "an information processing task that involves the discrimination and memory of visual pattern symbols."[c] "If you find that a child has a visual, hearing, attentional, or motor problem that may interfere with his or her ability to take one or more of the subtests,

| Table 11-4 | **Wechsler Intelligence Scale for Children-IV (WISC-IV)**
Subtests *(Source: The WISC-IV Technical and Interpretive Manual)* |

Indexes and Subtests	Ability Measured
Verbal Comprehension Index	
Similarities	Abstract reasoning, verbal categories and concepts
Vocabulary	Language development, word knowledge, verbal fluency
Comprehension	Social and practical judgment, common sense
Information (supplementary subtest)	Factual knowledge, long-term memory, recall
Word Reasoning (supplementary subtest)	Verbal comprehension, general reasoning ability
Working Memory	
Digit Span	Short-term auditory memory, mental manipulation
Letter-Number Sequencing	Sequencing, mental manipulation, attention
Arithmetic (supplementary subtest)	Attention and concentration, numerical reasoning
Perceptual Reasoning Index	
Block Design	Spatial analysis, abstract visual problem-solving
Picture Concepts	Abstract, categorical reasoning
Matrix Reasoning	Pattern recognition, classification, analogical reasoning
Picture Completion (supplementary subtest)	Alertness to detail, visual discrimination
Processing Speed Index	
Coding	Visual-motor coordination, speed, concentration
Symbol Search	Visual-motor quickness, concentration, persistence
Cancellation (supplementary subtest)	Processing speed, visual selective attention, vigilance

do not use these subtests in computing Index scores or a Full Scale IQ."[d] They also note that a left handed child may be penalized on the Coding subtest because the child will "have to lift his hand repeatedly during the task to view" the tested items.

Katie's scores are evidence that she could excel in discussions of complex literature in an honors English class because of her reasoning abilities, but she is unable to write what she knows. Since Katie could not write what she knew, she was placed in slow-paced remedial classes. Because her abilities were untapped, Katie concluded that she was stupid and wanted to quit school.

When you look at Katie's subtest scores, you see that several scores are in parentheses. On the WISC-IV, Information, Word Reasoning, Arithmetic, Picture Completion, and Cancellation are not included in the Full Scale IQ or the Index scores. These subtests are used to provide additional data about how a child learns.

☑ **When subtest scores are in (parentheses), the scores are not computed in the composite score.**

Test Categories and Descriptions

Tests administered to children fall into several categories: intellectual or cognitive tests; educational achievement tests; projective personality tests, questionnaires and surveys; speech and language tests; and neuropsychological tests.

For information about thousands of tests, go to Testlink from the Educational Testing Service (ETS) at www.ets.org/testcoll/index.html

Testlink has a library of more than 20,000 tests and other measurement devices from the early 1900s to the present. The collection makes information on standardized tests and research instruments available to researchers, graduate students, teachers, and others. After you review information at Testlink, you can visit the test publishers' websites for more information about specific tests.

By the time you read this chapter, new versions or editions will have replaced some of the tests that are described in this chapter. Like the law, tests are always changing.

For unparalleled expertise and wit on testing, visit the website published by John Willis and Ron Dumont at http://alpha.fdu.edu/psychology.

Intellectual or Cognitive Tests

When psychologists interpret IQ scores, they should look at other information about the child. The evaluator should consider previous and current assessment results, the developmental and educational history, health, behavioral challenges, and situational factors. Poor motivation, anxiety, depression, a lack of cultural opportunities, and poor attention/concentration can affect a child's performance on any given day.

Highly impulsive children may not be able to demonstrate what they know. They may blurt out responses before thinking. Impulsive children may be so busy moving about that they cannot devote their full attention to solving a problem. Evaluators should not report scores that do not accurately represent the skills being measured, and that do not provide an accurate picture of how a child functions.

Commonly used intellectual or cognitive tests are:

- Wechsler Intelligence Scale for Children, Fourth Edition (WISC-IV)
- Differential Ability Scales (DAS)
- Stanford-Binet Intelligence Scale – Fifth Edition (SB:V)
- Woodcock–Johnson III Tests of Cognitive Abilities (WJ III COG)
- Leiter International Performance Scale–Revised (Leiter-R)

Wechsler Intelligence Scale for Children, Fourth Edition_____

The Wechsler Intelligence Scale for Children, Fourth Edition (WISC-IV) is an individually administered test that is used to assess the problem solving skills of children ages 6 years through 16 years. It is used by evaluators to document styles of learning, strengths and weaknesses, and potential for success. The Wechsler Preschool and Primary Scale of Intelligence, Third Edition (WPPSI-III) is for children ages 2 years, 6 months to 7 years, 3 months of age. The Wechsler Adult Intelligence Scale, Third Edition (WAIS-III) is for adults aged 16 through 89.

The WISC-IV was published by the Psychological Corporation (www.psychcorp. com) in 2003 to replace the third edition (WISC-III) that was used for twelve years. Although the new test has much in common with the previous edition, there are differences that present new challenges in interpretation. You will learn about the differences between the WISC-III and WISC-IV and the important implications for educational decisions.

Structure of the WISC-IV

The WISC-IV consists of ten core subtests and five supplementary subtests. The core subtests contribute to the **Full Scale IQ**, a number that is thought (by some) to define intelligence. In contrast to the WISC-III, the WISC-IV does not provide a **Verbal IQ** and **Performance IQ**. The WISCI-IV uses a four factor (Index) model that describes different facets of how we think and solve problems. (See Table 11-5)

The Full Scale IQ is a measure of general intelligence, scholastic aptitude, and readiness to master school skills. The Full Scale IQ does not measure non-intellectual traits and abilities necessary for intelligent behavior, scholastic achievement, and school readiness. No single intelligence test measures all the intellectual abilities needed for such achievement. This is one reason why an individual's scores on different intelligence tests are likely to differ.

| Table 11-5 | **Structure of the Weschler Intelligence Scale for Children, Fourth Edition (WISC-IV)** |

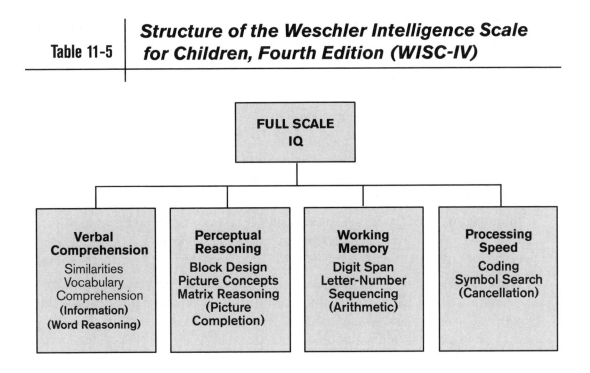

If there is a significant difference between Index scores or if there is significant scatter between subtests, the Full Scale IQ **may not** accurately represent the child's level of functioning. Let's look at the individual subtests. Note: Many of these descriptions were developed with assistance from John Willis, Ed.D.[e]

Verbal Comprehension Index

Vocabulary. Children are asked to provide oral definitions of words. Responses that are slightly tangential, or limited in their scope, may receive one point. Higher level, more comprehensive, or more precise definitions receive two points. Responses are not scored based on their grammar or word choice.

Similarities. Children are asked to identify how two words or concepts are alike. (Example: *How are a fork and a knife alike?*) Concrete responses, such as *they both are metal* or *you use them at meals* would earn one point. Higher level responses, such as *they are both eating utensils* or *they are both tools for eating* would receive two points.

Some children have a limited understanding of how word meanings relate to each other. Some may not know what the words mean. Others do poorly on this subtest because they are not able to retrieve the words needed to answer the questions.

Comprehension. Children are asked to explain the whys and wherefores of common social and governmental practices. Questions for younger children focus on social behaviors. (Example: *What should you do if you lose your mother or father in* *a store?*) Questions for older students focus on the role(s) of government institutions and education. (Example: *Why is literacy important in a society?*) Responses that are limited or that provide one reason receive one point; responses that are more comprehensive and detailed receive two points.

Children who fare poorly on the Comprehension subtest may have difficulty with abstract reasoning skill and inferential thinking. Some do poorly because they do not understand the language of the question. Others may have difficulty expressing their thoughts with sufficient precision for credit. Some items require two separate responses for full credit. The WISC-IV Comprehension subtest is not a measure of reading comprehension.

Information. Children are asked to recall factual information relating to history, geography, and the sciences as a measure of long-term memory. (Examples: *Who was George Washington? Where is the Nile River?*) This is now a supplementary subtest.

Word Reasoning. This new supplementary subtest measures verbal knowledge and reasoning ability. Children asked to make guesses in response to a series of clues. (Example: *This animal lives on a farm, and lays eggs, and males crow at the sun.*) Some children may have difficulty processing the language of the clues. Others may not be able to use the clues to derive an answer.

Perceptual Reasoning Index

Block Design. Children are asked to copy geometric designs with colored blocks while being timed. This subtest provides a measure of spatial relations, i.e. how shapes relate to each other in space, and abstract visual problem solving. Perception and understanding of spatial relations are important in understanding many basic math concepts and interpreting graphs, charts, and time lines.

Picture Concepts. This is a new subtest. Children are asked to select pictures (one from each of two or three rows) with common themes or characteristics. This subtest measures visual memory, verbal reasoning, and categorization ability. Some children do poorly because they have difficulty with abstract, categorical thinking. Some become overwhelmed by the number of pictures they have to scan. Others formulate a theory that they are unable to revise even when it becomes clear that their response is incorrect (for example, they picked two pictures, and they can't find a third).

Matrix Reasoning. This is a new subtest. Children are asked to discriminate visual detail, determine the pattern in a series of designs, and apply the rule(s) to select the missing design. Matrix Reasoning tasks correlate well with intelligence as a whole, and are often used to learn about the intellectual functioning in children with severe language-based learning disabilities.

Children who perform poorly on this task may have difficulty with novelty and with solving unique or unfamiliar problems, making rule-based decisions, and inferential thinking. These skills play a larger role at the middle school and high school level.

Picture Completion. Children are asked to identify the missing parts of pictures.

They may do so either by language (labeling the missing part) or by simply pointing to it. This task measures visual memory for meaningful objects and alertness to the environment. Children who rely heavily on vague, imprecise words, such as "thing" may show signs of poor vocabulary and word retrieval. This is now a supplementary subtest.

Working Memory Index

Digit Span. Children are asked to repeat orally presented numbers forward and in reverse order. Digits forward measures short-term memory (a temporary buffer zone where new learning is held briefly as a precursor to further processing). Digits in reverse measures working memory (a workspace in the brain where new learning is compared, contrasted and integrated into a cohesive product).

This subtest can be interpreted on different levels. For some children, the total subtest score provides a good description of short-term memory and working memory. If there is a discrepancy between short-term memory and working memory, the evaluator should provide the digits forward score and the digits in reverse score separately.

Letter-Number Sequencing. Children are asked to order randomly dictated numbers and letters alphanumerically (first the numbers, then the letters) as a measure of working memory. This is a new subtest.

Arithmetic. Children are asked to solve oral word problems while being timed. Children can have difficulty with this task for many different reasons. Math skills are highly dependent on the quality of the math instruction received in school. Some children do not know math facts. Others have difficulty processing the language of the word problems or performing mental math calculations. This is now a supplementary subtest.

Processing Speed Index

Coding. Children are asked to copy abstract symbols and pictures with pencil and paper while being timed. This subtest measures fine motor clerical skills (the ability to manipulate the pencil) and memory for abstract symbols.

Some children who do poorly have difficulty controlling their pencils with speed; other children may not be able to recall the symbols and lose time because they have to refer to the key more frequently. Children who have low scores on this subtest often have difficulty writing with enough speed to take notes. Their handwriting may be poor. There are two versions (one for children ages 6 and 7; one for children ages 8 through 16).

Symbol Search. Children are asked to identify whether symbols are alike or different (marking YES or NO) while being timed. This subtest measures visual memory for symbols and decision speed. There are two versions (one for children ages 6 and 7; one for children ages 8 through 16).

Cancellation. This is a new subtest. Children are asked to scan pictures that are presented in two formats, with structure and without structure, and mark pictures belonging to a particular category, such as vegetables and desserts, while being timed. This task measures visual attention, the ability to scan quickly and efficiently, and thinking speed.

Key Differences Between the WISC-III and WISC-IV

Studies conducted by the Psychological Corporation indicate that children who take the WISC-IV will receive slightly lower scores than the scores they earned on the WISC-III. The Full Scale and Index scores on the WISC-IV and the WISC-III cannot be compared easily in a meaningful fashion. This is because the WISC-IV and the WISC-III are different in their composition and do not contain the same subtests.

When IQ and Index scores on the WISC-IV and the WISC-III differ, it is important to compare the individual subtest scores, subtest by subtest. Even if you complete this comparison, you need to understand that the content of the subtests may have changed. When there is a decrease in scores, it is important to find out why.

Evaluators should check their protocols for scoring errors, then consider the changes in the test structure. It may be advisable to recheck the child's hearing and vision. Depression and anxiety can lower processing speed. For some children, verbal skills decline because their reading skills are poor. Keith Stanovich[f] called this decline the "Matthew Effect."[g] When differences cannot be explained, the child should be referred for a comprehensive neurological evaluation.

To learn about the Matthew Effect, read Chapter Three of the Executive Summary of the National Reading Panel at www.nichd.nih.gov/publications/nrp/ch3.pdf.

Other Measures of Intellectual Functioning

All IQ tests do not measure the same skills. As a result, children may earn different scores on different IQ tests. The evaluator needs to select an IQ test that will best demonstrate the child's potential for learning.

Differential Ability Scales (DAS)

Differential Ability Scales (DAS) is an individually administered IQ test that consists of twelve core subtests, five diagnostic subtests, and three achievement tests. The DAS provides a General Conceptual Ability (GCA) score that is a composite of subtests in three areas: Verbal Ability, Nonverbal Ability, and Spatial Ability.

Diagnostic subtests are not included in the GCA so it is a more appropriate measure of intelligence for students with deficits in short term memory, visual memory for pictures, and processing speed. The DAS offers a Special Nonverbal Composite, a measure of intellectual functioning that is appropriate for individuals with language-based disabilities and hearing impairments. The DAS is being revised and is published by the Psychological Corporation (www.psychcorp.com).

Stanford-Binet, Fifth Edition (SB:V)

Stanford-Binet, Fifth Edition (SB:V) is an individually administered test that provides a Full Scale IQ, a Verbal IQ, and Nonverbal IQ, and five composite index scores (Fluid Reasoning, Knowledge, Quantitative Reasoning, Visual-Spatial Processing, and Working Memory). The Nonverbal IQ does not require expressive language, so it may provide a valid measure of IQ for individuals with speech problems. The SB:V is available from Riverside Publishing. (www.riverpub.com)

Woodcock-Johnson III Tests of Cognitive Abilities (WJ III COG)

Woodcock-Johnson III Tests of Cognitive Abilities (WJ III COG) consists of two batteries: the WJ III Tests of Cognitive Abilities (WJ III COG) and the WJ III Tests of Achievement (WJ III ACH). The WJ III COG provides a measure of General Intellectual Ability, and cluster scores that describe Verbal Ability, Thinking Ability, and Cognitive Efficiency.

When the standard battery and the extended battery are combined, they provide data about phonemic awareness, working memory, broad attention, cognitive fluency, and executive processes. Because the WJ III COG was developed on the same population as the WJ III ACH, it is possible to directly compare a student's scores with a higher degree of accuracy than when using tests normed on different populations. The SB:V and the Woodcock-Johnson III are available from Riverside Publishing. (www.riverpub.com).

Leiter International Performance Scale, Revised (Leiter-R)

The *Leiter International Performance Scale, Revised (Leiter-R)* is an individually administered IQ test for individuals between the ages of 2 to 20 years. The Leiter provides a Full Scale IQ and three Composite scores (Fluid Reasoning, Fundamental Visualization, and Spatial Visualization). It also measures nonverbal attention and memory.

The Leiter-R was developed to provide a reliable, valid measure of intelligence in individuals who struggle with communication disorders, motor challenges, hearing impairments, cognitive delays, traumatic brain injury, attention-deficit disorder, and learning disabilities. The test is administered in pantomime without language. Children demonstrate their knowledge by pointing. The Leiter-R is published by Stoelting Co. (www.stoeltingco.com).

Educational Achievement Tests

Educational achievement tests measure the academic skills children acquire through instruction – reading, spelling, mathematics, writing, vocabulary, science, and social studies.

Screening Tests

There are two types of achievement tests: screening tests and comprehensive tests. Screening tests generally assess reading, math, and spelling with just one subtest per skill area. The Wide Range Achievement Test (WRAT3), for example, measures word reading, spelling, and arithmetic.

Screening tests may not reveal problems that warrant further investigation due to their limited scope and focus. Screening tests, such as the WRAT3, should not be used in place of a thorough evaluation. The Wide Range Achievement Test is published by Psychological Assessment Resources, Inc. (www3.parinc.com).

Comprehensive Achievement Tests

Comprehensive achievement tests are divided into two categories: multiple-subject tests and single-subject tests. School psychologists and special educators are more likely to use multiple-subject tests that provide information about the basic skills of reading, writing, and mathematics. Some multiple-subject tests also assess oral language skills, fluency, rapid naming, and phonological awareness.

Just because a multiple-subject test claims to be comprehensive does not mean that it is so. These tests do not have to be administered in their entirety, and evaluators may choose what subtests they want to use.

Multiple-subject achievement tests include:

- Kaufman Test of Educational Achievement, Second Edition (KTEA-II)
- Wechsler Individual Achievement Test, Second Edition (WIAT-II)
- Peabody Individual Achievement Test, Revised (PIAT-R)
- Woodcock-Johnson III Tests of Achievement (WJ III ACH)

Kaufman Test of Educational Achievement (KTEA-II)

The *Kaufman Test of Educational Achievement, Second Edition (KTEA-II)* measures Letter and Word Recognition, Reading Comprehension, Math Concepts and Applications, Math Computation, Written Expression, Spelling, Listening Comprehension, and Oral Language.

The KTEA-II provides valuable information on phonological awareness, nonsense words, oral fluency, and reading fluency. In addition to composite and subtest scores, the KTEA-II provides a detailed summary of the child's errors that is extremely useful in planning remedial instruction. The Listening Comprehension and the Oral Language subtests are not a substitute for a speech and language evaluation. There are two forms. The KTEA-II is published by AGS Publishing (www.agsnet.com).

Wechsler Individual Achievement Test, Second Edition (WIAT-II)

The *Wechsler Individual Achievement Test, Second Edition (WIAT-II)* measures Word Reading, Pseudoword Decoding (nonsense words), Reading Comprehension, Numerical Operations, Math Reasoning, Spelling, Written Expression, Listening Comprehension, and Oral Expression.

The WIAT-II also provides supplemental scores that describe reading accuracy, reading rate, word fluency, word count, and alphabet writing. The Listening Comprehension and the Oral Expression subtests are not a substitute for a speech and language evaluation. The WIAT is published by the Psychological Corporation (www.psychcorp.com).

Peabody Individual Achievement Test, Revised (PIAT-R)

The *Peabody Individual Achievement Test, Revised (PIAT-R)* measures General Information, Reading Recognition, Reading Comprehension, Mathematics, Spelling, and Written Expression. No oral language is required. Students demonstrate their knowledge on all subtests, with the exception of General Information and Reading Recognition, by pointing to one of four possible responses. This assessment can be valuable for students with severe expressive language challenges who cannot, or will have great difficulty, expressing their knowledge orally. The PIAT it is published by AGS Publishing (www.agsnet.com).

Woodcock-Johnson III Tests of Achievement (WJ-III ACH)

Woodcock-Johnson III Tests of Achievement (WJ-III ACH) include two batteries, a standard battery and an extended battery. Subtests are organized into clusters. The standard battery assesses Letter-Word Identification, Reading Fluency, Passage Comprehension, Story Recall, Understanding Directions, Calculation, Math Fluency, Applied Problems, Spelling Writing Fluency, and Writing Samples.

The extended battery measures Word Attack (nonsense words), Reading Vocabulary, Picture Vocabulary, Oral Comprehension, Quantitative Concepts, Editing, and Academic Knowledge. There are also supplemental subtests.

Because the WJ-III subtests are short, many subtests do not provide good qualitative information about what a child knows, can do, and where the child needs continued work. The WJ-III does not measure the child's ability to write a paragraph or an essay; it only examines the ability to formulate brief responses.

Cluster scores must be considered with caution when there is a significant difference between individual subtest scores. The WJ-III is scored by computer. There are two forms. Examiners may opt to use the alternate form for retesting in order to minimize the possibility that a child would demonstrate improvement solely because he or she was familiar with the test questions.

Single-Subject Tests

Single-subject tests include several subtests that measure different skills in one broad area. Single-subject tests allow the evaluator to obtain more information about the child's strengths and weaknesses in a specific area. Three single-subject tests, the Gray Oral Reading Test, the Woodcock Reading Mastery Test-Revised, and the Kaufman Test of Educational Achievement, are described in greater detail in Chapter 10.

Gray Oral Reading Tests, Fourth Edition (GORT-4)

The *Gray Oral Reading Tests, Fourth Edition (GORT-4)* provide an objective measure of growth in oral reading and an aid in the diagnosis of oral reading difficulties. Five scores provide information on a child's oral reading skills. The GORT is published by AGS Publishing (www.agsnet.com).

Woodcock-Johnson III, Diagnostic Reading Battery (WJ III DRB)

The *Woodcock-Johnson-III, Diagnostic Reading Battery (WJ III DRB)* assesses specific attributes of reading achievement and abilities related to reading, including the five essential components of Reading First instruction. The WJ III DRB is published by Riverside Publishing (www.riverpub.com)

Comprehensive Test of Phonological Processing (CTOPP)

The *Comprehensive Test of Phonological Processing (CTOPP)* measures phonological memory, phonological awareness, and rapid naming, the skills that make reading and spelling possible. These skills should be assessed when a child has difficulty learning to read.

Phonological memory is a temporary buffer zone where auditory data is held briefly as a precursor to further processing. Phonological awareness is the ability to discriminate speech sounds in words, hold them in memory, and manipulate them. Rapid naming is the ability to name objects, colors, letters, and numbers aloud quickly while being timed. The CTOPP is published by Riverside Publishing (www.riverpub.com).

Test of Written Language, Third Edition (TOWL-3)

The *Test of Written Language, Third Edition (TOWL-3)* focuses on two areas. The contrived portion of the test measures the child's ability to write dictated sentences with correct spelling, punctuation, and capitalization, read and use words in sentences, combine sentences, and edit nonsensical sentences to make sense. The spontaneous portion of the test assesses the child's ability to write a story based upon a picture prompt, while being timed. When testing written expression, it is important to use a lengthy writing sample that will demonstrate whether a child can plan and organize his or her thoughts on paper.

Some children can write individual sentences without being able to write a well constructed paragraph or essay. Other children struggle to express their thoughts grammatically on a sentence level. The TOWL-3 is published by Psychological Assessment Resources, Inc. (www3.parinc.com).

KeyMath Diagnostic Inventory, Revised (KeyMath-R)

The *KeyMath Diagnostic Inventory-Revised (KeyMath-R)* is organized into three areas: Basic Concepts, Operations, and Applications. Basic Concepts include Numeration, Rational Numbers, and Geometry. Operations includes basic written and mental computational skills. Applications provides information about Measurement, Time and Money, Estimation, Interpreting Data, and Problem Solving. The KeyMath-R can be administered to students between the ages of 5 to 21. This test does not measure many skills that are taught at the high school level, nor does it measure computational fluency. The KeyMath test is published by AGS Publishing (www.agsnet.com).

Comprehensive Mathematical Abilities Test (CMAT)

The *Comprehensive Mathematical Abilities Test (CMAT)* provides composite scores and individual subtest scores in Basic Calculations, Mathematical Reasoning, Practical Applications, and Advanced Calculations (Algebra, Geometry, Rational Numbers).

Although the test can be administered to children as young as seven years of age, it is particularly valuable at the high school level (through 18 years, 11 months). Although the manual indicates that some subtests can be administered with a calculator, the test was not normed in this way. The CMAT is published by Psychological Assessment Resources, Inc. (www3.parinc.com).

Personality Tests

Children experience intense frustration and unhappiness when they cannot succeed in school. Personality tests are designed to assess the child's mental state, degree of anxiety, and areas of stress. Personality tests often show that a child who is viewed as "emotionally disturbed," is often a reasonably healthy child who is experiencing intense stress and frustration because of chronic school failure.

Projective personality tests include:

- Children's Apperception Test (CAT)
- Draw-a-Person (DAP)
- House-Tree-Person (H-T-P)
- Kinetic Family Drawing
- Thematic Apperception Test (TAT)

Objective personality tests include:

- Minnesota Multiphasic Personality Inventory for Adolescents (MMPI-A)
- Millon Adolescent Clinical Inventory (MACI)

Behavior Rating Scales

Surveys and questionnaires provide norm-reference data about the child's behavior, how the child sees himself or herself, and how parents and teachers view the child.

Commonly administered questionnaires include the *Conners' Rating Scales-Revised* and the *Vineland Adaptive Behavior Scales, Second Edition (Vineland-II)*. The Conners' Rating Scales-Revised includes questionnaires for parents and teachers that focus on a wide range of problem behaviors including ADHD, impulsivity, anxiety, and social problems. The Conners' Scales is published by Psychological Assessment Resources, Inc. (www3.parinc.com)

The Vineland-II focuses on communication, daily living skills, socialization, and motor skills. It is used to help identify individuals with mental retardation, developmental delays, brain injuries, and other challenges. The Vineland is published by AGS Publishing (www.agsnet.com).

Speech and Language Tests

Oral language is the foundation for written language. Speech and language skills play a significant role in reading, written expression, and math. Children who have difficulty understanding the language they hear will experience those same challenges when working with language in print. Children who have difficulty expressing themselves with precision and style will have difficulty putting their thoughts on paper. Speech and language skills are not separate from academics, and they warrant careful consideration.

Many different speech and language tests can be useful in describing a child's strengths and weaknesses. Most speech and language tests examine listening and speaking skills. Some tests also examine higher level skills, including pragmatics (the ability to use language effectively), abstract and figurative language, and inferential thinking.

Commonly used speech and language tests include:

- Test of Language Development (TOLD-3)
- Clinical Evaluation of Language Fundamentals–Fourth Edition (CELF-4)
- Comprehensive Assessment of Spoken Language (CASL)
- Oral and Written Language Scales (OWLS)

Vocabulary Tests

There are also tests that measure vocabulary. The *Peabody Picture Vocabulary Test, Third Edition (PPCT-III)* assesses the child's understanding of word meanings. Children demonstrate what they know by pointing to the picture that best illustrates the word spoken by the examiner. The *Expressive Vocabulary Test (EVT)* measures spoken vocabulary, the ability to provide synonyms to words presented by the examiner. Because these tests were developed on the same population, they can be directly compared to assess word retrieval or word finding. Both tests are published by AGS Publishing (www.agsnet.com)

Neuropsychological Tests

Neuropsychological tests assess specific neurological issues that affect learning. Children who have difficulty processing information and have significant scatter often benefit from a neuropsychological evaluation. A comprehensive neuropsychological evaluation can be especially valuable if a child's eligibility for special education is disputed.

Charting Test Scores

Assume that three years ago, your child was tested with the Woodcock Johnson III Tests of Achievement (WJ III ACH). In the Word Identification subtest, your child scored at the 60th percentile. In Passage Comprehension, your child scored at the 10th percentile. The child's composite reading score was at the 35th percentile.

Recently, your child was reevaluated with the same form of the Woodcock-Johnson III. On Word Identification, your child scored at the 45th percentile. On Passage Comprehension, the child scored at the 5th percentile. The child's **composite reading score** was at the 25th percentile.

With these test results, you may conclude that your child needs a different, more intensive reading remediation program. The school may refuse because your child's composite reading score falls within the "average range." What can you do?

Creating Progress and Regression Charts

Graphs of your child's test scores are important tools. You can use test scores to create progress or regression graphs or charts. If you use computer software that can create graphs (i.e., MS Word, Excel, or PowerPoint), you can use the chart wizard to create graphs.

Use pre- and post-test scores to make graphs of your child's progress or regression. You can use the same data to make different types of graphs and charts. When you use a computer to make graphs, it is easy to change the display mode for your graphs (i.e., line and bar, portrait and landscape) Try different styles to find one that has a strong visual impact.

Visit Wrightslaw.com to view graphs and charts in PowerPoint

When parents make graphs that show a child's lack of progress, they can often persuade school personnel that the child needs a more intensive remediation program. The school may provide these services. On occasion, schools have reimbursed parents who paid for these services.

For more information about tuition reimbursement, see 20 U. S. C. § 1412(a)(10) in Chapter 16 and the *Burlington* and *Carter* cases in *Wrightslaw: Special Education Law, 2nd Edition*.

Using Test Scores in Your Child's IEPs

Assume that your child's IEP includes a keyboarding goal. The IEP goal purports to "measure" the child's progress by "teacher observation" with an 80 percent success rate. How can you write an IEP goal for keyboarding that includes objective scores?

By December 2005, the child will type 15 words-per-minute, with one word-per-minute deducted for each error, on a 5-minute timed typing test of text.

By June 2006, the child will type 30 words-per-minute, with five words per minute deducted for each error, on a 5-minute timed typing test of text.

This goal is Specific, Measurable, uses an Action word, is Realistic, and Time specific. You will learn more about "SMART" IEP goals in Chapter 12.

Your Homework Assignment

Read your Homework Assignment in Table 11-6. After you make a list of tests given to your child, select tests that have been given more than once. Use the Conversion Table (Table 11-2) to convert the repeated test scores from standard scores to percentile ranks. When you compare these scores, you should be able to tell if your child is making progress or regressing. Use your computer to create graphs. Experiment with the landscape (horizontal) appearance and the portrait (vertical) presentation to determine which style has the greater visual impact.

In Summation

In this chapter, you learned how to use pre- and post-tests to measure progress. You learned about norm-referenced and criterion-referenced tests, standard deviations, and standard scores. You learned how to convert standard scores into percentile ranks, and percentile ranks into standard scores.

You learned what the Index and subtests of the Wechsler Intelligence Scale for Children, Fourth Edition (WISC-IV) measure and how the WISC-IV is different from the WISC-III.

You learned about different types of IQ, achievement, speech and language, and personality tests. You learned how to chart your child's test scores and how to create graphs to display the child's progress or lack of progress. You learned how to use test scores in your child's IEP. You completed your Homework Assignment.

In the next chapter, you will learn about SMART IEPs that are specific, measurable, use action words, are realistic, and time-specific. You will learn how to use test scores in the present levels of performance and how to write measurable IEP goals.

Note: Melissa Farrall co-authored this chapter with Pete Wright.

Table 11-6 | *Parent's Homework Assignment*

1. Read these chapters about tests and measurement several times.

Use a highlighter or make margin notes to help you learn the information.

2. Make a list of all tests that have been given to your child. Arrange the list in chronological order.

Look for test results as standard scores and percentile ranks. Test scores may be reported as "ranges" (i.e., high-average, low-average) or as grade equivalent or age equivalent scores. If standard scores are not included in the evaluation, ask the school to provide this information. When you request your child's test data as standard scores, the school should comply with your request.

3. List all tests given more than once.

Using your list, make a new list of all tests that have been given more than once. Repeated tests will probably include the Wechsler Intelligence Scale, the Woodcock-Johnson, the Wechsler Individual Achievement Tests (WIAT), and/or the Kaufman Educational Achievement Tests.

4. Convert the standard scores into percentile ranks.

Make a list of the standard scores on the first test. Using the conversion chart in Table 11-2, convert the standard scores to percentile ranks. Make a list of the standard scores from the most recent test. Convert these standard scores to percentile ranks.

5. Compare scores.

When you compare the test results, you should know if your child is catching up (being remediated), staying in the same position, or falling behind (regression)

6. Make graphs of scores.

Find areas where your child has regressed or made minimal progress. Chart these test results. Computer software programs like MS Word, Excel and PowerPoint have "wizards" that will help you make your graphs. With these software programs, you can create dramatic visual presentations of test data. If you do not have a computer, you can use graph paper and colored markers to make graphs.

7. Consult with an independent expert.

Make an appointment to meet with the independent psychologist or educational diagnostician who evaluated your child. Gather your information – your list of test scores, the standard score/percentile rank conversion chart, the bell curve chart, and your child's evaluations – and take the information to your meeting.

Ask the private sector expert to use the bell curve chart with standard scores, standard deviations and percentile ranks to teach you about your child's test scores. Make a copy of the bell curve chart. If possible, it will be useful to tape-record the session so you can review it later along with the bell curve chart and test scores.

Endnotes

[a] Jerome M. Sattler, Ph.D., is widely regarded as one of the world's leading experts on assessment. He has published numerous articles and books, including *Assessment of Young Children*, which has been described as the "bible" of testing wisdom.

[b] Dr. Ron Dumont is an Associate Professor of Psychology at Fairleigh-Dickinson University in Teaneck, New Jersey who is well known for his expertise in cognitive assessment, learning disabilities, emotional disorders, and test reviews. With Jerome Sattler, he co-authored the *WISC-IV and WPPSI-III Supplement to Assessment for Children-Fourth Edition*. With John Willis, he co-authored a *Guide to the Identification of Learning Disabilities*.

[c] Sattler and Dumont, *WISC-IV and WPPSI-III Supplement to Assessment for Children-Fourth Edition*, page 73

[d] Sattler and Dumont, *WISC-IV and WPPSI-III Supplement to Assessment for Children-Fourth Edition*, page 48

[e] John O. Willis, Ed.D., SAIF, has been an assessment specialist at the Regional Services and Education Center, Amherst, NH since 1974. He has been a Lecturer in Assessment at Rivier College since 1981 and Senior Lecturer since 1989. He has been a volunteer, tutor, teacher, and administrator in special education since 1962. With Ron Dumont, he co-authored a *Guide to the Identification of Learning Disabilities*. He is a prolific writer about assessment.

[f] Dr. Keith Stanovich is the Research Chair of Applied Cognitive Science at the Department of Human Development and Applied Psychology at the University of Toronto in Canada. He is an expert not only in reading, but also in how reading helps to develop the mind.

[g] For additional information about the Matthew Effect, see Chapter Three of the Executive Summary of the National Reading Panel at www.nichd.nih.gov/publications/nrp/ch3.pdf

[h] Melissa Farrall, Ph.D, SAIF, M.Ed, is an independent evaluator and a founding director of The Reading Foundation in Amherst, New Hampshire (www.thereadingfoundation).

Dr. Farrall has always had a strong interest in language. She has designed text-to-speech algorithms enabling computers to read and talk, provided specialized instruction in the public schools, and taught graduate level courses in language, reading, and cognition at Rivier College.

Dr. Farrall received her doctorate from Brown University in 1981 in the area of Slavic Linguistics. She received her Master's Degree from Rivier College in Learning Disabilities in 1994, and her certification as a Specialist in the Assessment of Intellectual Functioning in 1999. She has served on the Board of Directors for the New Hampshire Branch of the International Dyslexia Association for several years.

Dr. Farrall lives in Merrimack, New Hampshire with her husband and two children, one of whom has a reading disability.

12 | SMART IEPs

> "If you're not sure where you're going, you're liable to end up someplace else. If you don't know where you're going, the best made maps won't help you get there."
>
> —Robert Mager, psychologist, writer, educator

If you are like many parents, you feel anxious and insecure at IEP meetings. What do you know? What can you offer? What should you do?

Some parents believe that if they are not educators, they have nothing of value to offer in planning their child's educational program. Other parents realize that their child's IEP is not appropriate but do not know how to resolve the problem. Diane belongs to this group:

I do not think my son's IEP is appropriate. The only goal is 'Commitment to academic success.' I imagine 'Commitment to academic success' is appropriate for all students. If 'Commitment to academic success' is not appropriate, what should I propose?

How are measurable goals defined? Can you give me an example of a well-written IEP? (Diane, parent of 15-year-old special education student)

Diane represents countless parents who are confused about IEP goals and objectives. If you are the parent of a child with a disability, you are probably confused too. How do you write IEP goals and objectives? Do you agree with Diane when she says, "Commitment to academic success is not an appropriate goal?"

Learning About SMART IEPs

The term SMART IEPs describes IEPs that are specific, measurable, use action words, are realistic and relevant, and time-limited.

S Specific

M Measurable

A Use Action Words

R Realistic and relevant

T Time-limited

Let's examine each of these concepts.

Specific

SMART IEPs have specific goals and objectives. Specific goals target areas of academic achievement and functional performance. They include clear descriptions of the knowledge and skills that will be taught and how the child's progress will be measured.

Look at these two goals. Which one is specific?

Dylan will increase study skills for academic success.

Dylan will demonstrate the following study skills: skimming written material and use reference materials in social studies class.

Measurable

SMART IEPs have measurable goals and objectives. Measurable means you can count or observe it. Measurable goals allow parents and teachers to know how much progress the child has made since the performance was last measured. With measurable goals, you will know when the child reaches the goal.

Which of these two goals is measurable and observable?

Owen will improve his reading skills.

Given second grade material, Owen will read a passage of text orally at 110-130 wpm with random errors.

Action Words

IEP goals include three components that must be stated in measurable terms:

(a) direction of behavior (increase, decrease, maintain, etc.)

(b) area of need (i.e., reading, writing, social skills, transition, communication, etc.)

(c) level of attainment (i.e., to age level, without assistance, etc.)

SMART IEPs use action words like: "The child will be able to . . ."

Which of these goals is specific, measurable and includes action words?

Betsy will decrease her anger and violation of school rules.

Provided with anger management training and adult support, Betsy will be able to remove herself from environments that cause her to lose control of her behavior so that she has no disciplinary notices.

Realistic and Relevant

SMART IEPs have realistic, relevant goals and objectives that address the child's unique needs that result from the disability. SMART IEP goals are not based on district curricula, state or district tests, or other external standards.

Which of these goals is specific, measurable and realistic?

Kelsey will demonstrate improved writing skills.

Kelsey will improve her writing and spelling skills so she can write a clear, cohesive, and readable paragraph consisting of at least 3 sentences, including compound and complex sentences that are clearly related.

Time-limited

SMART IEP goals and objectives are time-limited. What does the child need to know and be able to do after one year of special education? What is the starting point for each of the child's needs (present levels of academic achievement and functional performance)?

Time-limited goals and objectives enable you to monitor progress at regular intervals.

Assume your child is in the fifth grade. Alex's reading skills are at the early third grade level. Here is a specific, measurable, time-limited goal that tells you what Alex can do now and what he will be able to do after one year of special education:

Present Level of Performance: Given third grade material, Alex reads 50-70 wpm with 4-6 errors.

Annual Goal: Given fifth grade material, Alex will read 120 wpm with only random errors.

To ensure that Alex meets his goal, we will measure his progress at nine-week intervals (4 times during the school year).

After **9 weeks**, given third grade material, Alex will read 110 to 120 wpm with 1-3 errors.

After **18 weeks**, given fourth grade material, Alex will read 70-100 wpm with 1-3 errors.

After **27 weeks**, given fifth grade material, Alex will read 70-100 wpm with 1-3 errors.

At the **end of the year**, Alex will read 120 wpm with only random errors.

Smart IEP Goals and Objectives

IDEA 2004 requires your child's IEP to include:

a statement of the child's present levels of academic achievement and functional performance, including how the child's disability affects the child's involvement and progress in the general education curriculum . . . [and]

a statement of measurable annual goals, including academic and functional goals, designed to meet the child's needs that result from the child's disability to enable the child to be involved in and make progress in the general education curriculum; and . . . meet each of the child's other educational needs that result from the child's disability. (See Chapter 17: Section 1414 about IEPs)

Present Levels of Academic Achievement and Functional Performance

Begin by analyzing your child's present levels of performance. The present levels of performance describe "areas of need arising from the child's disability." The present levels of performance tell you what the child knows and is able to do.

How can you make your child's present levels of academic achievement and functional performance measurable? Here are some suggestions:

- You can specify performance at a grade or age level on objective tests.

- You can indicate a rate (i.e., 3 out of 4 times, 5 minutes out of every 10 minutes.)

Here are some things you need to consider when thinking about your child's IEPs:

- What is the relationship between the goal and the purpose of IDEA 2004, which is to prepare your child for further education, employment and independent living?

- What are your child's areas of need?

- How do these areas of need relate to your child's disability?

- How do these areas of need affect your child's progress in the general education curriculum?

- What does your child need to know or be able to do as a result of the IEP?

- What is it about the child's disability that is interfering with achieving this knowledge or skill?

- What is the measurable starting point for this knowledge or skill?

- How will you know if your child is learning this knowledge or skill?

- What will you see your child doing when s/he reaches this goal?

- What effect will reaching this goal have on your child's learning gaps as compared to his / her peers?

- How can this knowledge or skill be measured?

When you look at the test data from standardized testing and evaluations on your child, this will provide information about what your child knows and is able to do.

Here are some questions to help you identify your child's present levels of academic achievement:

- What is your child's level of academic achievement in reading, writing, spelling, and arithmetic?

- Can your child read the textbooks assigned to general education students in her grade?

- Are your child's reading skills two or three years below grade level on an individual educational achievement test of reading? (See Chapter 10 to learn about reading tests)

- Can your child read the grade level textbooks in core academic subjects?

Assume your child is in the tenth grade. Let's look at her functional performance in different areas.

- Can she read a job application? Can she complete the job application without assistance?
- Can she read the driver training manual? Can she pass the driving test without assistance?
- Can she read a map? A bus schedule? Can she balance a checkbook?
- Can she use the Internet to do research?

Developing the IEP

The Individuals with Disabilities Education Act of 2004 describes how IEPs should be developed. The IEP team **shall** consider:

- the child's strengths
- the parents' concerns for enhancing their child's education
- the results of the initial evaluation or most recent evaluation of the child
- the academic, developmental, and functional needs of the child.
  (20 USC §1414(d)(3)(A))

Use Baseline Data for Present Levels of Performance

The term "performance" describes what the child can do. What are your child's present levels of academic achievement and functional performance? What do your child's standard scores, percentile rank, grade equivalent and age equivalent scores mean? (If you completed the Homework Assignment in Chapter 11, you will be able to answer these questions.)

Present levels of academic achievement and functional performance include data from objective tests, including "criterion-referenced tests, standard achievement tests, diagnostic tests, or any combination of the above." (Source: Appendix A, Question 1, of the 1999 Regulations for IDEA 97)

If your child has reading problems, the baseline data for the present levels of academic achievement should include scores from educational achievement tests of reading. If your child has math problems, the present levels should include scores from achievement tests of math. (Note: The difference between subtest scores and composite scores is explained in Chapters 10 and 11.)

The purpose of using assessments is to determine the child's present levels of educational performance and areas of need arising from the child's disability so that approaches for ensuring the child's involvement and progress in the general curriculum and any needed adaptations or modifications to that curriculum can be identified. (Source: Appendix A, Question 1, of the 1999 Regulations for IDEA 97)

Measurable Academic and Functional Goals

IEP goals should enable the child to learn the basic skills that are necessary for the child to be independent and self-sufficient. These basic skills include:

- Communication skills

- Social skills and the ability to interact with others

- Reading skills

The child must learn to communicate. Most children communicate by expressive and receptive speech. Some children use assistive technology to communicate. The child must learn social skills so he or she can interact with other people. Finally, the child must learn to read. Reading is the gateway to all other knowledge.

"Teaching students to read by the end of third grade is the single most important task assigned to elementary schools." - American Federation of Teachers

The IEP should:

- Meet the child's academic, development, and functional needs that result from the disability;

- Enable the child to be involved in and progress in the general curriculum;

- Meet each of the child's other educational needs that result from the child's disability. (Source: 20 USC §1414(d))

IEP goals cannot be broad statements about what a child will accomplish in a year, but must address the child's academic achievement and functional performance. The IEP must identify all the child's needs, how the school will meet these needs, and how the school will measure the child's progress.

If the IEP is based on the child's present levels of academic achievement and related developmental needs, addresses the child's academic and functional needs, and includes research validated instructional methods, the IEP should pass muster under IDEA 2004.

If the IEP does not include measurable academic and functional goals, the IEP is defective and open to a challenge that it denies the child a FAPE.

SMART IEP Goals and Objectives

Write down several statements about what you want your child to know and be able to do. Revise these statements into goals that are specific, measurable, use action words, are realistic, and time-limited.

Break down each goal into a few measurable short-term steps. Describe what the child will know or be able to do. Focus on behavior that you can count or observe.

How will you know if your child is achieving these goals? Your child's progress should be assessed objectively and often. If your goals are measurable, you will be able to observe the child's behavior.

Here is a SMART IEP goal for a child who needs to learn to type:

At the end of the first semester, Mark will touch-type a passage of text at a speed of 20 words per minute, with no more than 10 errors, with progress measured on a five-minute timed test.

At the end of the second semester, Mark will touch-type a passage of text at a speed of 40 words per minute, with no more than 5 errors, with progress measured on a five-minute timed test.

This SMART goal is specific, measurable, and time-limited. It focuses on Mark's need to learn the functional skill of typing. You can measure Mark's progress by observing his typing speed and accuracy.

Short-term Objectives

In IDEA 2004, Congress eliminated requirements for short-term objectives and benchmarks in IEPs for students with disabilities, except for students who take alternate assessments.

By eliminating short-term objectives and benchmarks, Congress made teachers' jobs more difficult. Annual goals will have to be far more comprehensive than they were under IDEA 1997. Since short-term objectives and benchmarks were eliminated, this information will now have to be included in the annual goals.

Eliminating short-term objectives creates as many problems for educators as it does for parents. Short-term objectives and benchmarks are steps that measure the child's progress toward the annual goals in the IEP. When written correctly, short-term objectives provide teachers with a roadmap and a clear mechanism to evaluate the child's progress.

Pitfalls

As a parent, you must be vigilant. The danger is that the IEP team will propose annual goals that are not specific and measurable, do not meet the child's academic and functional needs, and do not describe how the child's progress will be measured.

Teachers will have to work harder and think more creatively to ensure that the annual goals address all the child's educational needs and that the goals are written in clear, measurable language.

Other IEP Issues

Advising Parents About Child's Progress

Did you know that the school must inform you about your child's educational progress at regular intervals? In fact, your child's IEP must include:

a description of how the child's progress toward meeting the annual goals ... will be measured and when periodic reports on the progress the child is making toward meeting the annual goals (such as through the use of quarterly or other periodic reports, concurrent with the issuance of report cards) will be provided. (Source: 20 U.S.C. § 1414(d)(A)(III))

Reviewing and Revising the IEP

As your child grows and changes, the child's educational needs will also change. The IEP team must meet at least once a year to review the child's IEP and determine whether the annual goals for the child are being achieved. The IEP team is to revise the IEP to address

- any lack of expected progress toward the annual goals and in the general education curriculum, where appropriate

- the results of any reevaluation

- information about the child provided to, or by, the parents

- the child's anticipated needs

- other matters

Learning to Write SMART Goals and Objectives

Are you still confused about SMART IEP goals and objectives? If you believe a parent cannot develop SMART goals and objectives, it is time to change your beliefs!

Change the facts. Assume that like many parents, inactivity and stress have caused you to gain weight. This extra weight came on gradually — so gradually that you did not realize how much weight you had gained until you went to the doctor for a check-up. When you weighed in, you discovered that you gained 50 pounds since your last checkup three years ago!

Your doctor has more bad news. You are "borderline diabetic" and your blood pressure is high. You must lose weight and change your lifestyle. If you do not take action, you are at risk to develop serious health problems within the next few years. The doctor advised you that children model their parent's behavior. If you do not change your behavior, your children are very likely to be obese and develop chronic health problems too.

When you go back to work, you think about what the doctor said. What can you do? You have been on fad diets. You lost weight but the loss was always temporary. When you went off the diet, you gained even more weight. You are worried and distracted. Fifty pounds!

Your friend Marie asks, "What's wrong?" You explain. Marie tells you that several of her friends used the Weight Watchers® Program to lose weight. She explains that Weight Watchers is not a crash-diet or fad. You hit the Internet and find the Weight Watchers web site. You learn that Weight Watchers programs are research-based by specialists in endocrinology, diabetes, nutrition, clinical and health psychology, and exercise physiology.

You talk to friends and do more research. You learn about low carb diets and low fat diets.

One night, you listened to a talk show on the way home from work. The guest was an engineer who became a physical fitness and nutrition expert. He said, "Successful weight loss is about a healthy diet and exercise." He explained, "One pound of fat is equal to 3,500 calories. If we reduce our daily caloric intake by 500 calories, we will lose one pound of fat in one week. If we burn 500 calories a day by exercising, we will lose one pound of fat a week. If we reduce our daily intake by 500 calories **and** burn 500 calories a day by exercising, we will lose two pounds a week.

The SMART Weight Loss Program

You decide to create a SMART Weight Loss Program that is tailored to your unique needs as an overweight, stressed-out parent. Your SMART Weight Loss Program will include goals and objectives that are specific, measurable, use action words, are realistic, relevant, and time-limited.

Present Levels: Baseline Data

You are 5 feet, 5 inches tall and weigh 190 pounds. You check height-weight charts on the Internet. According to these charts, you should weigh between 138 and 144 pounds. You plug your height (5 feet, 5 inches) and weight (190 pounds) to find your Body Mass Index. Your BMI is 32. A number of 30 or more "is considered obese – people in this range are at great risk for disease."

Measurable Goals and Objectives

Since you weigh 190 pounds, this is your starting point. Your goal is to lose 50 pounds. You decide to lose 10% of your body weight in 12 weeks. If you cut 800 calories a day, you should lose that 20 pounds in 12 weeks. You decide to reduce your daily caloric intake by 400 calories and burn another 400 calories a day through exercise.

> **Long-term Goal:** I will lose 50 pounds in nine months.
>
> **Short-term Objective:** I will lose 19 pounds (10% of my present weight) in 12 weeks.

Are your goals and objectives specific, measurable, use action words, realistic, relevant, and time-limited? Yes! An independent observer can quickly look at the data – your weight as measured by the bathroom scale – and determine if you are making progress toward your goal.

Revising Goals and Objectives

You were successful on your SMART Weight Loss Plan and lost 20 pounds in 12 weeks. At the end of 12 weeks, you weigh 170 pounds. You still need to lose 30 pounds to reach your goal of 140 pounds. If you continue at the rate of 1.5 pounds a week, you will reach your goal in approximately 20 weeks. You revise your goal:

> **Long-term Goal:** I will lose 30 pounds in 20 weeks.

> **Short-term Objective:** I will lose 15 pounds in 10 weeks. At the end of 10 weeks, my weight will be 155 pounds.

You are on a roll! At the end of 10 weeks, you weigh 155 pounds. Only 15 pounds to go! You revise your goal again:

> **Goal & Objective:** I will lose 15 pounds in 10 weeks. At the end of 10 weeks, my weight will be 140 pounds.

Are your goals and objectives specific, measurable, use action words, are realistic, and time-limited? Yes!

You designed a SMART Weight Loss Program to measure your progress objectively and often. When you broke down your long-term goal into short-term objectives, you gained control over the process. When you met the first objective of losing 10% of your body weight in 12 weeks, you realized that you could complete this weight loss program successfully.

You used SMART IEP principles to develop a SMART Weight Loss Program. Your SMART Weight Loss Program includes specific, measurable, active, realistic, time-limited goals and objectives.

Using Objective Data

When a doctor develops a treatment plan for a sick child, the doctor uses objective data from diagnostic tests. Medical specialists use objective data to measure the effectiveness of treatment plans. You want your doctor to use objective data to analyze the effectiveness of a treatment program, not subjective feelings and beliefs.

Your child's IEP is similar to a medical treatment plan. The IEP includes:

- Present levels of performance from objective tests and assessments
- Measurable goals and objectives
- A plan to address the child's educational problems
- A statement of how the child's progress will be measured

To Make Decisions

You are a member of your child's IEP team. The IEP team must identify and define your child's problems before the team can develop an appropriate educational plan.

The IEP team will gather information from different sources. This information may include observations of your child in different environments, including the home and classroom. This information includes objective test data that describes your child's problems, the severity of the problems, and measure your child's progress or lack of progress.

Let's look at a medical problem to see how progress should be assessed. Your son John complains that his throat is sore. His throat is red. His skin is hot to the touch. He is sleepy and lethargic. When you take John to the doctor, his temperature is 104 degrees. Lab tests show that John has an elevated white count. A strep test is positive. According to these tests, John has a strep infection.

Your doctor uses this objective test data to develop a treatment plan. When you return for a follow-up visit, the doctor is likely to order more tests. You need objective tests to know if John's infection is under control. Similarly, you need objective tests to know that your child is acquiring reading, writing and arithmetic skills.

To Measure Progress

Jay is an eight-year-old boy who received special education services for two years, beginning in kindergarten. Jay's parents felt that he was not learning how to read and write like other children his age. The school personnel assured the parents that Jay was making progress.

After two years, a child psychologist in the private sector tested Jay. While Jay's abilities were in the average to above average range, his reading and language skills were at the kindergarten level. Despite two years of special education, Jay had not learned to read or write.

When a teacher says a child is making progress, the teacher is offering an opinion based on subjective observations. In many cases, teacher opinions and subjective observations are not accurate. If you have concerns about your child's progress, get independent testing of your child's reading, writing, and mathematics skills by an expert in the private sector. These test results will tell you if your child is making progress.

Is your child receiving passing grades? Can you rely on grades to measure progress? No. Grades are not objective assessments of progress. Many factors influence grades, including grade inflation and the teacher's beliefs and perceptiona about the child's effort, attendance, behavior, and attitude.

You say, "The IEP for my child does not include objective measures of progress. How can the IEP be written differently? How can I tell if my child is actually making progress?"

Mike Trains for the Fitness Test

Change the facts. Your eight-year-old son, Mike, is upset because he did not pass the President's Physical Fitness Test. He wants to pass the test next year and asks for your help.

To pass the President's Physical Fitness Test, Mike must meet specific criteria. His performance on fitness skills is measured objectively. You check Mike's scores. He ran the 50-yard dash within the specified time. He completed only 12 out of an expected 25 sit-ups and could not complete a single pull-up.

You and Mike know what he needs to do to qualify for the President's Physical Fitness Award. You help him design a SMART training program with goals and objectives that target his weak areas (i.e. sit-ups, pull-ups) and maintain or improve his running ability.

When Mike takes the Fitness Test, his performance on the test is measured objectively. His running speed over a specified distance is measured with a stopwatch. His ability to do the required number of sit-ups and pull-ups is measured by counting. Because these measurements are objective, anyone who counts Mike's sit-ups and pull-ups will know if he meets the criteria for the Physical Fitness Award. The observer will focus on the outcome of the educational program, not the process of Mike's program.

Kevin Learns to Type

Let's look at a goal that is written to evaluate a child's progress subjectively. We will revise the goal to make it a SMART goal that is specific, measurable, uses action words, is realistic and relevant, and time-limited. Kevin is learning to type.

The school's proposed IEP goal says that Kevin will acquire keyboarding skills. Kevin's progress will be assessed by "Teacher Judgment," "Teacher Observation" and "Teacher-made Tests" with a score of "80%" as the criteria for success. This goal does not include information about words per minute or errors.

After we revise this goal to make it specific, measurable, active, realistic, relevant, and time-limited, the goal reads:

By the end of the first semester, Kevin will touch-type a passage of text at a rate of 15 words per minute with no more than 10 errors on a 5-minute test.

By the end of this academic year, Kevin will touch type a passage of text at a rate of 35 words per minute with no more than five errors on a 5-minute test.

Megan Learns to Read

Meet Megan, a fifth grader who has not learned to read. Megan's reading decoding skills are at the 10th percentile level. How will Megan's parents know if she is benefiting from the special education program? If Megan receives an appropriate education, her scores on reading subtests will improve.

According to Megan's SMART IEP goal:

After one year of specialized instruction, Megan will be able to decode words at the 25th percentile level as measured by the decoding score of the Gray Oral Reading Test (GORT).

When Megan's reading skills reach the 25th percentile level, she is making progress. Her progress will be measured with standardized tests. Megan's next IEP will include new goals and objectives to bring her reading skills up to the level of her peers.

Non-Goals: Attitude Statements

Earlier in this chapter, Diane asked if "commitment to academic success" was an appropriate goal. IEPs often include attitude statements, i.e., "have a good attitude," "display a cooperative spirit," or "develop healthy peer relationships."

You cannot measure an attitude. An attitude is a state of mind that exists within an individual. Attitudes are not measurable, nor are attitudes observable to outsiders.

You must be able to describe an outcome to know if the goal has been met. How will you know if an attitude goal is met? Can you measure Johnny's "better attitude?" No. Can you observe "commitment to academic success?" No.

Perhaps we agree that Johnny has a better attitude. On what do we base our opinions? Dr. Robert Mager, author of books about goal analysis and measuring educational outcomes, explains that we base our opinions on circumstantial evidence.

We use circumstantial evidence to decide if Johnny's attitude has improved. If Johnny displays behaviors that we associate with a good attitude, we conclude that Johnny's attitude has improved. Examples: Johnny smiles often. Johnny stopped yelling at the teacher and his classmates. Johnny offers to help others. These are observations, not subjective beliefs.

Strategies: How to Deal with Attitude Goals

Assume your son Johnny has behavior problems in class. The IEP team proposes to change Johnny's behavior. You agree that this is an appropriate goal but you have concerns about the educators' ability to devise specific, measurable, realistic goals to addresss the behavior. clear goals and objectives. What can you do?

Strategies: Ask Questions (the Columbo Strategy)

Use the Columbo Strategy. Ask questions —"5 Ws + H + E" questions. (Who, What, Why, Where, When, How, and Explain.) Tell the school staff that you are confused. You want to ask a stupid question. (Do you see why we call this the "Columbo Strategy?")

What is Johnny doing? How often? When? Ask more questions. Listen attentively to the answers. If you use "5 Ws + H + E" questions skillfully, you may be able to help school personnel shift from reporting their feelings and beliefs to reporting their observations. facts and observations.

From the team members' comments, you can make a list of behaviors. What behaviors will they observe? Who will observe these behaviors? When? How often? As you continue to ask questions, the team members will make statements that describe observable behavior—circumstantial evidence.

Finally, his teacher says, "Johnny pinches his classmates at least two times an hour." Good! Now you have data. You have Johnny's present levels of performance in pinching to use as a starting point.

You ask, "What change in Johnny's pinching behavior do we seek?"

The teacher may say, "Johnny should never pinch anyone." While this may be true, you need a baseline starting point before you can develop a goal and measure improved behavior.

After some discussion, the team formulates this goal: "During the next two weeks, Johnny will pinch classmates no more than once every two hours." Now you have a goal that allows you to measure changes in Johnny's pinching behavior.

Anticipate resistance from educators if you criticize abstract goals and request observable goals and objectives. When you encounter resistance, use this strategy suggested by Dr. Mager.

Ask the resistant person to describe the child's negative, undesirable observable behaviors. Make a list of these negative observable behaviors that need to be changed. When you finish your list, turn the list around and use the list to describe desired positive behaviors. These positive behaviors are "circumstantial evidence" that can be used to determine that the goal has been reached

Strategies: Make Behavior Measurable

You can make behavior measurable by defining the factors surrounding the behavior. These factors include:

- precipitating events ("when asked to work independently")
- environmental factors ("when dealing with female authority figures)
- other observable patterns ("after lunch," "always on the playground," "in math class")

You can also make behavior measurable by identifying the results of the behavior (i.e. "removal from the classroom increases this negative behavior.")

Non-Goals: States of Being

Many IEPs include goals that cannot be measured. Examples: to appreciate music, to understand weather, to have a better attitude, to develop a love of reading, to show respect for authority.

Non-Goal: The student will appreciate classical music.

To accomplish this non-goal, the student will listen to classical music three hours a day, for one month. How can you assess "appreciation of classical music?" How will independent observers know if the student appreciates classical music? The goal focuses on a state of being. You cannot measure a state of being.

Non-Goal: The student will understand the workings of a gasoline combustion engine.

Do you want the student to understand a gasoline combustion engine? How will you know if the student understands a gasoline combustion engine?

Do you really want the student to be able to repair a gasoline combustion engine? Do you want the student to be able to take an engine apart and put it back together? Do you want the student to be able to diagnose a malfunctioning engine?

Homework Assignment #1: You Learn to Write Goals

Make a list of statements that describe what you expect your child to know (knowledge) and what you expect your child to be able to do (performance).

Select one statement. Write one goal that is specific, measurable, uses action words, is realistic and relevant, and is time-limited. Use words that describe the intended outcome. For example, "Mary will be able to . . ."

Write the performances that will show that your child has mastered the goal. As you read these statements, you see how they become more specific:

- My child will learn to read.
- My child will learn to read at the fifth grade level.
- After one year of individualized tutoring an hour a day, my child will read at the fifth grade level.
- After one year of individualized tutoring an hour a day in the acquisition of reading skills, my child will read at the fifth grade level, as measured by the global composite score of the Gray Oral Reading Test.

Your independent consultant or evaluator can give you reasonable timeframes for remediation. Do not set your goals too low!

Homework Assignment #2: You Learn to Write SMART IEP Goals and Objectives

Go through the most recent testing on your child. Make a list of your child's educational achievement scores in reading, writing, mathematics, and spelling.

Revise your list and write your child's skills in objective measurable terms. Use data from tests (i.e., percentile ranks, standard scores, grade- or age-equivalent scores).

List your child's baseline skills as present levels of performance. Example: "My child reads a passage of text orally at the 10th percentile level as measured by the Gray Oral Reading Test."

After one year of special education, where should the skill be? Write this statement as a measurable goal. For example:

By May 15 [one year later], my child will be able to read a passage of text orally at the ___ [insert the appropriate increased percentile or grade equivalent level] as measured by the Gray Oral Reading Test.

Earlier in this book, we described the hierarchy of skills that children must acquire:

- Communication skills
- Social skills and the ability to interact with others
- Reading skills

Most children with disabilities have reading problems. In the last three chapters, you learned how to measure reading skills objectively.

You need to focus on the skills your child needs to acquire. These skills may include communication, social skills, academic skills, or knowledge and skills in other areas affected by your child's disability. You need to determine how you can objectively determine the child's baseline levels of performance and how to measure the child's progress.

To learn more about IEP goals that are appropriate for your child, you must learn about your child's disability. You must learn how to measure changes in skills. When you master these tasks, you will be able to write measurable goals and objectives.

In Summation

In this chapter, you learned about SMART IEPs that are specific, measurable, use action words, are realistic and relevant, and time-limited. You learned how to use baseline levels of performance to write measurable goals and objectives. It's time to learn about special education law.

Section Four

Special Education Law

As the parent of a child with a disability, you need to learn how to do legal research. If the school says, "The law says we cannot do what you ask us to do," you need to research the issue independently. After you read the statute, the regulation, and a case or two, you will know what the law says the school can and should do. Knowledge gives you power.

To understand a legal issue, you should study three types of law:

- Statutory law
- Regulatory law
- Judicial decisions, also known as case law

Read the statute first. Next, read the federal regulation and your state regulation. The regulation usually expands on the statute. Then, read cases that interpret your issue. After you read the statute, regulations, and cases, you will understand the law about your issue. Do not rely on legal advice provided by school personnel or articles written by others. In this book, you will read the law. In the beginning, this is more difficult than having the law interpreted for you. As you read, the law will begin to fit together in your mind. When you know how the law is organized, you can find sections or regulations that are relevant to your situation.

Each chapter in this Section begins with a short introduction, followed by selected portions of the statute. After the statute is a Wrightslaw discussion of the statute.

The Individuals with Disabilities Education Act of 2004 is divided into five parts:

Part A - General Provisions (includes Findings & Purposes, Definitions)

Part B - Assistance for Education of All Children with Disabilities (includes state responsibilities, evaluations, eligibility, IEPs, procedural safeguards)

Part C - Infants and Toddlers with Disabilities

Part D - National Activities to Improve Education of Children with Disabilities

Part E - National Center for Special Education Research

Parents, advocates, attorneys, and educators will refer most often to the following sections:

Section 1400 - Findings and Purposes

Section 1401 - Definitions

Section 1412 - State Responsibilities (the "Catch-all Statute)

Section 1414 - Evaluations, Eligibility, IEPs, Placements

Section 1415 - Procedural Safeguards

This section of the book includes the most important laws that govern the education of children with disabilities, including portions of :

The Individuals with Disabilities Education Act of 2004

Section 504 of the Rehabilitation Act of 1973

The No Child Left Behind Act of 2001

Wrightslaw: From Emotions to Advocacy is a tactics and strategy manual that includes this primer about special education law.

In the next chapters, you will find references to other Wrightslaw books: *Wrightslaw: No Child Left Behind*, a legal reference book about the federal law that was enacted to help disadvantaged children and *Wrightslaw: Special Education Law, 2nd Edition*, a legal reference book that includes tactics and strategies (expected publication date: Spring 2006).

13 | IDEA – Overview and Legislative Intent

"In these days, it is doubtful that any child may reasonably be expected to succeed in life if he is denied the opportunity of an education."
—*Brown v. Board of Education*, 347 U.S. 483 (1954)

In this chapter, you will learn about the factors that led Congress to enact the special education law in 1975 and the most recent amendment in 2004. You will also learn about statutory law, regulatory law, case law, and the Supremacy Clause.

Legislative Intent

On November 19, 1975, Congress enacted Public Law 94-142, also known as **The Education for All Handicapped Children Act of 1975.**

In May 1972, this legislation was introduced after several:

. . . landmark court cases establishing in law the right to education for all handicapped children . . .

In 1954, the Supreme Court of the United States (in *Brown v. Board of Education*) established the principle that all children be guaranteed equal educational opportunity.

In these days, it is doubtful that any child may reasonably be expected to succeed in life if he is denied the opportunity of an education. Such an opportunity . . . is a right which must be made available to all on equal terms.

Congress described the high social and economic costs that society paid for failing to provide an appropriate education:

Yet, the most recent statistics provided by the Bureau of Education for the Handicapped estimated that of the more than 8 million children . . . with handicapping conditions requiring special education and related services, only 3.9 million such children are receiving an appropriate education. 1.75 million handicapped children are receiving no educational services at all, and 2.5 million handicapped children are receiving an inappropriate education.

The long-range implications of these statistics are that public agencies and taxpayers will spend billions of dollars over the lifetimes of these individuals to *maintain such persons as dependents and in a minimally acceptable lifestyle. With proper education services, many would be able to **become productive citizens**, contributing to society instead of being **forced to remain burdens**. Others, through such services, would **increase their independence**, thus **reducing their dependence on society**.*

*There is no pride in being forced to receive economic assistance. Not only does this have **negative effects upon the handicapped person**, but it has far reaching effects for such person's family.*

*Providing educational services will ensure against persons needlessly being **forced into institutional settings**. One need only look at public residential institutions to find thousands of persons whose families are no longer able to care for them and who themselves have received no educational services. Billions of dollars are expended each year to maintain persons in these subhuman conditions . . .*

*Parents of handicapped children all too frequently are **not able to advocate the rights of their children** because they have been **erroneously led to believe that their children will not be able to lead meaningful lives** . . .*

It should not . . . be necessary for parents throughout the country to continue utilizing the courts to assure themselves a remedy . . .

The Individuals with Disabilities Education Act of 2004

Congress amended the Individuals with Disabilities Education Act several times since 1975. On December 3, 2004, Congress amended the Individuals with Disabilities Education Act again. The newly amended statute is the Individuals with Disabilities Education Improvement Act of 2004 (IDEA 2004).

The amended statute is in Volume 20 of the United States Code (U.S.C.), beginning at Section 1400. The special education regulations will be published in Volume 34 of the Code of Federal Regulations, (C.F.R.) beginning at Section 300.

Each state has special education statutes and regulations that must be consistent with federal law. State laws may not diminish or reduce the rights of special education children but may provide children with more rights and protections. The rules of procedure vary from state to state. When state law conflicts with federal law, federal law is supreme, pursuant to the Supremacy Clause of the U. S. Constitution.

In Summation

In this chapter, you learned about the legislative history of the special education law. In the next chapter, you will learn about the Findings and Purposes of the Individuals with Disabilities Education Act.

14 | IDEA– Section 1400: Findings and Purposes

"If the children are untaught, their ignorance and vices will in future life cost us much dearer in their consequences than it would have done in their correction by a good education."   —Thomas Jefferson

The most important statutes in the Individuals with Disabilities Education Act are Findings and Purposes in Section 1400. The history and findings that led Congress to pass the Education for All Handicapped Children Act of 1975 (Public Law 94-142), now called the Individuals with Disabilities Education Improvement Act, are in Section 1400(c).

The most important statute in IDEA is Purposes in Section 1400(d): "to ensure that all children with disabilities have available to them a free appropriate public education that emphasizes special education and related services designed to **meet their unique needs** and **prepare them for further education, employment and independent living**" and "to ensure that the **rights of children** with disabilities **and parents** of such children are protected ..." When you are confused about a term or section in the law, go back and re-read Section 1400, especially Purposes in Section 1400(d).

Note: When you see this * * * it signifies that a portion of the statute is not included. For the full text of a specific statute in IDEA 2004, you will want to refer to *Wrightslaw: IDEA 2004* or *Wrightslaw: Special Education Law, 2nd Edition.*

A Wrightslaw discussion of these issues follows Section 1400.

20 U.S.C. § 1400 Congressional Findings and Purposes

(c) Findings.

Congress finds the following:

(1) Disability is a natural part of the human experience and in no way diminishes the right of individuals to participate in or contribute to society. **Improving educational**

results for children with disabilities **is an essential element of our national policy** of ensuring equality of opportunity, full participation, independent living, and economic self-sufficiency for individuals with disabilities.

(2) Before the date of enactment of the Education for All Handicapped Children Act of 1975 (Public Law 94-142), the educational needs of millions of children with disabilities were not being fully met because--

(A) the children did not receive appropriate educational services;

(B) the children were excluded entirely from the public school system and from being educated with their peers;

(C) undiagnosed disabilities prevented the children from having a successful educational experience; or

(D) a lack of adequate resources within the public school system forced families to find services outside the public school system.

(3) Since the enactment and implementation of the Education for All Handicapped Children Act of 1975, this title has been successful in ensuring children with disabilities and the families of such children access to a free appropriate public education and in improving educational results for children with disabilities.

(4) However, the implementation of this title has been **impeded by low expectations, and an insufficient focus on applying replicable research on proven methods of teaching and learning for children with disabilities.**

(5) Almost 30 years of research and experience has demonstrated that the education of children with disabilities can **be made more effective by -**

(A) **having high expectations** for such children and **ensuring their access to the general education curriculum in the regular classroom,** to the maximum extent possible, in order to -

(i) **meet developmental goals** and, **to the maximum extent possible, the challenging expectations that have been established for all children;** and

(ii) be **prepared to lead productive and independent adult lives,** to the maximum extent possible;

(B) **strengthening the role and responsibility of parents** and ensuring that families of such children have meaningful opportunities to participate in the education of their children at school and at home;

(C) coordinating this title with other local, educational service agency, State, and Federal school improvement efforts, including improvement efforts under the Elementary and Secondary Education Act of 1965, in order to ensure that such children benefit from such efforts and that **special education can become a service for such children rather than a place where such children are sent;**

(D) **providing appropriate special education and related services,** and aids and supports **in the regular classroom,** to such children, whenever appropriate;

(E) supporting **high-quality, intensive preservice preparation and professional development** for all personnel who work with children with disabilities in order to **ensure that such personnel have the skills and knowledge** necessary to improve the academic achievement and functional performance of children with disabilities, including the **use of scientifically based instructional practices,** to the maximum extent possible;

(F) providing incentives for whole-school approaches, **scientifically based early reading programs, positive behavioral interventions and supports, and early intervening services** to reduce the need to label children as disabled in order to address the learning and behavioral needs of such children;

(G) focusing resources on teaching and learning while reducing paperwork and requirements that do not assist in improving educational results; and

(H) supporting the development and use of technology, including assistive technology devices and assistive technology services, to maximize accessibility for children with disabilities.

* * *

(d) Purposes. The purposes of this title are –

(1)

(A) to ensure that **all children with disabilities have** available to them **a free appropriate public education** that emphasizes special education and related services **designed to meet their unique needs and prepare them for further education, employment, and independent living;**

(B) to ensure that the **rights of children with disabilities and parents** of such children **are protected;** and

(C) to assist States, localities, educational service agencies, and Federal agencies to provide for the education of all children with disabilities;

(2) to assist States in the implementation of a statewide, comprehensive, coordinated, **multidisciplinary, interagency system of early intervention services** for infants and toddlers with disabilities and their families;

(3) to ensure that educators and parents have the necessary tools to improve educational results   for children with disabilities by supporting system improvement activities; coordinated research and personnel preparation; coordinated technical assistance, dissemination, and support; and technology development and media services; and

(4) **to assess, and ensure the effectiveness of, efforts to educate children with disabilities.**

Wrightslaw Discussion of Findings and Purposes

When we feel overwhelmed by a daunting task before us, it is helpful to look at the progress we have made.

Findings

When Congress enacted the Education for All Handicapped Children Act (Public Law 94-142) in 1975, fewer than half of all children with disabilities were receiving an appropriate education. More than one million children were excluded from school. Initially, the law focused on ensuring that children had access to an education and due process of law.

Accountability and Improved Outcomes

When Congress reauthorized the law in 2004, they focused on accountability and improved outcomes by bringing IDEA 2004 into conformity with the No Child Left Behind Act. IDEA 2004 includes new requirements for early intervening services, research-based instruction, and highly qualified special education teachers.

Research-Based Instruction: "Proven Methods of Teaching and Learning"

IDEA 2004 requires schools to use "proven methods of teaching and learning" based on "replicable research." Many schools continue to use educational methods that are not research-based. Pressure from litigation, legal rulings requiring schools to use research-based methods, and No Child Left Behind are forcing school districts to adopt research-based methods of teaching.

Purposes: The Mission Statement of IDEA

Purposes in Section 1400(d) is the mission statement of IDEA. The purpose of special education is to prepare children with disabilities for further education, employment, and independent living. When you develop IEPs, use this "mission statement" as your long-term goal.

Stop. Go back and re-read the Purpose in Section 1400(d)(1)(A). Mark this in your book so you can find it easily. This is the most important part of IDEA.

In Summation

In this chapter, you learned about the findings and purposes of the special education law. In the next chapter, you will learn the definitions of key terms.

15 | IDEA–Section 1401: Definitions

"Loyalty to a petrified opinion never broke a chain or freed a human soul." – Mark Twain, author

Six new definitions were added to IDEA 2004: core academic subjects, highly qualified teacher, homeless children, limited English proficient, universal design, and ward of the state. In this chapter, you will become familiar with the legal definitions of eight of the 36 terms defined in the reauthorized law. This chapter will help you understand, apply, and use these terms used in the statute.

Note: When you see this * * * it signifies that a portion of the statute is not included in this book. For the full. text of a specific statute in IDEA 2004, you will want to read *Wrightslaw: IDEA 2004* or *Wrightslaw: Special Education Law, 2nd Edition*.

A Wrightslaw discussion of these issues follows Section 1401.

20 U.S.C. § 1401 Definitions

Except as otherwise provided, in this title:

* * *

(3) Child With A Disability.

(A) In General. The term 'child with a disability' means a child–

(i) with mental retardation, hearing impairments (including deafness), speech or language impairments, visual impairments (including blindness), serious emotional disturbance (referred to in this title as 'emotional disturbance'), orthopedic impairments, autism, traumatic brain injury, other health impairments, or specific learning disabilities; and

(ii) **who, by reason thereof, needs special education and related services.**

(B) Child Aged 3 Through 9. The term 'child with a disability' for a child aged 3 through 9 (or any subset of that age range, including ages 3 through 5), may, at the discretion of the State and the local educational agency, include a child–

(i) experiencing developmental delays, as defined by the State and as measured by appropriate diagnostic instruments and procedures, in 1 or more of the following areas: physical development; cognitive development; communication development; social or emotional development; or adaptive development; and

(ii) **who, by reason thereof, needs special education and related services.**

* * *

(9) Free Appropriate Public Education. The term 'free appropriate public education' means special education and related services that–

(A) have been provided at public expense, under public supervision and direction, and without charge;

(B) meet the standards of the State educational agency;

(C) include an appropriate preschool, elementary school, or secondary school education in the State involved; and

(D) are provided in conformity with the individualized education program required under section 1414(d) of this title.

* * *

(23) Parent. The term '**parent**' means–

(A) a natural, adoptive, or foster parent of a child (unless a foster parent is prohibited by State law from serving as a parent);

(B) a guardian (but not the State if the child is a ward of the State);

(C) an individual acting in the place of a natural or adoptive parent (including a grandparent, stepparent, or other relative) with whom the child lives, or an individual who is legally responsible for the child's welfare; or

(D) except as used in sections 1415(b)(2) and 1439(a)(5), an individual assigned under either of those sections to be a surrogate parent.

* * *

(26) Related Services.

(A) In General. The term '**related services**' means **transportation**, and such **developmental, corrective, and other supportive services** (including speech-language pathology and audiology services, interpreting services, psychological services, physical and occupational therapy, recreation, including therapeutic recreation, social work services, school nurse services designed to enable a child with a disability to receive a free appropriate public education as described in the individualized education program of the child, counseling services, including rehabilitation counseling, orientation and mobility services, and medical services, except that such medical services shall be for diagnostic and evaluation purposes only) as may be required **to assist a child with a disability to benefit from special education,** and includes the early identification and assessment of disabling conditions in children.

(B) Exception. The term does not include a medical device that is surgically implanted, or the replacement of such device.

* * *

(29) Special Education. The term 'special education' means specially designed instruction, at no cost to parents, to meet the unique needs of a child with a disability, including -

(A) instruction conducted in the classroom, in the home, in hospitals and institutions, and in other settings; and

(B) instruction in physical education.

* * *

(30) Specific Learning Disability.

(A) In General. The term 'specific learning disability' means a disorder in 1 or more of the basic psychological processes involved in understanding or in using language, spoken or written, which disorder may manifest itself in the imperfect ability to listen, think, speak, read, write, spell, or do mathematical calculations.

(B) Disorders Included. Such term includes such conditions as perceptual disabilities, brain injury, minimal brain dysfunction, dyslexia, and developmental aphasia.

(C) Disorders Not Included. Such term does not include a learning problem that is primarily the result of visual, hearing, or motor disabilities, of mental retardation, of emotional disturbance, or of environmental, cultural, or economic disadvantage.

* * *

(33) Supplementary Aids and Services. The term 'supplementary aids and services' means aids, services, and other supports that are provided **in regular education classes** or other education-related settings to enable children with disabilities to be educated with nondisabled children to the maximum extent appropriate in accordance with section 1412(a)(5) of this title.

(34) Transition Services. The term 'transition services' means a coordinated set of activities for a child with a disability that–

(A) is designed to be within a results-oriented process, that is focused on improving the academic and functional achievement of the child with a disability to facilitate the child's movement from school to post-school activities, including post-secondary education, vocational education, integrated employment (including supported employment), continuing and adult education, adult services, independent living, or community participation;

(B) is based on the individual child's needs, taking into account the child's strengths, preferences, and interests; and

(C) includes instruction, related services, community experiences, the development of employment and other post-school adult living objectives, and, when appropriate, acquisition of daily living skills and functional vocational evaluation.

Wrightslaw Discussion of Definitions

For the parent of a child with a disability, the most important definition is "child with a disability." Your child's classification as a "child with a disability" controls your child's eligibility for special education under the Individuals with Disabilities Education Act.

Child with a Disability

A child with a disability is not automatically eligible for special education and related services under IDEA. The key phrase is "who, by reason thereof, needs special education and related services." Does the child's disability adversely affect educational performance? To be eligible for a free, appropriate public education under the IDEA, the child must meet both criteria.

If a child has a disability but does not need special education services, the child will not be eligible under IDEA but may be eligible for protections under Section 504 of the Rehabilitation Act.

Free Appropriate Public Education (FAPE)

The term free appropriate public education (FAPE) has been litigated extensively since the IDEA was enacted. In *Board of Education v. Rowley*, 458 U.S. 176 (1982), the U. S. Supreme Court concluded that the child with a disability is not entitled to the "best" education, nor to an education that maximizes the child's potential.

Highly Qualified

Special educators who teach core academic subjects must meet the highly qualified teacher requirements in NCLB and must demonstrate competence in the core academic subjects they teach. Special educators who do not provide instruction in core academic subjects do not have to meet the highly qualified teacher requirements.

The full text of Section 1401(10) about highly qualified teachers is in *Wrightslaw: IDEA 2004* and *Wrightslaw: Special Education Law, 2nd Edition.*

While the lengthy definition of "highly qualified teacher" is not included in this book, it is located in IDEA 2004 at Section 1401(10), in Title IX of No Child Left Behind (NCLB) at Section 7801(23) and also referenced in NCLB Section 6311(b)(1).

The full text of the No Child Left Behind Act is in *Wrightslaw: No Child Left Behind*. For guidance about how NCLB applies to special educators, read Chapter 6, "NCLB for Teachers, Principals and Paraprofessionals" in *Wrightslaw: No Child Left Behind.* Dozens of resources for educators are included in the NCLB CD-ROM in *Wrightslaw: No Child Left Behind.*

Parent

IDEA 2004 expanded the definition of "parent" to include natural, adoptive, and foster parents, guardians, individuals who act in the place of a parent, individuals who are legally responsible for the child, and surrogate parents.

Special Education

Special education is defined as "specially designed instruction, at no cost to the parents, to meet the unique needs of a child with a disability . . ."

Special education encompasses a range of services and may include one-on-one tutoring, intensive academic remediation, and 40-hour Applied Behavioral Analysis (ABA) programs. Special education is provided in different settings, including the child's home.

Specific Learning Disability

Congress did not change the definition of "specific learning disability" in IDEA 2004. However, Congress did change the language about evaluations for specific learning disabilities. Schools do not have to find a discrepancy between IQ and educational achievement to find a child eligible for special education services as a child with a specific learning disability. (See Chapter 17: Section 1414)

Many terms used to describe disabilities in IDEA are those used during the 1970's when Congress enacted Public Law 94-142. The term "minimal brain dysfunction" is now "Attention Deficit Disorder." "Dyslexia" is a language learning disability in reading, writing, spelling, and/or math. From a legal perspective, dyslexia is a learning disability that adversely affects educational performance.

Supplementary Aids and Services

Supplementary aids and services are provided in general education classes so children with disabilities can be educated with their non-disabled peers. Compare "supplementary aids and services" with "related services" in Section 1401(26).

Transition Services

Congress changed the definition of transition services, emphasizing that transition is "a results-oriented process that is focused on improving the child's academic and functional achievement. The goal is to facilitate the child's movement to life after school.

Remember the language in "Purposes" about preparing disabled children for "further education, employment and independent living?" IDEA 2004 includes new language about IEPs about "measurable postsecondary goals" and "courses of study" to reach those goals (Section 1414(d)) and in Findings about "effective transition services to promote successful post-school . . . education." (Section § 1400(c)(14))

In Summation

In this chapter, you learned the definitions of legal terms that are often litigated. When Congress passes legislation that includes vague terms, this is usually because the legislators could not agree on definitions t hat were acceptable to all. By using vague terms, they ensured that courts would define the terms. This is true in many areas of law.

To understand the definitions that may affect your child's situation, read the statute. Definitions and legal terms are often ambiguous and must be interpreted in light of the purposes of IDEA 2004. It may help to go back and re-read "Purposes" in Section 1400(d).

In the next chapter, you will learn about Section 1412, State Eligibility, often called the "catch-all statute." You will learn about the right to a free appropriate education, child find, least restrictive environment and mainstreaming, reimbursement for private placements, and and new requirements about participation in state and district assessments, accommodations guidelines, and alternate assessments.

16 | IDEA–Section 1412: LRE, ESY, Child Find, Private Placement, Assessments

"Most schools function – with stunning efficiency – to stop real learning."
—George Leonard, author

Section 1412 about State Eligibility is often called the "Catch-All" statute because it includes such diverse topics: child find, least restrictive environment, transition to preschool programs, equitable services to children in private schools, unilateral placements in private programs, tuition reimbursement, new requirements about participation in assessments, accommodations guidelines, and alternate assessments.

Although Extended School Year (ESY) is not cited in the IDEA statute, the special education regulations that interpret Section 1412 clarify ESY.

To receive federal funds, States must provide assurances to the U. S. Department of Education that they have policies and procedures in place to ensure that all children with disabilities receive a free appropriate public education. The right to a free, appropriate public education extends to children with disabilities who have been suspended or expelled from school.

Note: When you see this * * * it signifies that a portion of the statute is not included in this book. For the full. text of a specific statute in IDEA 2004, you will want to read *Wrightslaw: IDEA 2004* or *Wrightslaw: Special Education Law, 2nd Edition*.

A Wrightslaw discussion of these issues follows Section 1412.

20 U.S.C. § 1412: State Eligibility

(a) **In General.** A State is eligible for assistance under this part for a fiscal year if the State submits a plan that provides assurances to the Secretary that the State has in effect policies and procedures to ensure that the State meets each of the following conditions:

(1) **Free Appropriate Public Education.**

(A) **In General.** A free appropriate public education is available to **all children with disabilities** residing in the State **between the ages of 3 and 21**, inclusive, **including** children with disabilities who have been suspended or expelled from school.
* * *

(3) **Child Find.**

(A) **In General. All children with disabilities** residing in the State, including children with disabilities who are homeless children or are wards of the State and children with disabilities attending private schools, regardless of the severity of their disabilities, and who are in need of special education and related services, are **identified, located, and evaluated** and a practical method is developed and implemented to determine which children with disabilities are currently receiving needed special education and related services.

(B) **Construction. Nothing** in this title **requires that children be classified by their disability** so long as each child who has a disability listed in section 1401 of this title and who, by reason of that disability, needs special education and related services is regarded as a child with a disability under this part.
* * *

(5) **Least Restrictive Environment.**

(A) **In General. To the maximum extent appropriate,** children with disabilities, including children in public or private institutions or other care facilities, **are educated with children who are not disabled,** and special classes, separate schooling, or other removal of children with disabilities from the regular educational environment **occurs only when the nature or severity** of the disability of a child is such that education in regular classes with the use of supplementary aids and services cannot be achieved satisfactorily.
* * *

(6) **Procedural Safeguards.**

(A) **In General.** Children with disabilities and their parents are afforded the procedural safeguards required by section 1415 of this title.

(B) **Additional Procedural Safeguards.** Procedures to ensure that **testing and evaluation materials and procedures** utilized for the purposes of evaluation and placement of children with disabilities for services under this title will be selected and administered so as **not to be racially or culturally discriminatory.** Such materials or procedures shall be provided and administered **in the child's native language or mode of communication,** unless it clearly is not feasible to do so, and **no single procedure shall be the sole criterion** for determining an appropriate educational program for a child.
* * *

(10) Children in Private Schools.

(A) Children Enrolled in Private Schools by Their Parents.

(i) In General. To the extent consistent with the number and location of children with disabilities in the State who are enrolled by their parents in private elementary schools and secondary schools in the school district served by a local educational agency, provision is made for the participation of those children in the program assisted or carried out under this part by providing for such children special education and related services in accordance with the following requirements, unless the Secretary has arranged for services to those children under subsection (f) . . .

* * *

(ii) Child Find Requirement.

(I) In General. The requirements of paragraph (3) (relating to child find) **shall apply** with respect to children with disabilities in the State who are **enrolled in private, including religious, elementary schools and secondary schools.**

* * *

(iii) Consultation. To ensure timely and meaningful consultation, a local educational agency, or where appropriate, a State educational agency, **shall consult with private school representatives and representatives of parents of parentally placed private school children** with disabilities during the design and development of special education and related services for the children, including regarding -

* * *

(B) Children Placed in, or Referred to, Private Schools by Public Agencies.

(i) In General. Children with disabilities in private schools and facilities are provided special education and related services, in accordance with an individualized education program, at no cost to their parents, if such children are placed in, or referred to, such schools or facilities by the State or appropriate local educational agency as the means of carrying out the requirements of this part or any other applicable law requiring the provision of special education and related services to all children with disabilities within such State.

* * *

(C) Payment for Education of Children Enrolled in Private Schools Without Consent of or Referral by the Public Agency.

(i) In General. Subject to subparagraph (A), this part does not require a local educational agency to pay for the cost of education, including special education and related services, of a child with a disability at a private school or facility if that agency made a free appropriate public education available to the child and the parents elected to place the child in such private school or facility.

(ii) Reimbursement for Private School Placement. If the parents of a child with a disability, who previously received special education and related services under the authority of a public agency, enroll the child in a private elementary school or secondary school without the consent of or referral by the public agency, a court or a hearing officer may require the agency to reimburse the parents for the cost of that enrollment **if** the court or hearing officer finds that the agency had not made a free appropriate public education available to the child in a timely manner prior to that enrollment.

(iii) Limitation on Reimbursement. The cost of reimbursement described in clause (ii) **may be reduced or denied**

(I) **if** (aa) at the most recent IEP meeting that the parents attended prior to removal of the child from the public school, the **parents did not inform the IEP Team that they were rejecting the placement** proposed by the public agency to provide a free appropriate public education to their child, including **stating their concerns and their intent to enroll their child in a private school at public expense; or** (bb) **10 business days** (including any holidays that occur on a business day) prior to the removal of the child from the public school, the **parents did not give written notice** to the public agency of the information described in item (aa);

(II) **if,** prior to the parents' removal of the child from the public school, the public agency informed the parents, through the notice requirements described in section 1415(b)(3) of this title, of its intent to evaluate the child (including a statement of the purpose of the evaluation that was appropriate and reasonable), but the **parents did not make the child available for such evaluation; or**

(III) upon a **judicial finding of unreasonableness** with respect to actions taken by the parents.

(iv) Exception. Notwithstanding the notice requirement in clause (iii)(I), the cost of reimbursement

(I) shall not be reduced or denied for failure to provide such notice if (aa) the school prevented the parent from providing such notice; (bb) the parents had not received notice, pursuant to section 1415 of this title, of the notice requirement in clause (iii)(I); or (cc) compliance with clause (iii)(I) would likely result in physical harm to the child; and

(II) may, in the discretion of a court or a hearing officer, not be reduced or denied for failure to provide such notice if (aa) the parent is illiterate or cannot write in English; or (bb) compliance with clause (iii)(I) would likely result in serious emotional harm to the child.

* * *

(14) Personnel Qualifications.

(A) In General. The State educational agency has established and maintains qualifications to ensure that personnel necessary to carry out this part are appropriately and adequately prepared and trained, including that those **personnel have the content knowledge and skills to serve children with disabilities.**

(B) Related Services Personnel and Paraprofessionals. The qualifications under subparagraph (A) include qualifications for related services personnel and paraprofessionals that

(i) are consistent with any State-approved or State-recognized certification, licensing, registration, or other comparable requirements that apply to the professional discipline in which those personnel are providing special education or related services;

(ii) ensure that related services personnel who deliver services in their discipline or profession meet the requirements of clause (i) and have not had certification or licensure requirements waived on an emergency, temporary, or provisional basis; and

(iii) allow paraprofessionals and assistants who are appropriately trained and supervised, in accordance with State law, regulation, or written policy, in meeting the requirements of this part to be used to assist in the provision of special education and related services under this part to children with disabilities.

(C) Qualifications for Special Education Teachers. The qualifications described in subparagraph (A) shall ensure that each person employed as a special education teacher in the State who teaches elementary school, middle school, or secondary school is highly qualified by the deadline established in section 6319(a)(2) of this title.

(D) Policy. In implementing this section, a State shall adopt a policy that includes a requirement that local educational agencies in the State take measurable steps to recruit, hire, train, and retain highly qualified personnel to provide special education and related services under this part to children with disabilities.

(E) Rule of Construction. Notwithstanding any other individual right of action that a parent or student may maintain under this part, nothing in this paragraph shall be construed to create a right of action on behalf of an individual student for the failure of a particular State educational agency or local educational agency staff person to be highly qualified, or to prevent a parent from filing a complaint about staff qualifications with the State educational agency as provided for under this part.

* * *

(16) Participation in Assessments.

(A) In General. All children with disabilities are included in all general State and districtwide assessment programs, including assessments described under section 6311 of this title, **with appropriate accommodations and alternate assessments where necessary** and as indicated in their respective individualized education programs.

(B) Accommodation Guidelines. The State (or, in the case of a districtwide assessment, the local educational agency) has developed guidelines for the provision of appropriate accommodations.

(C) Alternate Assessments.

(i) In General. The State (or, in the case of a districtwide assessment, the local educational agency) has developed and implemented guidelines for the participation of children with disabilities in alternate assessments for those children who cannot participate in regular assessments under subparagraph (A) with accommodations as indicated in their respective individualized education programs.

(ii) Requirements for Alternate Assessments. The guidelines under clause (i) shall provide for alternate assessments that (I) are aligned with the State's challenging academic content standards and challenging student academic achievement standards; and (II) if the State has adopted alternate academic achievement standards permitted under the regulations promulgated to carry out section 6311(b)(1) of this title, measure the achievement of children with disabilities against those standards.

(iii) Conduct of Alternate Assessments. The State conducts the alternate assessments described in this subparagraph.

* * *

(25) Prohibition on Mandatory Medication.

(A) In General. The State educational agency shall prohibit State and local educational agency personnel from requiring a child to obtain a prescription for a substance covered by the Controlled Substances Act (21 U.S.C. 801 et seq.) as a condition of attending school, receiving an evaluation under subsection (a) or (c) of section 1414 of this title, or receiving services under this title.

(B) Rule of Construction. Nothing in subparagraph (A) shall be construed to create a Federal prohibition against teachers and other school personnel consulting or sharing classroom-based observations with parents or guardians regarding a student's academic and functional performance, or behavior in the classroom or school, or regarding the need for evaluation for special education or related services under paragraph (3).

* * *

Wrightslaw Discussion of State Eligibility (the "Catch-All Statute")

Free Appropriate Public Education

All children who are eligible for special education services under IDEA are entitled to a free, appropriate public education (FAPE), including children who have been suspended or expelled from school. Before Congress enacted Public Law 94-142 in 1975, millions of children with disabilities were not allowed to attend public schools. (See Findings in Section 1400(c) and Discipline in Section 1415(k)).

Child Find

Child find requires school districts to identify, locate, and evaluate all children with disabilities, including children who are home schooled, homeless, wards of the state, and children who attend private schools. See also Section 1412(a)(10) regarding the requirements that public schools consult with private school officials.

If a child is eligible for special education services under Section 1401(3), the child does not have to have a specific disability label in order to receive special education services. The school does not have to determine the child's "label" before providing services. Schools often spend months evaluating a child before providing any special education services. During this time, the child falls further behind. See also Section 1414(a)(1)(C)(i)(I) about the new 60 calendar day timeline between parental consent and completion of the evaluation process.

Least Restrictive Environment (LRE) and Mainstreaming

The definition of "least restrictive environment" did not change in IDEA 2004. Schools are required to educate children with disabilities in the least restrictive environment. Judicial decisions about "mainstreaming" and "least restrictive environment" (LRE) vary, even within the same state.

Some school districts claim the law requires them to mainstream all children with disabilities, even children who need individualized instruction that cannot be delivered in general education classrooms. In other districts, parents must fight to have their disabled child "included" in general education classes.

The law takes a commonsense approach to this issue: children with disabilities should be educated with children who are not disabled "to the maximum extent appropriate." However, children can receive one-to-one or small group instruction outside of regular classes if this is necessary for them to learn.

Special Education Services to Children Who Attend Private Schools

Court decisions about whether school districts (LEAs) must provide special education and related services at a child's private school differ around the country. Many courts have held that the public school must make these services available, but that services do not have to be provided at the private school. IDEA 2004 may cause a shift in future legal rulings.

If a public school places a child in a private school, the child has the same rights under IDEA as if the child attended a public school.

Reimbursement

The law about reimbursement for parental placements in private schools is unchanged in IDEA 2004. If the parent removes the child from a public school program and places the child in a private program, the parent may be reimbursed for the costs of the private program if a hearing officer or court determines that the public school did not offer FAPE "in a timely manner."

The language that reimbursement "shall not be reduced . . ." was modified in IDEA 2004 (the language in IDEA 97 said "may not be reduced . . .") Changing the language to "shall not be reduced" eliminates the discretion of the hearing officer. Now hearing officers shall not reduce or deny reimbursement if the subsequent conditions are met.

Qualifications of Special Education Teachers

The requirements about qualifications of special education teachers in Section 1412(a)(14) are new and track the highly qualified teacher requirements in No Child Left Behind. (20 U.S.C. § 6319)

Teachers of core academic subjects must be highly qualified by the end of the 2005-2006 school year. (NCLB, Section 6319(a)(2)) The requirements for related services personnel and paraprofessionals did not change in IDEA 2004.

IDEA 2004 requires states to take measurable steps "to recruit, hire, train, and retain highly qualified personnel to provide special education and related services." (Section 1412(a)(14)(D))

For more information about requirements for teachers and paraprofessionals under No Child Left Behind, read Chapter 6, "NCLB for Teachers, Principals and Paraprofessionals" in *Wrightslaw: No Child Left Behind.*

There is no right of action, i.e., right to sue a state or school district because a teacher is not highly qualified. However, parents may file complaints about inadequately trained teachers with the State Department of Education.

Participation in Assessments, Accommodations Guidelines, Alternate Assessments

Congress changed the language about participation in assessments in IDEA 2004 to: "**All** children with disabilities are included in **all** general State and districtwide assessment programs... with appropriate accommodations and alternate assessments where necessary. The child's IEP team, including the parents, makes all decisions about accommodations and alternate assessments.

The requirements that schools include **all** children with disabilities in all State and district assessments may have a negative impact on those schools that fail to use research based methods to teach children to read, write, spell, and do arithmetic, and that fail to assess children's progress frequently.

The requirements about accommodations guidelines and alternate assessments are new in IDEA 2004. Alternate assessments must be aligned with the State's academic content standards and student academic achievement standards. States and school districts must report the performance of children with disabilities to the public.

Mandatory Medication Prohibited

The requirements that prohibit school personnel from requiring a child to obtain a prescription for a controlled substance (i.e., Ritalin, Adderal, etc.) in order to attend school, receive an evaluation, or receive special education services are new in IDEA 2004.

In Summation

In this chapter, you learned that states must ensure that all children with disabilities receive a free, appropriate public education. You learned that schools must provide FAPE to disabled children who are suspended and expelled from school.

You learned about child find, least restrictive environment and mainstreaming and inclusion, and private school placements. You learned that IDEA 2004 requires states and schools to test all children with disabilities in state and district assessments, and provide appropriate accommodations. You learned about accommodations guidelines and alternate assessments.

In the next chapter about Section 1414, you will learn about evaluations, parental consent, reevaluations, eligibility, Individualized Educational Programs (IEPs), IEP teams, reviewing and revising IEPs, and placement decisions.

Your Notes Here

17 | IDEA–Section 1414: Evaluation, Eligibility, IEPs, and Placement

> "The greatest danger for most of us is not that we aim too high and we miss, but that we aim too low and we reach it." —Author unknown

In this chapter, you will learn about requirements for evaluations, reevaluations, parental consent, eligibility, Individualized Educational Programs (IEPs), IEP teams, review and revisions of IEPs, and decisions about placement.

The new requirements for initial evaluations, parental consent, the new 60-day timeline to complete evaluations, and new limits on reevaluations are in Section 1414(a). Section 1414(b) includes new requirements for evaluation procedures, determining educational needs, and the movement away from using discrepancy models to identify children with specific learning disabilities.

Congress also made significant changes in Section 1414(d) about Individualized Education Programs (IEPs), IEP team attendance, and how to review and revise IEPs. Section 1414(e) clarifies that the parent is a member of any group that makes decisions about a child's educational placement.

Note: When you see this * * * it signifies that a portion of the statute is not included in this book. For the full. text of a specific statute in IDEA 2004, you will want to read *Wrightslaw: IDEA 2004* or *Wrightslaw: Special Education Law, 2nd Edition*.

A Wrightslaw discussion of these issues follows Section 1414.

20 U.S.C. § 1414. Evaluations, Consent, Eligibility, Individualized Education Programs, Placements

(a) Evaluations, Parental Consent, and Reevaluations.

(1) Initial Evaluations.

(A) In General. A State educational agency, other State agency, or local educational agency **shall conduct a full and individual initial evaluation** in accordance with this paragraph and subsection (b), before the initial provision of special education and related services to a child with a disability under this part.

(B) Request for Initial Evaluation. Consistent with subparagraph (D), either a parent of a child, or a State educational agency, other State agency, or local educational agency may initiate a request for an initial evaluation to determine if the child is a child with a disability.

(C) Procedures.

(i) In General. Such initial evaluation shall consist of procedures (I) to determine whether a child is a child with a disability (as defined in section 1401 of this title) within 60 days of receiving parental consent for the evaluation, or, if the State establishes a timeframe within which the evaluation must be conducted, within such timeframe; and (II) to determine the educational needs of such child.

(ii) Exception. The relevant timeframe in clause (i)(I) shall not apply to a local educational agency if

(I) a child enrolls in a school served by the local educational agency after the relevant timeframe in clause (i)(I) has begun and prior to a determination by the child's previous local educational agency as to whether the child is a child with a disability (as defined in section 1401 of this title), but only if the subsequent local educational agency is making sufficient progress to ensure a prompt completion of the evaluation, and the parent and subsequent local educational agency agree to a specific time when the evaluation will be completed; or

(II) the parent of a child repeatedly fails or refuses to produce the child for the evaluation.

(D) Parental Consent.

(i) In General.

(I) Consent for Initial Evaluation. The agency proposing to conduct an initial evaluation to determine if the child qualifies as a child with a disability as defined in section 1401 of this title shall obtain informed consent from the parent of such child before conducting the evaluation. Parental consent for evaluation shall not be construed as consent for placement for receipt of special education and related services.

(II) Consent for Services. An agency that is responsible for making a free appropriate public education available to a child with a disability under this part shall seek to obtain informed consent from the parent of such child before providing special education and related services to the child.

(ii) Absence of Consent.

(I) For Initial Evaluation. If the parent of such child does not provide consent for an initial evaluation under clause (i)(I), or the parent fails to respond to a request to provide the consent, the local educational agency may pursue the initial evaluation of the child by utilizing the procedures described in section 1415 of this title, except to the extent inconsistent with State law relating to such parental consent.

(II) For Services. If the parent of such child refuses to consent to services under clause (i)(II), the local educational agency shall not provide special education and related services to the child by utilizing the procedures described in section 1415 of this title.

(III) Effect on Agency Obligations. If the parent of such child refuses to consent to the receipt of special education and related services, or the parent fails to respond to a request to provide such consent (aa) the local educational agency shall not be considered to be in violation of the requirement to make available a free appropriate public education to the child for the failure to provide such child with the special education and related services for which the local educational agency requests such consent; and (bb) the local educational agency shall not be required to convene an IEP meeting or develop an IEP under this section for the child for the special education and related services for which the local educational agency requests such consent.

(iii) Consent for Wards of the State.

(I) In General. If the child is a ward of the State and is not residing with the child's parent, the agency shall make reasonable efforts to obtain the informed consent from the parent (as defined in section 1401 of this title) of the child for an initial evaluation to determine whether the child is a child with a disability.

(II) Exception. The agency shall not be required to obtain informed consent from the parent of a child for an initial evaluation to determine whether the child is a child with a disability if (aa) despite reasonable efforts to do so, the agency cannot discover the whereabouts of the parent of the child; (bb) the rights of the parents of the child have been terminated in accordance with State law; or (cc) the rights of the parent to make educational decisions have been subrogated by a judge in accordance with State law and consent for an initial evaluation has been given by an individual appointed by the judge to represent the child.

(E) Rule of Construction. The screening of a student by a teacher or specialist to determine appropriate instructional strategies for curriculum implementation shall not be considered to be an evaluation for eligibility for special education and related services.

(2) Reevaluations.

(A) In General. A local educational agency shall ensure that a reevaluation of each child with a disability is conducted in accordance with subsections (b) and (c) -

(i) if the local educational agency determines that the educational or related services needs, including improved academic achievement and functional performance, of the child warrant a reevaluation; or

(ii) if the child's parents or teacher requests a reevaluation.

(B) Limitation. A reevaluation conducted under subparagraph (A) shall occur -

(i) not more frequently than once a year, unless the parent and the local educational agency agree otherwise; and

(ii) at least once every 3 years, unless the parent and the local educational agency agree that a reevaluation is unnecessary.

(b) Evaluation Procedures.

(1) Notice. The local educational agency shall provide notice to the parents of a child with a disability, in accordance with subsections (b)(3), (b)(4), and (c) of section 1415 of this title, that describes any evaluation procedures such agency proposes to conduct.

(2) Conduct of Evaluation. In conducting the evaluation, the local educational agency shall -

(A) use a **variety of assessment tools and strategies** to gather **relevant functional, developmental, and academic information, including information provided by the parent,** that may assist in determining -

(i) whether the child is a child with a disability; and

(ii) the **content of the child's individualized education program,** including information related to enabling the child to be involved in and **progress in the general education curriculum,** or, for preschool children, to participate in appropriate activities;

(B) **not use any single measure or assessment as the sole criterion** for determining whether a child is a child with a disability or determining an appropriate educational program for the child; and

(C) use technically sound instruments that may assess the relative contribution of cognitive and behavioral factors, in addition to physical or developmental factors.

(3) Additional Requirements. Each local educational agency **shall ensure** that

(A) assessments and other evaluation materials used to assess a child under this section -

(i) are selected and administered so as **not to be discriminatory** on a racial or cultural basis;

(ii) are provided and **administered in the language and form most likely to yield accurate information on what the child knows and can do academically, developmentally, and functionally,** unless it is not feasible to so provide or administer;

(iii) are used for purposes for which the assessments or measures are valid and reliable;

(iv) are administered by **trained and knowledgeable personnel;** and

(v) are administered in accordance with any instructions provided by the producer of such assessments;

(B) the child is **assessed in all areas of suspected disability;**

(C) assessment tools and strategies that provide relevant information that directly assists persons in **determining the educational needs** of the child are provided; and

(D) assessments of children with disabilities who transfer from 1 school district to another school district in the same academic year are coordinated with such children's prior and subsequent schools, as necessary and as expeditiously as possible, to ensure prompt completion of full evaluations.

(4) Determination of Eligibility and Educational Need. Upon completion of the administration of assessments and other evaluation measures -

(A) the determination of whether the child is a child with a disability as defined in section 1401(3) of this title and the educational needs of the child shall be made by a team of qualified professionals and the parent of the child in accordance with paragraph (5); and

(B) a copy of the evaluation report and the documentation of determination of eligibility shall be given to the parent.

(5) Special Rule for Eligibility Determination. In making a determination of eligibility under paragraph (4)(A), a child shall not be determined to be a child with a disability if the determinant factor for such determination is -

(A) lack of appropriate instruction in reading, including in the essential components of reading instruction (as defined in section 6368(3) of this title);

(B) lack of instruction in math; or

(C) limited English proficiency.

(6) Specific Learning Disabilities.

(A) In General. Notwithstanding section 1407(b) of this title, when determining whether a child has a specific learning disability as defined in section 1401 of this title, a local educational agency **shall not be required** to take into consideration **whether a child has a severe discrepancy between achievement and intellectual ability** in oral expression, listening comprehension, written expression, basic reading skill, reading comprehension, mathematical calculation, or mathematical reasoning.

(B) Additional Authority. In determining whether a child has a specific learning disability, a local educational agency may use a process that determines if the child **responds to scientific, research-based intervention** as a part of the evaluation procedures described in paragraphs (2) and (3).

(c) Additional Requirements for Evaluation and Reevaluations.

(1) Review of Existing Evaluation Data. As part of an initial evaluation (if appropriate) and as part of any reevaluation under this section, the IEP Team and other qualified professionals, as appropriate, shall -

(A) **review existing evaluation data** on the child, including -

(i) **evaluations** and **information provided by the parents** of the child;

(ii) current classroom-based, local, or State **assessments**, and classroom-based observations; and

(iii) **observations** by teachers and related services providers; and

(B) on the basis of that review, and input from the child's parents, identify what additional data, if any, are needed to determine -

(i) whether the child is a child with a disability as defined in section 1401(3) of this title, and the educational needs of the child, or, in case of a reevaluation of a child, whether the child continues to have such a disability and such educational needs;

(ii) the **present levels of academic achievement and related developmental needs** of the child;

(iii) whether the child **needs special education and related services,** or in the case of a reevaluation of a child, whether the child continues to need special education and related services; and

(iv) whether any **additions or modifications** to the special education and related services are **needed to enable the child to meet the measurable annual goals** set out in the individualized education program of the child and to participate, as appropriate, in the general education curriculum.

(2) Source of Data. The local educational agency shall administer such assessments and other evaluation measures as may be needed to produce the data identified by the IEP Team under paragraph (1)(B).

(3) Parental Consent. Each local educational agency shall obtain **informed parental consent,** in accordance with subsection (a)(1)(D), prior to conducting any reevaluation of a child with a disability, except that such informed parental consent need not be obtained if the local educational agency can demonstrate that it had taken reasonable measures to obtain such consent and the child's parent has failed to respond.

(4) Requirements If Additional Data Are Not Needed. If the IEP Team and other qualified professionals, as appropriate, determine that no additional data are needed to determine whether the child continues to be a child with a disability and to determine the child's educational needs, the local educational agency -

(A) shall notify the child's parents of -

(i) that determination and the reasons for the determination; and

(ii) the right of such parents to request an assessment to determine whether the child continues to be a child with a disability and to determine the child's educational needs; and

(B) shall not be required to conduct such an assessment **unless requested to by the child's parents.**

(5) **Evaluations Before Change in Eligibility.**

(A) **In General.** Except as provided in subparagraph (B), a local educational agency shall evaluate a child with a disability in accordance with this section before determining that the child is no longer a child with a disability.

(B) **Exception.**

(i) **In General.** The evaluation described in subparagraph (A) shall not be required before the termination of a child's eligibility under this part due to graduation from secondary school with a regular diploma, or due to exceeding the age eligibility for a free appropriate public education under State law.

(ii) **Summary of Performance.** For a child whose eligibility under this part terminates under circumstances described in clause (i), a local educational agency shall provide the child with a summary of the child's academic achievement and functional performance, which shall include recommendations on how to assist the child in meeting the child's postsecondary goals.

(d) Individualized Education Programs.

(1) **Definitions.** In this title:

(A) **Individualized Education Program.**

(i) **In General.** The term 'individualized education program' or IEP' means a written statement for each child with a disability that is developed, reviewed, and revised in accordance with this section and that **includes -**

(I) a statement of the **child's present levels of academic achievement and functional performance,** including (aa) how the child's disability affects the child's involvement and progress in the general education curriculum; (bb) for preschool children, as appropriate, how the disability affects the child's participation in appropriate activities; and (cc) for children with disabilities who take alternate assessments aligned to alternate achievement standards, a description of benchmarks or short-term objectives;

(II) a **statement of measurable annual goals, including academic and functional goals,** designed to (aa) meet the child's needs that result from the child's disability to enable the child to be involved in and make progress in the general education curriculum; and (bb) meet each of the child's other educational needs that result from the child's disability;

(III) a description of **how the child's progress toward meeting the annual goals** described in subclause (II) **will be measured** and when periodic reports on the progress the child is making toward meeting the annual goals (such as through the use of quarterly or other periodic reports, concurrent with the issuance of report cards) will be provided;

(IV) a **statement of the special education and related services and supplementary aids and services, based on peer-reviewed research** to the extent practicable, to be provided to the child, or on behalf of the child, and a **statement of the program modifications or supports for school personnel that will be provided** for the child (aa) to advance appropriately toward attaining the annual goals; (bb) to be involved in and make progress in the general education curriculum in accordance with subclause (I) and to participate in extracurricular and other nonacademic activities; and (cc) to be educated and participate with other children with disabilities and nondisabled children in the activities described in this subparagraph;

(V) an explanation of the extent, if any, to which the child will not participate with nondisabled children in the regular class and in the activities described in subclause (IV)(cc);

(VI) (aa) a **statement of any individual appropriate accommodations** that are **necessary to measure the academic achievement and functional performance** of the child on State and districtwide assessments consistent with section 1412(a)(16)(A) of this title; and (bb) if the IEP Team determines that the child shall take an alternate assessment on a particular State or districtwide assessment of student achievement, a statement of why (AA) the child cannot participate in the regular assessment; and (BB) the particular alternate assessment selected is appropriate for the child;

(VII) the projected **date for the beginning of the services** and modifications described in subclause (IV), and the anticipated **frequency, location, and duration of those services and modifications**; and

(VIII) beginning not later than the first IEP to be in effect when the child is 16, and updated annually thereafter (aa) **appropriate measurable postsecondary goals based upon age appropriate transition assessments** related to training, education, employment, and, where appropriate, independent living skills; (bb) the transition services (including courses of study) needed to assist the child in reaching those goals; and (cc) beginning not later than 1 year before the child reaches the age of majority under State law, a statement that the child has been informed of the child's rights under this title, if any, that will transfer to the child on reaching the age of majority under section 1415(m) of this title.

(ii) **Rule of Construction.** Nothing in this section shall be construed to require (I) that additional information be included in a child's IEP beyond what is explicitly required in this section; and (II) the IEP Team to include information under 1 component of a child's IEP that is already contained under another component of such IEP.

(B) **Individualized Education Program Team.** The term 'individualized education program team' or IEP Team' means a group of individuals composed of -

(i) the parents of a child with a disability;

(ii) not less than 1 regular education teacher of such child (if the child is, or may be, participating in the regular education environment);

(iii) not less than 1 special education teacher, or where appropriate, not less than 1 special education provider of such child;

(iv) a representative of the local educational agency who (I) is qualified to provide, or supervise the provision of, specially designed instruction to meet the unique needs of children with disabilities; (II) is knowledgeable about the general education curriculum; and (III) is knowledgeable about the availability of resources of the local educational agency;

(v) an individual who can interpret the instructional implications of evaluation results, who may be a member of the team described in clauses (ii) through (vi);

(vi) at the discretion of the parent or the agency, other individuals who have knowledge or special expertise regarding the child, including related services personnel as appropriate; and

(vii) whenever appropriate, the child with a disability.

(C) IEP Team Attendance.

(i) **Attendance Not Necessary.** A member of the IEP Team shall not be required to attend an IEP meeting, in whole or in part, if the parent of a child with a disability and the local educational agency agree that the attendance of such member is not necessary because the member's area of the curriculum or related services is not being modified or discussed in the meeting.

(ii) **Excusal.** A member of the IEP Team may be excused from attending an IEP meeting, in whole or in part, when the meeting involves a modification to or discussion of the member's area of the curriculum or related services, if (I) the parent and the local educational agency consent to the excusal; and (II) the member submits, in writing to the parent and the IEP Team, input into the development of the IEP prior to the meeting.

(iii) **Written Agreement and Consent Required.** A parent's agreement under clause (i) and consent under clause (ii) shall be in writing.

(D) IEP Team Transition.
In the case of a child who was previously served under part C, an invitation to the initial IEP meeting shall, at the request of the parent, be sent to the part C service coordinator or other representatives of the part C system to assist with the smooth transition of services.

(2) Requirement That Program Be in Effect.

(A) **In General.** At the beginning of each school year, each local educational agency, State educational agency, or other State agency, as the case may be, shall have in effect, for each child with a disability in the agency's jurisdiction, an individualized education program, as defined in paragraph (1)(A).

(B) **Program for Child Aged 3 Through 5.** In the case of a child with a disability aged 3 through 5 (or, at the discretion of the State educational agency, a 2-year-old child with a disability who will turn age 3 during the school year), the IEP Team shall consider the individualized family service plan that contains the material described in section 1436 of this title, and <u>that is developed in accordance with this</u> section, and the individualized family service plan may serve as the IEP of the child if using that plan as the IEP is -

(i) consistent with State policy; and

(ii) agreed to by the agency and the child's parents.

(C) Program for Children Who Transfer School Districts.

(i) In General.

(I) Transfer within the Same State. In the case of a child with a disability who transfers school districts within the same academic year, who enrolls in a new school, and who had an IEP that was in effect in the same State, the local educational agency **shall provide** such child with a free appropriate public education, including **services comparable to those described in the previously held IEP**, in consultation with the parents until such time as the local educational agency adopts the previously held IEP or develops, adopts, and implements a new IEP that is consistent with Federal and State law.

(II) Transfer Outside State. In the case of a child with a disability who transfers school districts within the same academic year, who enrolls in a new school, and who had an IEP that was in effect in another State, the local educational agency shall provide such child with a free appropriate public education, including services comparable to those described in the previously held IEP, in consultation with the parents until such time as the local educational agency conducts an evaluation pursuant to subsection (a)(1), if determined to be necessary by such agency, and develops a new IEP, if appropriate, that is consistent with Federal and State law.

(ii) Transmittal of Records. To facilitate the transition for a child described in clause (i) (I) the new school in which the child enrolls shall take reasonable steps to **promptly obtain the child's records, including the IEP and supporting documents** and any other records relating to the provision of special education or related services to the child, from the previous school in which the child was enrolled, pursuant to section 99.31(a)(2) of title 34, Code of Federal Regulations; and (II) the previous school in which the child was enrolled shall take reasonable steps to promptly respond to such request from the new school.

(3) Development of IEP.

(A) In General. In developing each child's IEP, the IEP Team, subject to subparagraph (C), shall consider

(i) the **strengths** of the child;

(ii) the **concerns of the parents** for enhancing the education of their child;

(iii) the **results of** the initial evaluation or **most recent evaluation** of the child; and

(iv) the **academic, developmental, and functional needs** of the child.

(B) Consideration of Special Factors. The IEP Team shall -

(i) in the case of a child whose **behavior** impedes the child's learning or that of others, consider the use of **positive behavioral interventions and supports,** and other strategies, to address that behavior;

(ii) in the case of a child with **limited English proficiency,** consider the language needs of the child as such needs relate to the child's IEP;

(iii) in the case of a child who is **blind or visually impaired,** provide for instruction in Braille and the use of Braille unless the IEP Team determines, after an evaluation of the child's reading and writing skills, needs, and appropriate reading and writing media (including an evaluation of the child's future needs for instruction in Braille or the use of Braille), that instruction in Braille or the use of Braille is not appropriate for the child;

(iv) consider the **communication needs** of the child, and in the case of a child who is **deaf or hard of hearing,** consider the child's language and communication needs, opportunities for direct communications with peers and professional personnel in the child's language and communication mode, academic level, and full range of needs, including opportunities for direct instruction in the child's language and communication mode; and

(v) consider whether the child needs **assistive technology devices and services.**

(C) Requirement with Respect to Regular Education Teacher. A regular education teacher of the child, as a member of the IEP Team, shall, to the extent appropriate, participate in the development of the IEP of the child, including the determination of appropriate positive behavioral interventions and supports, and other strategies, and the determination of supplementary aids and services, program modifications, and support for school personnel consistent with paragraph (1)(A)(i)(IV).

(D) Agreement. In making changes to a child's IEP after the annual IEP meeting for a school year, the parent of a child with a disability and the local educational agency may agree not to convene an IEP meeting for the purposes of making such changes, and instead may develop a written document to amend or modify the child's current IEP.

(E) Consolidation of IEP Team Meetings. To the extent possible, the local educational agency shall encourage the consolidation of reevaluation meetings for the child and other IEP Team meetings for the child.

(F) Amendments. Changes to the IEP may be made either by the entire IEP Team or, as provided in subparagraph (D), by amending the IEP rather than by redrafting the entire IEP. Upon request, a parent shall be provided with a revised copy of the IEP with the amendments incorporated.

(4) Review and Revision of IEP.

(A) In General. The local educational agency shall ensure that, subject to subparagraph (B), the IEP Team -

(i) reviews the child's IEP periodically, but **not less frequently than annually,** to determine whether the annual goals for the child are being achieved; and

(ii) **revises the IEP** as appropriate to address (I) **any lack of expected progress** toward the annual goals and in the general education curriculum, where appropriate; (II) the **results of any reevaluation** conducted under this section; (III) **information** about the child **provided to, or by, the parents,** as described in subsection (c)(1)(B); (IV) the child's **anticipated needs;** or (V) other matters.

(B) Requirement with Respect to Regular Education Teacher. A regular education teacher of the child, as a member of the IEP Team, shall, consistent with paragraph (1)(C), participate in the review and revision of the IEP of the child.

(5) Multi-Year IEP Demonstration.

* * *

(6) Failure to Meet Transition Objectives. If a participating agency, other than the local educational agency, fails to provide the transition services described in the IEP in accordance with paragraph (1)(A)(i)(VIII), the local educational agency shall reconvene the IEP Team to identify alternative strategies to meet the transition objectives for the child set out in the IEP.

(7) Children with Disabilities in Adult Prisons.

* * *

(e) Educational Placements.

Each local educational agency or State educational agency shall ensure that the parents of each child with a disability are members of any group that makes decisions on the educational placement of their child.

(f) Alternative Means of Meeting Participation.

When conducting IEP team meetings and placement meetings pursuant to this section, section 1415(e) of this title, and section 1415(f)(1)(B) of this title, and carrying out administrative matters under section 1415 of this title (such as scheduling, exchange of witness lists, and status conferences), the parent of a child with a disability and a local educational agency may agree to use alternative means of meeting participation, such as video conferences and conference calls.

Wrightslaw Discussion of Evaluations, Eligibility, IEPs, IEP Teams, and Placements

This section in IDEA about Evaluations, Reevaluations, Eligibility, and IEPs is the second most important statute in this book. (The most important is Purposes in Section 1400(d))

Initial Evaluations

Section 1414(a)(1)(B) is new and states that the parents, the state department of education, other state agencies, and the school district may request an initial evaluation. IDEA 2004 includes a new requirement that initial evaluations and eligibility be completed within 60 days of receiving parental consent. When federal law and regulations create a timeline of "days," this means calendar days, not school days. Some states may have statutes or regulations that permit longer timelines.

Parental Consent

The school must obtain parental consent before conducting the initial evaluation. Parental consent for an evaluation is not consent for the child to receive special education services. The school must obtain informed parental consent before providing special education services.

"Absence of Consent" is new in IDEA 2004. If the parent does not consent to an evaluation, the district may request a due process hearing against the parent. However, if the parent does not consent to special education services, the district may not pursue a due process hearing against the parent. The "Effect on Agency Obligations" section is also new. If the parent refuses consent for services, the district has not violated the IDEA and is not required to convene an IEP meeting or develop an IEP for the child.

Reevaluations

The language about reevaluations changed in IDEA 2004. The school is not required to reevaluate a child more often than once a year, unless the parent and school agree otherwise. The school shall evaluate at least every three years, unless the parent and school agree that a reevaluation is unnecessary. The school must reevaluate if the child's educational needs change or if the child's parent or teacher request a reevaluation.

These limits on the frequency of reevaluations are likely to cause difficulties in developing IEPs. The law requires that the IEP include "a statement of the child's present levels of academic achievement and functional performance" (Section 1414(d)(1)(A)(i)). If the child has not been evaluated for a year or more, the IEP team will not have valid information about the child's present levels of academic achievement and functional performance.

Evaluation Procedures

The language about evaluation procedures changed in IDEA 2004. The school "shall use a variety of assessment tools and strategies to gather relevant functional, developmental, and academic information" about the child. Information from the evaluation is to be used in determining the contents of the child's IEP, and how to help the child make progress in the general education curriculum.

The school shall "not use any single measure or assessment as the sole criterion" for determining if a child is eligible. The language about assessing children "in all areas of suspected disability" and that assessments shall provide relevant information to determine the child's educational needs are unchanged. A "screening" by a teacher or educational diagnostician to determine instructional strategies does not comply with the requirements for evaluations in Section 1414.

IDEA 2004 includes additional new requirements about assessments. The school must ensure that assessments "are provided and administered in the language and form most likely to yield accurate information on what the child knows and can do academically, developmentally, and functionally . . ."

Determining Eligibility and Educational Need

In IDEA 2004, the heading, "Determination of Eligibility" was changed to "Determination of Eligibility and Educational Need." (Section 1414(b)(4)) A team of qualified professionals and the parent determine "whether the child is a child with a disability . . . and the educational needs of the child . . ." The requirements about providing the parent with copies of the evaluation report and documentation of eligibility are unchanged.

If the school decides that a child with a disability is not eligible for special education services under IDEA, or if the parent disagrees with the school's classification of the child's disability, the parent should obtain a comprehensive psycho-educational evaluation from an expert in the private sector.

Lack of Appropriate Instruction in Reading

The new language about "lack of appropriate instruction in reading, including the essential components of reading instruction" brings IDEA into conformity with NCLB.

The essential components of reading instruction are defined as explicit and systematic instruction in (A) phonemic awareness; (B) phonics; (C) vocabulary development; (D) reading fluency, including oral reading skills; and (E) reading comprehension strategies." (See 20 U.S.C. § 6368 in *Wrightslaw: No Child Left Behind.*)

Severe Discrepancy Not Required for Eligibility

Schools are not required to determine if a child has a severe discrepancy between achievement and intellectual ability to determine that a child has a specific learning disability and needs special education services, nor are schools prohibited from using a discrepancy model.

Response to Intervention

Schools may use Response to Intervention (RTI) to determine if the child responds to scientific, research-based intervention as part of the evaluation process.

The legal definition of "scientifically based reading research" is in No Child Left Behind, 20 U.S.C. § 6368(6). (See also *Wrightslaw: No Child Left Behind*, the "Glossary of Terms" in *Wrightslaw: IDEA 2004* and *Wrightslaw: Special Education Law, 2nd Edition*.)

The law includes new language that allows school personnel to decide that "no additional data are needed" to determine the child's educational needs or eligibility. (Section 1414(c)(4)) This language is at odds with the requirement that the school reevaluate "at least once every 3 years." (Section 1414 (a)(2)(B)(ii))

Present Levels of Academic Achievement and Related Developmental Needs

The IEP must include "a statement of the child's present levels of academic achievement and functional performance. . ." The IEP team must determine the child's "educational needs" and "present levels of academic achievement and related developmental needs." For children who take alternate assessments, the IEP must include "a description of benchmarks or short-term objectives."

If a child is not evaluated at frequent intervals, information about the child's educational needs, "present levels of academic achievement" and "related developmental needs" will not be available. (Section 1414(d)(1)(A)(i)(I))

Parental Request for an Evaluation

The parent has a right to request that the school conduct an assessment to determine the child's educational needs. (Section 1414(a)(4)(ii)). To ensure that your request is honored, be sure to make your request for an assessment of your child's educational needs in writing.

To learn what the scores in your child's evaluations mean (i.e., standard scores, percentile ranks, age and grade equivalent scores), re-read Chapters 10 and 11 about "Tests and Measurements" in this book. To learn how to write IEPs that are Specific, Measurable, use Action words, are Realistic and Time specific, re-read Chapter 11 about SMART IEPs.

IEPs Must Include Measurable Goals

Your child's IEP must include measurable annual goals that address the child's "present levels of academic achievement and functional performance."

Congress added new language about research based instruction to IDEA 2004. The child's IEP must include "a statement of the special education and related services and supplementary aids and services, **based on peer-reviewed research** to the extent practicable, to be provided to the child...and a statement of the program modifications or supports for school personnel that will be provided..."

Individual Appropriate Accommodations

IDEA contains new language about "individual appropriate accommodations" on state and district tests and new requirements for alternate assessments. Your child's IEP must include: "a statement of any individual appropriate accommodations that are necessary to measure the academic achievement and functional performance of the child on State and districtwide assessments..."

Why an Alternate Assessment Is Appropriate

If the IEP Team recommends that your child shall take an alternate assessment on a State or district assessment, the team must include a statement about "why the child cannot participate in the regular assessment" and [why] "the particular alternate assessment selected is appropriate for the child..."

Transition Requirements

The requirements for transition in IEPs changed. The first IEP after the child is 16 (and updated annually) must include "appropriate measurable postsecondary goals based upon age appropriate transition assessments related to training, education, employment, and, where appropriate, independent living skills...and the transition services (including courses of study) needed to assist the child in reaching these goals."

IEP Team Members

A member of the IEP team may be excused from attending an IEP meeting if their area of curriculum or service will not be discussed or modified during the meeting. An IEP team member may also be excused from an IEP meeting that involves their area of curriculum or service **if** they submit input in writing and **if** the parent and school consents. The parent's consent must be in writing.

IEPs must be in effect at the beginning of the school year for all children with disabilities, including children who attend private programs. Under IDEA 2004, public schools may be responsible for offering IEPs to students who attend private schools.

See Sections 1412(a)(3)+(10) about child find and private schools.

Children Who Transfer Schools

The subsection about programs for children who transfer is new. If the child transfers to a district in the same state or another state, the receiving school must provide comparable services to those in the sending district's IEP until they develop and implement a new IEP.

Parental Concerns

In developing the IEP, the IEP team must consider the parent's concerns about the child's education, including concerns about inadequate progress. The IEP Team shall include "not less than one regular education teacher" of the child who will participate in developing the IEP.

Reviewing and Revising IEPs

IDEA 2004 made significant changes to the law about how IEPs will be reviewed and revised. If the parent and school decide to amend or modify the IEP that was developed at an annual IEP meeting, and they do not want to convene another IEP meeting, they may revise the IEP by agreement.

The IEP team must create a written document to amend or modify the IEP. This document must describe the changes or modifications in the IEP and note that, by agreement of the parties, an IEP meeting was not convened. The parent should be provided with a copy of the revised IEP.

Multi-Year IEPs

IDEA 2004 added a multi-year IEP pilot project. The parent has a right to "opt-out" of this program.

Placement Decisions

Decisions about the child's placement cannot be made until after the IEP team, including the child's parent, meets and reaches consensus about the IEP goals. Although the law is clear on this issue, school personnel often decide on the child's program and placement before the IEP meeting. These unilateral actions prevent parents from "meaningful participation" in the educational decision-making process. When Congress added this provision to the IDEA in 1997, they sent a message that unilateral educational placement decisions by school officials are illegal.

New Ways to Meet

School meetings do not have to be face-to-face but can be convened by conference calls or video conferences. IEP and placement meetings (Sections 1414(d)+(e)), mediation meetings (Section 1415(e)) and due process (IEP) resolution sessions (Section 1415(f)(1)(B)).

In Summation

In this chapter, you learned about initial evaluations, reevaluations, parental consent, evaluation procedures, and requirements for evaluations. You learned about the required components of your child's IEP, IEP team members and when team members may be excused. You learned about transition requirements and how to review and revise your child's IEP.

The next chapter is about Section 1415, Procedural Safeguards. You will learn about the procedural safeguards designed to protect the rights of children with disabilities and their parents. These safeguards include the right to participate in all meetings, to examine all educational records, and to obtain an independent educational evaluation (IEE) of your child.

You have the right to written notice whenever the school proposes to change or refuses to change your child's identification, evaluation or placement, and the right to participate in mediation, to present a complaint, and to request a due process hearing.

In the next chapter, you will also learn about new requirements for due process hearings and the Resolution Session that may allow the parties to resolve disputes before a due process hearing. There are new requirements for due process hearings and hearing officers, and new timelines, including a new two-year statute of limitations.

18 IDEA–Section 1415: Procedural Safeguards, Due Process, Discipline, etc.

"... whether the IEP and the FAPE requirements were put there out of mistrust of the parents, or out of mistrust of school authorities. It seems to me they were put there to make sure that the school authorities did not give the disabled child second-rate treatment. "

– Transcript of Oral Argument, statement by Supreme Court Justice,
Florence County School District IV. v. Shannon Carter (October 6, 1993)

In Section 1415, you will learn about the safeguards designed to protect the rights of children with disabilities and their parents. These safeguards include the right to participate in all meetings, to examine all educational records, and to obtain an independent educational evaluation (IEE) of the child. You will learn about prior written notice, procedural safeguards notice, mediation, legally binding mediation agreements, the new Resolution Sessions, due process hearings, "stay put," the new two-year statute of limitation, appeals, attorney's fees, discipline, and age of majority.

IDEA is like other laws, with rules of procedure and issues that relate to substance. In many cases, both issues are present. Substantive issues usually involve eligibility and the adequacy of the child's IEP. Procedural issues focus on notice, timelines, and remedies if the school district fails to obey the law.

The discipline statute is in Section 1415(k). This statute includes manifestation determinations, placement as determined by the IEP team, appeals, authority of the hearing officer, and transfer of rights at the age of majority.

Unless your child is labeled with an emotional disturbance, behavior disorder, or ADD/ADHD, or is facing suspension or expulsion, you are advised to skim "Placement in Alternative Educational Setting" about the rules for suspending and expelling children with disabilities.

Note: When you see this * * * it signifies that a portion of the statute is not included in this book. For the full. text of a specific statute in IDEA 2004, you will want to read *Wrightslaw: IDEA 2004* or *Wrightslaw: Special Education Law, 2nd Edition*.

A Wrightslaw discussion of these issues follows the statute.

20 U.S.C. § 1415 – Procedural Safeguards_____

(a) Establishment of Procedures. Any state educational agency, State agency, or local educational agency that receives assistance under this part shall establish and maintain procedures in accordance with this section to ensure that children with disabilities and their parents are guaranteed procedural safeguards with respect to the provisions of free appropriate public education by such agencies.

(b) Types of Procedures. The procedures required by this section shall include the following:

(1) An opportunity for the parents of a child with a disability to **examine all records** relating to such child and **to participate in meetings with respect to the identification, evaluation, and educational placement of the child,** and the provision of a free appropriate public education to such child, and **to obtain an independent educational evaluation of the child.**

(2)

(A) Procedures to protect the rights of the child whenever the parents of the child are not known, the agency cannot, after reasonable efforts, locate the parents, or the child is a ward of the State, including the assignment of an individual to act as a surrogate for the parents, which surrogate shall not be an employee of the State educational agency, the local educational agency, or any other agency that is involved in the education or care of the child. In the case of -

(i) a child who is a ward of the State, such surrogate may alternatively be appointed by the judge overseeing the child's care provided that the surrogate meets the requirements of this paragraph; and

(ii) an unaccompanied homeless youth as defined in section 11434a(6) of title 42, the local educational agency shall appoint a surrogate in accordance with this paragraph.

(B) The State shall make reasonable efforts to ensure the assignment of a surrogate not more than 30 days after there is a determination by the agency that the child needs a surrogate.

(3) **Written prior notice to the parents of the child,** in accordance with subsection (c)(1), whenever the local educational agency -

(A) **proposes to initiate or change;** or

(B) **refuses to initiate or change,** the identification, evaluation, or educational placement of the child, or the provision of a free appropriate public education to the child.

(4) Procedures designed to ensure that the notice required by paragraph (3) is **in the native language of the parents,** unless it clearly is not feasible to do so.

(5) An opportunity for **mediation,** in accordance with subsection (e).

(6) An opportunity for any party to **present a complaint**

(A) with respect to any matter relating to the identification, evaluation, or educational placement of the child, or the provision of a free appropriate public education to such child; and

(B) which sets forth an alleged **violation that occurred not more than 2 years before the date the parent or public agency knew or should have known** about the alleged action that forms the basis of the complaint, or, if the State has an explicit time limitation for presenting such a complaint under this part, in such time as the State law allows, except that the exceptions to the timeline described in subsection (f)(3)(D) shall apply to the timeline described in this subparagraph.

(7)

(A) Procedures that require either party, or the attorney representing a party, **to provide due process complaint notice** in accordance with subsection (c)(2) (which shall remain confidential) -

(i) to the other party, in the complaint filed under paragraph (6), and forward a copy of such notice to the State educational agency; and

(ii) that **shall include** (I) the name of the child, the address of the residence of the child (or available contact information in the case of a homeless child), and the name of the school the child is attending; (II) in the case of a homeless child or youth (within the meaning of section 11434a(2) of title 42), available contact information for the child and the name of the school the child is attending; (III) a description of the nature of the problem of the child relating to such proposed initiation or change, including facts relating to such problem; and
(IV) a proposed resolution of the problem to the extent known and available to the party at the time.

(B) A requirement that a party **may not have a due process hearing** until the party, or the attorney representing the party, files a notice that meets the requirements of subparagraph (A)(ii).

(8) Procedures that require the State educational agency to develop a **model form to assist parents in filing a complaint and due process complaint notice** in accordance with paragraphs (6) and (7), respectively.

(c) Notification Requirements.

(1) **Content of Prior Written Notice.** The notice required by subsection (b)(3) shall include -

(A) a description of the action proposed or refused by the agency;

(B) an explanation of why the agency proposes or refuses to take the action and a description of each evaluation procedure, assessment, record, or report the agency used as a basis for the proposed or refused action;

(C) a statement that the parents of a child with a disability have protection under the procedural safeguards of this part and, if this notice is not an initial referral for evaluation, the means by which a copy of a description of the procedural safeguards can be obtained;

(D) sources for parents to contact to obtain assistance in understanding the provisions of this part;

(E) a description of other options considered by the IEP Team and the reason why those options were rejected; and

(F) a description of the factors that are relevant to the agency's proposal or refusal.

(2) **Due Process Complaint Notice.**

(A) Complaint. The due process complaint notice required under subsection (b)(7)(A) shall be deemed to be sufficient unless the party receiving the notice notifies the hearing officer and the other party in writing that the receiving party believes the notice has not met the requirements of subsection (b)(7)(A).

(B) Response to Complaint.

(i) Local Educational Agency Response.

(I) In General. If the local educational agency has not sent a prior written notice to the parent regarding the subject matter contained in the parent's due process complaint notice, such local educational agency shall, within 10 days of receiving the complaint, send to the parent a response that shall include -(aa) an explanation of why the agency proposed or refused to take the action raised in the complaint; (bb) a description of other options that the IEP Team considered and the reasons why those options were rejected; (cc) a description of each evaluation procedure, assessment, record, or report the agency used as the basis for the proposed or refused action; and (dd) a description of the factors that are relevant to the agency's proposal or refusal.

(II) Sufficiency. A response filed by a local educational agency pursuant to subclause (I) shall not be construed to preclude such local educational agency from asserting that the parent's due process complaint notice was insufficient where appropriate.

(ii) Other Party Response. Except as provided in clause (i), the non-complaining party shall, within 10 days of receiving the complaint, send to the complainant a response that specifically addresses the issues raised in the complaint.

(C) Timing. The party providing a hearing officer notification under subparagraph (A) shall provide the notification **within 15 days** of receiving the complaint.

(D) Determination. Within 5 days of receipt of the notification provided under subparagraph (C), the hearing officer **shall** make a determination on the face of the notice of whether the notification meets the requirements of subsection (b)(7)(A), and shall immediately notify the parties in writing of such determination.

(E) Amended Complaint Notice.

(i) In General. A party may amend its due process complaint notice only if

(I) the other party consents in writing to such amendment and is given the opportunity to resolve the complaint through a meeting held pursuant to subsection (f)(1)(B); or (II) the hearing officer grants permission, except that the hearing officer may only grant such permission at any time not later than 5 days before a due process hearing occurs.

(ii) Applicable Timeline. The applicable timeline for a due process hearing under this part shall recommence at the time the party files an amended notice, including the timeline under subsection (f)(1)(B).

(d) Procedural Safeguards Notice.

(1) In General.

(A) Copy to Parents. A copy of the procedural safeguards available to the parents of a child with a disability shall be given to the parents only 1 time a year, except that a copy also shall be given to the parents -

(i) upon initial referral or parental request for evaluation;

(ii) upon the first occurrence of the filing of a complaint under subsection (b)(6); and

(iii) upon request by a parent.

(B) Internet Websites. A local educational agency may place a current copy of the procedural safeguards notice on its Internet website if such website exists.

(2) Contents. The procedural safeguards notice shall include a full explanation of the procedural safeguards, written **in the native language of the parents** (unless it clearly is not feasible to do so) and **written in an easily understandable manner**, available under this section and under regulations promulgated by the Secretary relating to -

(A) independent educational evaluation;

(B) prior written notice;

(C) parental consent;

(D) access to educational records;

(E) the opportunity to present and resolve complaints, including -

(i) the time period in which to make a complaint;

(ii) the opportunity for the agency to resolve the complaint; and

(iii) the availability of mediation;

(F) the child's placement during pendency of due process proceedings;

(G) procedures for students who are subject to placement in an interim alternative educational setting;

(H) requirements for unilateral placement by parents of children in private schools at public expense;

(I) due process hearings, including requirements for disclosure of evaluation results and recommendations;

(J) State-level appeals (if applicable in that State);

(K) civil actions, including the time period in which to file such actions; and

(L) attorneys' fees.

(e) Mediation.

(1) **In General.** Any State educational agency or local educational agency that receives assistance under this part shall ensure that procedures are established and implemented to allow parties to disputes involving any matter, including matters arising prior to the filing of a complaint pursuant to subsection (b)(6), to resolve such disputes through a mediation process.

(2) **Requirements.** Such procedures shall meet the following requirements:

(A) The procedures shall ensure that the mediation process -

(i) is voluntary on the part of the parties;

(ii) is not used to deny or delay a parent's right to a due process hearing under subsection (f), or to deny any other rights afforded under this part; and

(iii) is conducted by a qualified and impartial mediator who is trained in effective mediation techniques.

(B) **Opportunity to Meet with a Disinterested Party.** A local educational agency or a State agency may establish procedures to offer to parents and schools that choose not to use the mediation process, an opportunity to meet, at a time and location convenient to the parents, with a disinterested party who is under contract with -

(i) a parent training and information center or community parent resource center in the State established under section 1471 of this title or 1472 of this title; or

(ii) an appropriate alternative dispute resolution entity, to encourage the use, and explain the benefits, of the mediation process to the parents.

(C) **List of Qualified Mediators.** The State shall maintain a list of individuals who are qualified mediators and knowledgeable in laws and regulations relating to the provision of special education and related services.

(D) **Costs.** The State shall bear the cost of the mediation process, including the costs of meetings described in subparagraph (B).

(E) **Scheduling and Location.** Each session in the mediation process shall be scheduled in a timely manner and shall be held in a location that is convenient to the parties to the dispute.

(F) **Written Agreement.** In the case that a resolution is reached to resolve the complaint through the mediation process, the parties shall execute a legally binding agreement that sets forth such resolution and that -

(i) states that all discussions that occurred during the mediation process shall be confidential and may not be used as evidence in any subsequent due process hearing or civil proceeding;

(ii) is signed by both the parent and a representative of the agency who has the authority to bind such agency; and

(iii) is enforceable in any State court of competent jurisdiction or in a district court of the United States.

(G) Mediation Discussions. Discussions that occur during the mediation process shall be confidential and may not be used as evidence in any subsequent due process hearing or civil proceeding.

(f) Impartial Due Process Hearing.

(1) In General.

(A) Hearing. Whenever a complaint has been received under subsection (b)(6) or (k), the parents or the local educational agency involved in such complaint shall have an opportunity for an impartial due process hearing, which shall be conducted by the State educational agency or by the local educational agency, as determined by State law or by the State educational agency.

(B) Resolution Session.

(i) **Preliminary Meeting.** Prior to the opportunity for an impartial due process hearing under subparagraph (A), the local educational agency shall convene a meeting with the parents and the relevant member or members of the IEP Team who have specific knowledge of the facts identified in the complaint (I) **within 15 days of receiving notice of the parents' complaint;** (II) which shall include a representative of the agency who has decisionmaking authority on behalf of such agency; (III) which may not include an attorney of the local educational agency unless the parent is accompanied by an attorney; and (IV) where the parents of the child discuss their complaint, and the facts that form the basis of the complaint, and the local educational agency is provided the opportunity to resolve the complaint, unless the parents and the local educational agency agree in writing to waive such meeting, or agree to use the mediation process described in subsection (e).

(ii) **Hearing.** If the local educational agency has not resolved the complaint to the satisfaction of the parents **within 30 days of the receipt of the complaint,** the due process hearing may occur, and all of the applicable timelines for a due process hearing under this part shall commence.

(iii) **Written Settlement Agreement.** In the case that a resolution is reached to resolve the complaint at a meeting described in clause (i), the parties shall execute a **legally binding agreement** that is (I) signed by both the parent and a representative of the agency who has the authority to bind such agency; and (II) **enforceable in any State court of competent jurisdiction or in a district court of the United States.**

(iv) **Review Period.** If the parties execute an agreement pursuant to clause (iii), a party may void such agreement within 3 business days of the agreement's execution.

(2) Disclosure of Evaluations and Recommendations.

(A) In General. Not less than 5 business days prior to a hearing conducted pursuant to paragraph (1), each party shall disclose to all other parties all evaluations completed by that date, and recommendations based on the offering party's evaluations, that the party intends to use at the hearing.

(B) Failure to Disclose. A hearing officer may bar any party that fails to comply with subparagraph (A) from introducing the relevant evaluation or recommendation at the hearing without the consent of the other party.

(3) Limitations on Hearing.

(A) Person Conducting Hearing. A hearing officer conducting a hearing pursuant to paragraph (1)(A) shall, at a minimum -

(i) not be (I) an employee of the State educational agency or the local educational agency involved in the education or care of the child; or (II) a person having a personal or professional interest that conflicts with the person's objectivity in the hearing;

(ii) possess knowledge of, and the ability to understand, the provisions of this title, Federal and State regulations pertaining to this title, and legal interpretations of this title by Federal and State courts;

(iii) possess the knowledge and ability to conduct hearings in accordance with appropriate, standard legal practice; and

(iv) possess the knowledge and ability to render and write decisions in accordance with appropriate, standard legal practice.

(B) Subject Matter of Hearing. The party requesting the due process hearing shall not be allowed to raise issues at the due process hearing that were not raised in the notice filed under subsection (b)(7), unless the other party agrees otherwise.

(C) Timeline for Requesting Hearing. A parent or agency shall request an impartial due process hearing within 2 years of the date the parent or agency knew or should have known about the alleged action that forms the basis of the complaint, or, if the State has an explicit time limitation for requesting such a hearing under this part, in such time as the State law allows.

(D) Exceptions to the Timeline. The timeline described in subparagraph (C) shall not apply to a parent if the parent was prevented from requesting the hearing due to -

(i) specific misrepresentations by the local educational agency that it had resolved the problem forming the basis of the complaint; or

(ii) the local educational agency's withholding of information from the parent that was required under this part to be provided to the parent.

(E) Decision of Hearing Officer.

(i) **In General.** Subject to clause (ii), a decision made by a hearing officer shall be made on substantive grounds based on a determination of whether the child received a free appropriate public education.

(ii) **Procedural Issues.** In matters alleging a procedural violation, a hearing officer may find that a child did not receive a free appropriate public education only if the procedural inadequacies -(I) impeded the child's right to a free appropriate public education; (II) significantly impeded the parents' opportunity to participate in the decisionmaking process regarding the provision of a free appropriate public education to the parents' child; or (III) caused a deprivation of educational benefits.

(iii) **Rule of Construction.** Nothing in this subparagraph shall be construed to preclude a hearing officer from ordering a local educational agency to comply with procedural requirements under this section.

(F) **Rule of Construction.** Nothing in this paragraph shall be construed to affect the right of a parent to file a complaint with the State educational agency.

(g) Appeal.

(1) **In General.** If the hearing required by subsection (f) is conducted by a local educational agency, any party aggrieved by the findings and decision rendered in such a hearing may appeal such findings and decision to the State educational agency.

(2) **Impartial Review and Independent Decision.** The State educational agency shall conduct an impartial review of the findings and decision appealed under paragraph (1). The officer conducting such review shall make an independent decision upon completion of such review.

(h) Safeguards. Any party to a hearing conducted pursuant to subsection (f) or (k), or an appeal conducted pursuant to subsection (g), shall be accorded -

(1) the right to be accompanied and advised by counsel and by individuals with special knowledge or training with respect to the problems of children with disabilities;

(2) the right to present evidence and confront, cross-examine, and compel the attendance of witnesses;

(3) the right to a written, or, at the option of the parents, electronic verbatim record of such hearing; and

(4) the right to written, or, at the option of the parents, electronic findings of fact and decisions, which findings and decisions -

(A) shall be made available to the public consistent with the requirements of section 1417(b) of this title (relating to the confidentiality of data, information, and records); and

(B) shall be transmitted to the advisory panel established pursuant to section 1412(a)(21) of this title.

(i) Administrative Procedures.

(1) **In General.**

(A) **Decision Made in Hearing.** A decision made in a hearing conducted pursuant to subsection (f) or (k) shall be final, except that any party involved in such hearing may appeal such decision under the provisions of subsection (g) and paragraph (2).

(B) Decision Made at Appeal. A decision made under subsection (g) shall be final, except that any party may bring an action under paragraph (2).

(2) Right to Bring Civil Action.

(A) In General. Any party aggrieved by the findings and decision made under subsection (f) or (k) who does not have the right to an appeal under subsection (g), and any party aggrieved by the findings and decision made under this subsection, shall have the right to bring a civil action with respect to the complaint presented pursuant to this section, which action may be brought in any State court of competent jurisdiction or in a district court of the United States, without regard to the amount in controversy.

(B) Limitation. The party bringing the action shall have 90 days from the date of the decision of the hearing officer to bring such an action, or, if the State has an explicit time limitation for bringing such action under this part, in such time as the State law allows.

(C) Additional Requirements. In any action brought under this paragraph, the court

(i) shall receive the records of the administrative proceedings;

(ii) shall hear additional evidence at the request of a party; and

(iii) basing its decision on the preponderance of the evidence, shall grant such relief as the court determines is appropriate.

(3) Jurisdiction of District Courts; Attorneys' Fees.

(A) In General. The district courts of the United States shall have jurisdiction of actions brought under this section without regard to the amount in controversy.

(B) Award of Attorneys' Fees.

(i) In General. In any action or proceeding brought under this section, the court, in its discretion, may award reasonable attorneys' fees as part of the costs – (I) to a prevailing party who is the parent of a child with a disability; (II) to a prevailing party who is a State educational agency or local educational agency against the attorney of a parent who files a complaint or subsequent cause of action that is frivolous, unreasonable, or without foundation, or against the attorney of a parent who continued to litigate after the litigation clearly became frivolous, unreasonable, or without foundation; or (III) to a prevailing State educational agency or local educational agency against the attorney of a parent, or against the parent, if the parent's complaint or subsequent cause of action was presented for any improper purpose, such as to harass, to cause unnecessary delay, or to needlessly increase the cost of litigation.

(ii) Rule of Construction. Nothing in this subparagraph shall be construed to affect section 327 of the District of Columbia Appropriations Act, 2005.

(C) Determination of Amount of Attorneys' Fees. Fees awarded under this paragraph shall be based on rates prevailing in the community in which the action or proceeding arose for the kind and quality of services furnished. No bonus or multiplier may be used in calculating the fees awarded under this subsection.

(D) Prohibition of Attorneys' Fees and Related Costs for Certain Services.

(i) In General. Attorneys' fees may not be awarded and related costs may not be reimbursed in any action or proceeding under this section for services performed subsequent to the time of a written offer of settlement to a parent if (I) the offer is made within the time prescribed by Rule 68 of the Federal Rules of Civil Procedure or, in the case of an administrative proceeding, at any time more than 10 days before the proceeding begins; (II) the offer is not accepted within 10 days; and (III) the court or administrative hearing officer finds that the relief finally obtained by the parents is not more favorable to the parents than the offer of settlement.

(ii) IEP Team Meetings. Attorneys' fees may not be awarded relating to any meeting of the IEP Team unless such meeting is convened as a result of an administrative proceeding or judicial action, or, at the discretion of the State, for a mediation described in subsection (e).

(iii) Opportunity to Resolve Complaints. A meeting conducted pursuant to subsection (f)(1)(B)(i) shall not be considered -(I) a meeting convened as a result of an administrative hearing or judicial action; or (II) an administrative hearing or judicial action for purposes of this paragraph.

(E) Exception to Prohibition on Attorneys' Fees and Related Costs Notwithstanding subparagraph (D), an award of attorneys' fees and related costs may be made to a parent who is the prevailing party and who was substantially justified in rejecting the settlement offer.

(F) Reduction in Amount of Attorneys' Fees. Except as provided in subparagraph (G), whenever the court finds that

(i) the parent, or the parent's attorney, during the course of the action or proceeding, unreasonably protracted the final resolution of the controversy;

(ii) the amount of the attorneys' fees otherwise authorized to be awarded unreasonably exceeds the hourly rate prevailing in the community for similar services by attorneys of reasonably comparable skill, reputation, and experience;

(iii) the time spent and legal services furnished were excessive considering the nature of the action or proceeding; or

(iv) the attorney representing the parent did not provide to the local educational agency the appropriate information in the notice of the complaint described in subsection (b)(7)(A), the court shall reduce, accordingly, the amount of the attorneys' fees awarded under this section.

(G) Exception to Reduction in Amount of Attorneys' Fees. The provisions of subparagraph (F) shall not apply in any action or proceeding if the court finds that the State or local educational agency unreasonably protracted the final resolution of the action or proceeding or there was a violation of this section.

(j) Maintenance of Current Educational Placement.

Except as provided in subsection (k)(4), during the pendency of any proceedings conducted pursuant to this section, unless the State or local educational agency and the parents otherwise agree, the child shall remain in the then-current educational placement of the child, or, if applying for initial admission to a public school, shall, with the consent of the parents, be placed in the public school program until all such proceedings have been completed.

(k) Placement in Alternative Educational Setting.

(1) **Authority of School Personnel.**

(A) **Case-by-Case Determination.** School personnel may consider any unique circumstances on a case-by-case basis when determining whether to order a change in placement for a child with a disability who violates a code of student conduct.

(B) **Authority.** School personnel under this subsection may remove a child with a disability who violates a code of student conduct from their current placement to an appropriate interim alternative educational setting, another setting, or suspension, for not more than 10 school days (to the extent such alternatives are applied to children without disabilities).

(C) **Additional Authority.** If school personnel seek to order a change in placement that would exceed 10 school days and the behavior that gave rise to the violation of the school code is determined not to be a manifestation of the child's disability pursuant to subparagraph (E), the relevant disciplinary procedures applicable to children without disabilities may be applied to the child in the same manner and for the same duration in which the procedures would be applied to children without disabilities, except as provided in section 1412(a)(1) of this title although it may be provided in an interim alternative educational setting.

(D) **Services.** A child with a disability who is removed from the child's current placement under subparagraph (G) (irrespective of whether the behavior is determined to be a manifestation of the child's disability) or subparagraph (C) shall –

(i) continue to receive educational services, as provided in section 1412(a)(1) of this title, so as to enable the child to continue to participate in the general education curriculum, although in another setting, and to progress toward meeting the goals set out in the child's IEP; and

(ii) receive, as appropriate, a functional behavioral assessment, behavioral intervention services and modifications, that are designed to address the behavior violation so that it does not recur.

(E) **Manifestation Determination.**

(i) **In General.** Except as provided in subparagraph (B), within 10 school days of any decision to change the placement of a child with a disability because of a violation of a code of student conduct, the local educational agency, the parent, and relevant members of the IEP Team (as determined by the parent and the local educational agency) shall review all relevant information in the student's file, including the child's IEP, any teacher observations, and any relevant information provided by the parents to determine - (I) if the conduct in question was caused by, or had a direct and substantial relationship to, the child's disability; or (II) if the conduct in question was the direct result of the local educational agency's failure to implement the IEP.

(ii) **Manifestation.** If the local educational agency, the parent, and relevant members of the IEP Team determine that either subclause (I) or (II) of clause (i) is applicable for the child, the conduct shall be determined to be a manifestation of the child's disability.

(F) Determination That Behavior Was a Manifestation. If the local educational agency, the parent, and relevant members of the IEP Team make the determination that the conduct was a manifestation of the child's disability, the IEP Team **shall -**

(i) **conduct a functional behavioral assessment, and implement a behavioral intervention plan** for such child, provided that the local educational agency had not conducted such assessment prior to such determination before the behavior that resulted in a change in placement described in subparagraph (C) or (G);

(ii) in the situation where a behavioral intervention plan has been developed, review the behavioral intervention plan if the child already has such a behavioral intervention plan, and **modify it**, as necessary, **to address the behavior;** and

(iii) except as provided in subparagraph (G), **return the child to the placement from which the child was removed,** unless the parent and the local educational agency agree to a change of placement as part of the modification of the behavioral intervention plan.

(G) Special Circumstances. School personnel **may remove a student to an interim alternative educational setting** for **not more than 45 school days** without regard to whether the behavior is determined to be a manifestation of the child's disability, in cases where a child -

(i) **carries or possesses a weapon** to or at school, on school premises, or to or at a school function under the jurisdiction of a State or local educational agency;

(ii) **knowingly possesses or uses illegal drugs, or sells or solicits the sale of a controlled substance,** while at school, on school premises, or at a school function under the jurisdiction of a State or local educational agency; or

(iii) has **inflicted serious bodily injury** upon another person while at school, on school premises, or at a school function under the jurisdiction of a State or local educational agency.

(H) Notification. Not later than the date on which the decision to take disciplinary action is made, the local educational agency shall notify the parents of that decision, and of all procedural safeguards accorded under this section.

(2) Determination of Setting. The interim alternative educational setting in subparagraphs (C) and (G) of paragraph (1) **shall be determined by the IEP Team.**

(3) Appeal.

(A) In General. The parent of a child with a disability who disagrees with any decision regarding placement, or the manifestation determination under this subsection, or a local educational agency that believes that maintaining the current placement of the child is substantially likely to result in injury to the child or to others, may request a hearing.

(B) Authority of Hearing Officer.

(i) In General. A hearing officer shall hear, and make a determination regarding, an appeal requested under subparagraph (A).

(ii) Change of Placement Order. In making the determination under clause (i), the hearing officer may order a change in placement of a child with a disability. In such situations, the hearing officer may (I) return a child with a disability to the placement from which the child was removed; or (II) order a change in placement of a child with a disability to an appropriate interim alternative educational setting for not more than 45 school days if the hearing officer determines that maintaining the current placement of such child is substantially likely to result in injury to the child or to others.

(4) Placement During Appeals. When an appeal under paragraph (3) has been requested by either the parent or the local educational agency -

(A) the child shall remain in the interim alternative educational setting pending the decision of the hearing officer or until the expiration of the time period provided for in paragraph (1)(C), whichever occurs first, unless the parent and the State or local educational agency agree otherwise; and

(B) the State or local educational agency shall arrange for an **expedited hearing,** which shall occur **within 20 school days** of the date the hearing is requested and shall result in a determination within 10 school days after the hearing.

(5) Protections for Children Not Yet Eligible for Special Education and Related Services.

(A) In General. A child who has not been determined to be eligible for special education and related services under this part and who has engaged in behavior that violates a code of student conduct, may assert any of the protections provided for in this part if the local educational agency had knowledge (as determined in accordance with this paragraph) that the child was a child with a disability before the behavior that precipitated the disciplinary action occurred.

(B) Basis of Knowledge. A local educational agency shall be deemed to have knowledge that a child is a child with a disability if, before the behavior that precipitated the disciplinary action occurred -

(i) the parent of the child has expressed concern in writing to supervisory or administrative personnel of the appropriate educational agency, or a teacher of the child, that the child is in need of special education and related services;

(ii) the parent of the child has requested an evaluation of the child pursuant to section 1414(a)(1)(B) of this title; or

(iii) the teacher of the child, or other personnel of the local educational agency, has expressed specific concerns about a pattern of behavior demonstrated by the child, directly to the director of special education of such agency or to other supervisory personnel of the agency.

(C) Exception. A local educational agency shall not be deemed to have knowledge that the child is a child with a disability if the parent of the child has not allowed an evaluation of the child pursuant to section 1414 of this title or has refused services under this part or the child has been evaluated and it was determined that the child was not a child with a disability under this part.

(D) Conditions that Apply if No Basis of Knowledge.

(i) In General. If a local educational agency does not have knowledge that a child is a child with a disability (in accordance with subparagraph (B) or (C)) prior to taking disciplinary measures against the child, the child may be subjected to disciplinary measures applied to children without disabilities who engaged in comparable behaviors consistent with clause (ii).

(ii) Limitations. If a request is made for an evaluation of a child during the time period in which the child is subjected to disciplinary measures under this subsection, the evaluation shall be conducted in an expedited manner. If the child is determined to be a child with a disability, taking into consideration information from the evaluation conducted by the agency and information provided by the parents, the agency shall provide special education and related services in accordance with this part, except that, pending the results of the evaluation, the child shall remain in the educational placement determined by school authorities.

(6) Referral to and Action by Law Enforcement and Judicial Authorities.

(A) Rule of Construction. Nothing in this part shall be construed to prohibit an agency from reporting a crime committed by a child with a disability to appropriate authorities or to prevent State law enforcement and judicial authorities from exercising their responsibilities with regard to the application of Federal and State law to crimes committed by a child with a disability.

(B) Transmittal of Records. An agency reporting a crime committed by a child with a disability shall ensure that copies of the special education and disciplinary records of the child are transmitted for consideration by the appropriate authorities to whom the agency reports the crime.

(7) Definitions. In this subsection:

(A) Controlled Substance. The term 'controlled substance' means a drug or other substance identified under schedule I, II, III, IV, or V in section 812(c) of title 21, United States Code.

(B) Illegal Drug. The term 'illegal drug' means a controlled substance but does not include a controlled substance that is legally possessed or used under the supervision of a licensed health-care professional or that is legally possessed or used under any other authority under that Act or under any other provision of Federal law.

(C) Weapon. The term 'weapon' has the meaning given the term 'dangerous weapon' under section 930(g)(2) of title 18, United States Code.

(D) Serious Bodily Injury. The term 'serious bodily injury' has the meaning given the term 'serious bodily injury' under paragraph (3) of subsection (h) of section 1365 of title 18, United States Code.

(l) Rule of Construction.

Nothing in this title shall be construed to restrict or limit the rights, procedures, and remedies available under the Constitution, the Americans with Disabilities Act of 1990, [42 U.S.C. § 12101] title V of the Rehabilitation Act of 1973, [29 U.S.C. § 790] or other Federal laws protecting the rights of children with disabilities, except that before the filing of a civil action under such laws seeking relief that is also available under this part, the procedures under subsections (f) and (g) shall be exhausted to the same extent as would be required had the action been brought under this part.

(m) Transfer of Parental Rights at Age of Majority.

(1) In General. A State that receives amounts from a grant under this part may provide that, when a child with a disability reaches the age of majority under State law (except for a child with a disability who has been determined to be incompetent under State law) -

(A) the agency shall provide any notice required by this section to both the individual and the parents;

(B) all other rights accorded to parents under this part transfer to the child;

(C) the agency shall notify the individual and the parents of the transfer of rights; and

(D) all rights accorded to parents under this part transfer to children who are incarcerated in an adult or juvenile Federal, State, or local correctional institution.

(2) Special Rule. If, under State law, a child with a disability who has reached the age of majority under State law, who has not been determined to be incompetent, but who is determined not to have the ability to provide informed consent with respect to the educational program of the child, the State shall establish procedures for appointing the parent of the child, or if the parent is not available, another appropriate individual, to represent the educational interests of the child throughout the period of eligibility of the child under this part.

(n) Electronic Mail.

A parent of a child with a disability may elect to receive notices required under this section by an electronic mail (e-mail) communication, if the agency makes such option available.

(o) Separate Complaint.

Nothing in this section shall be construed to preclude a parent from filing a separate due process complaint on an issue separate from a due process complaint already filed.

Wrightslaw Discussion of Section 1415 - Procedural Safeguards, Notices, Due Process, Discipline

Procedural Safeguards

Parents have the right to examine all educational records, including test data. The right to examine records may include personal notes, if notes have been shared with other staff. Parents should request test data (i.e., standard scores, percentile ranks, age equivalent scores, and grade equivalent scores) in writing. The school district is to provide the parent, in writing, with the reason for refusing to evaluate a child or change the educational program.

Independent Educational Evaluations

Parents have the right to obtain an Independent Educational Evaluation of their child. Many school districts attempt to restrict the parent's choice of evaluators to a list of approved evaluators selected by the school. The Office of Special Education Programs issued a policy letter clarifying that parents have the right to choose their independent evaluator. (See OSEP, Letter to Parker, 2004 on the Wrightslaw website.)

Due Process Notice

The party who requests a due process hearing must provide a detailed notice to the other party that includes identifying information about the child, the nature of the problem, facts, and proposed resolution. The party that requests the due process hearing may not have the hearing until they provide this notice.

Prior Written Notice (PWN)

If the school district proposes to initiate or change, or refuses to change the identification, evaluation, or educational placement of your child, the district must provide you with prior written notice (PWN). Prior written notice must describe the district's rationale, describe other options that were considered, and describe the evaluations, tests, records and/or reports that were used as the basis of their decision. Prior written notice must be in writing and easily understood.

Procedural Safeguards Notice

The purpose of the Procedural Safeguards Notice is to provide parents with information about their rights and protections under the law. The Procedural Safeguards Notice includes rights about mediation, "stay put," discipline, reimbursement for private placements, and attorneys' fees.

Mediation

Mediation is a process that allows parties to resolve disputes without litigation. Before you enter into mediation, you should understand your rights and the law. When you mediate, your goals are to resolve the dispute and protect the parent-school relationship.

The mediator's role is to facilitate the communication process. Mediators should not take positions or take sides. In mediation, discussions and admissions by the parties are confidential. Legally binding written settlement agreements are new in IDEA 2004 and allow a party to use the power of federal courts to ensure that settlement agreements are honored.

If you have a dispute with the school, you need to learn how to resolve disputes and develop win-win solutions to problems.

Recommended Resources: *Getting to Yes* by Roger Fisher, *Getting Past No* by William Ury, and *You Can Negotiate Anything* by Herb Cohen. (See Bibliography)

Due Process Hearings

Parents and school districts may resolve disputes about special education issues by requesting due process hearings. Due process hearings are conducted differently in different states. Many pre-trial procedures and timelines for due process hearings are new in IDEA 2004.

Ultimately, your success in a hearing will depend on the law and facts, the preparedness of the attorneys, and the life experiences of the hearing officer, Administrative Law Judge, or other decision-maker. The pre-existing beliefs and opinions of the decision-maker are more controlling of outcome than the facts and the law. This is true in most litigation and is not unique to special education disputes. Be sure to read Chapter 21 about the Rules of Adverse Assumptions

To see a due process hearing, you may want to view *Surviving Due Process: When Parents and the School Board Disagree*, a DVD video available from Wrightslaw.

Resolution Session

The Resolution Session provides the parties with an opportunity to resolve their complaint before the due process hearing. The school district must send "the relevant member or members of the IEP team" who have knowledge about the facts in the parent's complaint and a school district representative who has decision-making authority (settlement authority).

Written Settlement Agreements

The requirements for legally binding written Settlement Agreements are new in IDEA 2004. Previously, when a party breached a settlement agreement, the other party had to enforce the agreement by filing suit under a breach of contract theory. Now the power of the federal courts may be used to ensure that settlement agreements are honored.

Exhibits and Evaluations

IDEA 2004 requires that evaluations and recommendations be disclosed no later than 5 business days before a due process hearing. Most state statutes and regulations require that all exhibits (including evaluations and recommendations), exhibit lists, and witness lists, be disclosed at least 5 days prior to a hearing. Failure to comply with these requirements may lead to dismissal of the case.

Your exhibit list may include:

- Letters, journals, logs
- Evaluations and reports
- Research, journal articles, book chapters
- Other documents that are relevant to your case

Two-Year Statute of Limitations

The two-year statute of limitations to present a complaint is new in IDEA 2004. If your state does not have a statute of limitations, you must request a due process hearing within two years. The two-year statute of limitations may not apply if the parent was prevented from requesting a hearing because of misrepresentations by the school district or because the district withheld information it was required to provide.

Rulings by Hearing Officers

Rulings by hearing officers should be based substantive issues, not procedural issues, unless the procedural violation impeded the child's right to a free appropriate public education, significantly impeded the parents' opportunity to participate in decision-making, or deprived the child of educational benefit. This language in the statute is new and incorporates existing caselaw about procedural and substantive issues.

Safeguards

In a due process hearing, parents or their attorney have the right to present evidence and cross-examine witnesses, and to issue subpoenas for witnesses. Parents have a right to a written verbatim record (transcript) of the hearing and to written findings of fact and decisions. In some states you can be represented by a lay advocate.

Attorneys' Fees

Parents who prevail can recover attorneys fees from school districts. Now, school districts may recover attorneys' fees from the parent's attorney or the parent under specific, limited circumstances. If the parent or parent's attorney files a complaint that is frivolous, unreasonable, or for an improper purpose (i.e., to harass, cause unnecessary delay, or needlessly increase the cost of litigation), the Court may award attorneys' fees to the school district.

"Stay Put"

The "Stay Put" statute explains that during the due process hearing and appeals, the child will remain (stay put) in the current educational placement. Many courts have held that the "current educational placement" is not the physical location of services, but the nature of the educational program.

Discipline

Many school administrators and school boards refuse to exercise discretion in disciplinary matters. In IDEA 2004, Congress added language that school personnel "may consider any unique circumstances on a case-by-case basis" in determining whether to order a change of placement in IDEA 2004.

Suspensions and Expulsions

If a child with a disability violates a code of student conduct, school officials may suspend the child for up to 10 days. Codes of Conduct are usually written policies adopted by the School Board. If the school suspends the child with a disability for more than 10 days and determines that the child's behavior was not a manifestation of the disability, they may use the same procedures as with non-disabled children, but must continue to provide the child with a free appropriate public education. (FAPE)

If the school district suspends a child with a disability for more than 10 days, regardless of severity of the child's misconduct (i.e. violation of a code of conduct v. possession of a weapon), the school must continue to provide FAPE so the child can participate in the general education curriculum, make progress on the IEP goals, and receive a functional behavioral assessment, behavioral intervention services and modifications to prevent the behavior from reoccurring.

Manifestation Reviews

The IEP team must review all information about the child and determine if the negative behavior was caused by the child's disability, had a direct and substantial relationship to the disability, or was the result of the school's failure to implement the IEP.

The IEP team must answer several questions. Is the child's IEP appropriate? Is the child's placement appropriate? Did the school provide appropriate behavior intervention strategies? Did the child's disability impair the child's ability to understand the impact and consequences of the behavior?

If the child's behavior was a manifestation of the disability, the IEP Team shall conduct a Functional Behavioral Assessment and implement a Behavioral Intervention Plan (BIP). If a Behavior Intervention Plan was developed previously, it should be modified to address behavior as necessary. If the child's behavior did not involve weapons, drugs, or seriously bodily injury, the child should return to the prior placement.

Dangerous Weapon, Illegal Drugs, Serious Bodily Harm

If the child's behavior involves a dangerous weapon, illegal drugs, or serious bodily injury, the child may be suspended for 45 school days even if the behavior was a manifestation of the disability. The child is still entitled to FAPE.

The term 'dangerous weapon' means a weapon, device, instrument, material, or substance, animate or inanimate, that is used for, or is readily capable of, causing death or serious bodily injury, except that such term does not include a pocket knife with a blade of less than 2 1/2 inches in length." The term 'serious bodily injury' means bodily injury which involves (A) a substantial risk of death; (B) extreme physical pain; (C) protracted and obvious disfigurement; or (D) protracted loss or impairment of the function of a bodily member, organ, or mental faculty . . ."

Prescribed Medications Are Not Illegal Drugs

Using "zero tolerance" anti-drug policies, many school districts have labeled over-the-counter-medication as "drugs," branded children as drug violators, and expelled children from school. IDEA 2004 clarifies that over-the-counter medications are not illegal drugs nor controlled substances.

If a doctor prescribes a controlled substance, and the child has possession of the medication at school, the school may not expel or suspend the child for possessing this prescribed medication. If the child attempts to sell or solicit the sale of the controlled substance, this "special circumstance" warrants a suspension for 45 school days and possible criminal prosecution.

Interim Alternative Placement

The decision to place a child into an interim alternative educational setting shall be made by the IEP Team, not by an administrator or school board member. The educational setting is an interim placement, not a permanent placement.

Strategies: Discipline Issues

Get a Comprehensive Evaluation

If you are dealing with a discipline issue, you need to obtain a comprehensive psycho-educational evaluation of the child by an evaluator in the private sector who has expertise in the disability. If there is a causal relationship between the child's disability and misbehavior, the evaluator should write a report that describes the child's disability, the basis for determining that the behavior was a manifestation of the disability, and recommendations for an appropriate program.

Put Your Concerns in Writing

If you are concerned that your child may have a disability, you must put your concerns in writing. Describe the disability and how, in your opinion, it adversely affects educational performance. If you report your concerns orally, for the purposes of law and litigation, you said nothing. Follow up your conversations, meetings, and telephone calls with letters that restate what you discussed and your concerns.

In Summation

In this chapter, you learned about the safeguards designed to protect the rights of children with disabilities and their parents. These safeguards include the right to participate in all meetings, to examine all educational records, and to obtain an independent educational evaluation (IEE) of the child.

You learned about prior written notice, procedural safeguards notice, mediation, legally binding mediation agreements, the new Resolution Sessions, due process hearings, "stay put," the new two-year statute of limitation, appeals, discipline, and age of majority.

In the next chapter, you will learn about Section 504 of the Rehabilitation Act and how it is different from the Individuals with Disabilities Education Act.

19 | Section 504 of The Rehabilitation Act of 1973 and the Americans with Disabilities Act

Morality cannot be legislated but behavior can be regulated. Judicial decrees may not change the heart, but they can restrain the heartless. — Martin Luther King, civil rights activist

Section 504 is a portion of the ADA (Americans w/ Disabilities Act)

IEPs are related to a different piece of legislation (IDEA)

In this chapter, you will learn about Section 504 of the Rehabilitation Act and the Americans with Disabilities Act, as contrasted with the Individuals with Disabilities Education Act (IDEA).

The key portion of **Section 504 of the Rehabilitation Act** states:

Section 794. Nondiscrimination under Federal grants and programs

(a) Promulgation of nondiscriminatory rules and regulations

No otherwise qualified individual with a disability in the United States, as defined in Sec. 705(20) of this title, shall, solely by reason of her or his disability, be excluded from the participation in, be denied the benefits of, or be subjected to discrimination under any program or activity receiving Federal financial assistance or under any program or activity conducted by any Executive agency or by the United States Postal Service . . .

The Americans with Disabilities Act, as it applies to public entities, is identical. The Americans with Disabilities Act states:

Section 12132. Discrimination

Subject to the provisions of this subchapter, no qualified individual with a disability shall, by reason of such disability, be excluded from participation in or be denied the benefits of the services, programs, or activities of a public entity, or be subjected to discrimination by any such entity.

Section 12133. Enforcement

The remedies, procedures, and rights set forth in section 794a of title 29 shall be the remedies, procedures, and rights this subchapter provides to any person alleging discrimination on the basis of disability in violation of section 12132 of this title.

The language of ADA tracks Section 504 and explains that the remedies, procedures and rights under the ADA are the same as under the Rehabilitation Act. Except for accessibility of buildings, and modifications and accommodations in testing, compared to IDEA 2004, Section 504 and ADA provide fewer protections and benefits to children with disabilities.

The key benefit related to legal remedies if a school district retaliates against a parent or child for exercising their rights.

Wrightslaw Discussion of Section 504, ADA and IDEA

Section 504 is a civil rights law. The purpose of Section 504 is to protect individuals with disabilities from discrimination for reasons related to their disabilities. ADA broadened the agencies and businesses that must comply with the non-discrimination and accessibility provisions of the law.

Unlike IDEA, Section 504 and ADA do not ensure that a child with a disability will receive an individualized educational program that is designed to meet the child's unique needs and provide the child with educational benefit, so the child will be prepared for "for employment and independent living."

Eligibility

If a child has a disability but does not need special education services, the child will not qualify for special education and related services under the Individuals with Disabilities Education Act but may receive protections under Section 504 of the Rehabilitation Act.

To be eligible for protections under Section 504, the child must have a physical or mental impairment. This impairment must substantially limit at least one major life activity. Major life activities include walking, seeing, hearing, speaking, breathing, learning, reading, writing, performing math calculations, working, caring for oneself, and performing manual tasks. The key is whether the child has an "impairment" that "substantially limits . . . one or more . . . major life activities."

Section 504 requires an evaluation that draws information from a variety of sources.

Protection from Discrimination

Section 504 protects children with disabilities from discrimination. Children who receive special education services under IDEA are automatically covered under Section 504. If your child does not receive special education services under IDEA, your child does not have the procedural protections that are available under the IDEA statute.

Accommodations and Modifications

Under Section 504, the child with a disability may receive accommodations and modifications that are not available to children who are not disabled. These accommodations and modifications are available to all children who receive special education services under IDEA.

Confusion about Benefits and Rights

Some parents and educators believe that under IDEA, the child must be placed in a special education class, but if the child has a 504 plan, the child may remain in the regular classroom. For these reasons, parents are often advised that Section 504 is more desirable. This is incorrect. "Special education" under IDEA is a services, not a place or placement.

The child with a Section 504 Plan has fewer rights and protections than the child who receives special education services under the IDEA. The child who receives special education services under the IDEA is automatically protected under Section 504.

Access v. Educational Benefit

Let's change the facts to clarify the differences between these two laws. Assume that your special needs child is in a wheel chair. Under Section 504, your child shall not be discriminated against because of the disability. Your child shall be provided with access to an education, to and through the schoolhouse door. Reasonable modifications may be made to the building and other "reasonable" accommodations may be made for your child.

Under Section 504 regulations, a free appropriate public education is defined as "the provision of regular or special education and related aids and services that . . . are designed to meet individual educational needs of persons with disabilities as adequately as the needs of persons without disabilities are met and . . . are based upon adherence to specified procedures." (34 C.F.R. § 104.33(b)(1))

Now assume that your child in a wheelchair also has neurological problems that adversely affect the child's ability to learn. Under the IDEA, if your child has a disability that adversely affects educational performance, your child is entitled to an education that is designed to meet the child's unique needs and from which your child receives educational benefit. Section 504 includes no guarantee that your wheelchair-bound child will receive an education from which the child will derive educational benefit.

Under Section 504, your child simply has access to the same free appropriate public education that is available to all children who are not disabled.

Discipline

If the Section 504 child misbehaves and the school decides the child's behavior is not a manifestation of the disability, the child can be expelled from school permanently. The IDEA child has the right to FAPE, even if expelled from school. Section 504 and ADA do not provide these protections.

Procedural Safeguards

In Chapter 18, you learned about the procedural safeguards in IDEA that protect children with disabilities and their parents. Section 504 does not include many of these protections.

The procedural safeguards in IDEA include the right to written notice before any change of placement and the right to an independent educational evaluation at public expense. IDEA requires that parents be participants in all meetings about their child's eligibility, special education program, and placement. Section 504 does not require a meeting before a change in placement.

Impartial Hearings

Section 504 and IDEA require school districts to conduct impartial hearings for parents who disagree with identification, evaluation, or placement. Under Section 504, the parent has an opportunity to participate and obtain representation by counsel, but other details are left to the discretion of the school district.

In Summation

In this chapter, you learned about Section 504 of the Rehabilitation Act and the Americans with Disabilities Act. You learned that these statutes relate to accommodations and modifications in testing situations and programs, and improved building accessibility.

You also learned that Section 504 and ADA do not require public schools to provide an educational program that is individualized to meet the needs of a disabled child with the goal of enabling the child to become independent and self-sufficient. You learned that the child with a Section 504 plan does not have the protections available to the child who has an IEP under the IDEA.

In the next chapter, you will learn about important features in the No Child Left Behind Act and how Congress aligned the Individuals with Disabilities Act with No Child Left Behind.

20 | No Child Left Behind Act of 2001 (NCLB)

"Education is a critical national security issue for our future, and politics must stop at the schoolhouse door." — Bill Clinton, former president, in his 1997 State of the Union Address

When you read the Findings and Purposes of the Individuals with Disabilities Education Act, you learned that the Purpose is the most important statute in a law.

Read the Purpose of the No Child Left Behind Act:

> The purpose of this title is to ensure that all children have a fair, equal, and significant opportunity to obtain a high-quality education and reach, at a minimum, proficiency on challenging State academic achievement standards and state academic assessments. (emphasis added) (20 U.S.C. § 6301)

For the full text of the No Child Left Behind statute, see *Wrightslaw: No Child Left Behind.*

The No Child Left Behind Act requires schools and school districts to meet the educational needs of all children, including children with disabilities, English language learners, minority and migratory children, and other neglected groups of children, and to publicly report their progress in educating these children every year.

The key requirements of the law include annual proficiency tests in grades 3-8, highly qualified teachers in every classroom, research-based instruction, increased parental rights, public school choice, and public reporting of progress by states, school districts and schools. These requirements are all strategies to accomplish the purpose of the law.

No Child Left Behind is not a new law. When Congress reauthorized the Elementary and Secondary Education Act of 1965 (ESEA), they gave that law a new name — the No Child Left Behind Act.

Wrightslaw Discussion of NCLB

When the No Child Left Behind was enacted, millions of children were leaving school without the basic skills they need to make it in the real world.

According to the Nation's Report Card:

- Only 36 percent of 12th graders are proficient in reading
- Only 18 percent of 12th graders are proficient in science
- Only 17 percent of 12th graders are proficient in math
- Only 11 percent of 12th graders are proficient in U. S. history

Closing the Gap

Nationally, there is a significant gap between the achievement test scores of children from low-income families, racial minorities, children with disabilities, English language learners, and the test scores of other children. Children with disabilities are one of the groups that have often been left behind.

No Child Left Behind seeks to close the achievement gap by holding states, local school districts, and schools accountable for improving the academic achievement of all children. The provisions in No Child Left Behind that affect children and their parents include:

- Annual proficiency testing
- Research based reading programs
- Highly qualified teachers
- Parents' right to know qualifications of their child's teachers
- Supplemental educational services and public school choice
- Parent involvement and empowerment.

Annual Proficiency Testing

Beginning in 2005, schools must test all children in grades 3-8 every year in math and reading. By 2007, schools must test all children in science.

Annual assessments or proficiency tests will give you information about the school's progress in teaching your child and other groups of children. This information will help you ensure that your child is not left behind or trapped in a failing school.

Annual testing also provides useful information to your child's teachers. Teachers will know the strengths and weaknesses of their students. This information will help teachers develop lessons and ensure that all students meet or exceed state standards.

Research Based Reading Programs

No Child Left Behind focuses on teaching young children, including children with disabilities, to read. One goal of NCLB is that all children will be reading at grade level by the end of third grade. According to the Nation's Report Card:

- 32 percent of 4th graders are proficient readers
- 33 percent of 8th graders are proficient readers.
- 36 percent of 12th graders are proficient readers.

If you are a parent, you know that the reading skills of most children with disabilities are deficient. Sadly, many schools continue to use reading programs that are not effective in teaching children with disabilities to read.

NCLB provides funds for states and school districts to use "in establishing reading programs for students in kindergarten through grade 3 that are based on scientifically based reading research, to ensure that every student can read at grade level or above not later than the end of grade 3." (20 U. S. C. § 6361)

NCLB includes the legal definitions of reading, the essential components of reading instruction, diagnostic reading assessments, and reading research.

Reading

No Child Left Behind includes the legal definition of reading.

"Reading is a complex system of deriving meaning from print that requires all of the following:

(A) The skills and knowledge to understand how phonemes, or speech sounds, are connected to print,

(B) The ability to decode unfamiliar words,

(C) The ability to read fluently,

(D) Sufficient background information and vocabulary to foster reading comprehension,

(E) The development of appropriate active strategies to construct meaning from print,

(F) The development and maintenance of a motivation to read." (20 U. S. C. § 6368(5))

Essential Components of Reading Instruction

No Child Left Behind defines the five essential components of reading instruction.

"The term 'essential components of reading instruction' means explicit and systematic instruction in-

(A) phonemic awareness,

(B) phonics,

(C) vocabulary development,

(D) reading fluency, including oral reading skills, and

(E) reading comprehension strategies." (20 U. S. C. § 6368(3))

Diagnostic Reading Assessments

No Child Left Behind defines diagnostic reading assessments.

"The term 'diagnostic reading assessment' means an assessment that is-

(i) valid, reliable, and based on scientifically based reading research; and

(ii) used for the purpose of-

(I) identifying a child's specific areas of strengths and weaknesses so that the child has learned to read by the end of grade 3;

(II) determining any difficulties that a child may have in learning to read and the potential cause of such difficulties; and

(III) helping to determine possible reading intervention strategies and related special needs." (20 U. S. C. § 6368(7))

Scientifically Based Reading Research

No Child Left Behind defines scientifically based reading research.

"The term 'scientifically based reading research' means research that-

(A) applies rigorous, systematic, and objective procedures to obtain valid knowledge relevant to reading development, reading instruction, and reading difficulties; and

(B) includes research that-

(i) employs systematic, empirical methods that draw on observation or experiment;

(ii) involves rigorous data analyses that are adequate to test the stated hypotheses and justify the general conclusions drawn;

(iii) relies on measurements or observational methods that provide valid data across evaluators and observers and across multiple measurements and observations; and

(iv) has been accepted by a peer-reviewed journal or approved by a panel of independent experts through a comparably rigorous, objective, and scientific review." (20 U. S. C. § 6368(6))

Highly Qualified Teachers

The requirements for highly qualified special educators are new in IDEA 2004 and bring the law into conformity with the No Child Left Behind Act.

A "highly qualified teacher" has full State certification (no waivers), holds a license to teach, and meets the State's requirements. The requirements are somewhat different for new and veteran teachers, for elementary, middle school, and high school teachers, for teachers of multiple subjects, and for teachers who teach to alternate standards. (Section 1401(10)(B))

Special educators who teach core academic subjects must meet the highly qualified teacher requirements in NCLB and must demonstrate competence in the core academic subjects they teach. Special educators who do not provide instruction in core academic subjects do not have to meet the highly qualified teacher requirements.

Parents' Right to Know Qualifications of Their Child's Teachers

Parents whose children attend Title I schools have more options than parents of children who attend schools that do not receive Title I funds. At the beginning of each school year, school districts that receive Title I funds must notify parents that they may request specific information about the qualifications of their children's teachers.

At a minimum, you have a right to know–

- if the teacher is certified or licensed to teach the grade levels and subjects she is teaching
- if the teacher's certification or licensure was waived under an emergency or provisional status
- the teacher's college major and any graduate degree or certification
- if the child received services from a paraprofessional, the qualifications of that paraprofessional (20 U. S. C. § 6311)

See the Sample letter to request information about your child's teacher at the end of this chapter.

Public School Choice

If your child attends a Title I School that fails to meet its Adequate Yearly Progress goal for **two consecutive years**, your child may transfer to a non-failing school within the district. If all schools in your district fail to meet their AYP goals for two consecutive years, your child may attend a better-performing school in another school district. If your child transfers to a better-performing school, the child may remain there until he or she completes the highest grade in that school.

Supplemental Educational Services

If your child attends a Title I school that fails to meet its Adequate Yearly Progress goal for **three consecutive years**, the school must provide supplemental educational services to the students from low-income families who remain in the school. Supplemental educational services include tutoring, after-school programs, and summer programs. Supplemental services must be free to parents.

Parents may choose a tutor or other supplemental service provider from a list of approved providers maintained by the state. The state must ensure that all providers on the list have a history of success. The district may give preference to the lowest-achieving children from low-income families who request supplemental services.

Providers of supplemental services must give information about student progress to the parents and the school. Providers must ensure that instruction meets state and local standards, including state student academic achievement standards. Providers must also comply with health, safety, and civil rights laws.

Your Child's IEP

As you develop your child's IEPs, you need to be familiar with the essential components of reading instruction. The definitions of reading and research based reading programs apply to all programs, all schools, all children, all the time. These terms define and describe the minimum requirements for your child's reading program at school.

Don't forget that the timeline for teaching a child to read fluently is at the end of grade three.

Participation in Assessments

In IDEA 2004, the language about who will participate in assessments was changed to "**All** children with disabilities are included in **all** general State and district-wide assessment programs...**with appropriate accommodations**, where necessary and as indicated in their respective individualized education programs." (emphasis added)

Adaptations and Accommodations

For children with disabilities who receive services under the Individuals with Disabilities Education Act and have an Individualized Education Program (IEP), NCLB mandates that the child will receive "the reasonable adaptations and accommodations for students with disabilities ... necessary to measure the academic achievement of such students relative to State academic content and State student academic achievement standards."

IDEA 2004 requires the child's IEP to include:

"a statement of any individual appropriate accommodations that are necessary to measure the academic achievement and functional performance of the child on State and districtwide assessments... [and] if the IEP Team determines that the child shall take an alternate assessment on a particular State or districtwide assessment of student achievement, a statement of why...the child cannot participate in the regular assessment; and... [why] the particular alternate assessment selected is appropriate for the child..." (Section 1414(d)(1)(A)(i)(VI))

In Summation

In this chapter, you learned about key provisions of the No Child Left Behind Act and how these provisions apply to children with disabilities. You learned about reading, the essential components of reading programs, reading assessments, and scientifically based reading research.

You learned that NCLB and IDEA require schools to provide children with disabilities with appropriate accommodations on all state and district tests.

On the next page is a sample letter to request information about the qualifications of your child's teachers that you can adapt to your circumstances.

In the next section, you will learn how to use tactics and strategies to anticipate problems, negotiate for services, and avoid crises. If you have a disagreement or dispute with your child's school, these tactics and strategies will help you influence the outcome.

Sample Letter to Request Information about Teachers' Qualifications

Debra Pratt
17456 Wake Road
Deltaville, Virginia 23043
899-555-1234
March 1, 2006

Dr. Deborah Harrison, Principal
Deltaville Middle School
1000 Main Street
Deltaville, Virginia 23043

Re: Crystal Pratt (DOB: 01/01/93)
School: Deltaville Middle School

Dear Dr. Harrison:

My daughter Crystal is an eighth grade student at Deltaville Middle School. She has four teachers: Ms. Adams, Mr. Brown, Ms. Canady, and Ms. Davis, a substitute math teacher. Crystal also receives tutoring from Ms. Evans, a paraprofessional.

When I read the publication "Teacher Quality Guide Supports Parents' Right to Know" from the U. S. Department of Education, I realized that that I am entitled to information about Crystal's teachers, including:

(1) Whether the teacher has met State qualification and licensing criteria for the grade levels and subject areas in which the teacher provides instruction;

(2) Whether the teacher is teaching under emergency or other provisional status through which State qualification or licensing criteria have been waived.

(3) The baccalaureate degree major of the teacher and any other graduate certification or degree held by the teacher, and the field of discipline of the certification or degree.

(4) Whether the child is provided services by paraprofessionals and, if so, their qualifications.

I am requesting this information about the qualifications of Crystal's teachers and paraprofessional. I believe the information will help me work more effectively with her teachers.

If you have questions about my request, please call me at work (899-555-9876) or at home (899-555-1234) after 6 p.m., or you may email me at debrapratt@deltavilleva.com.

Thanks in advance for your help.

Sincerely,

Debra Pratt

Section Five

Tactics and Strategies

In this section, you will learn how to use tactics and strategies to anticipate problems, negotiate for services, and avoid crises. If you have a dispute with the school, tactics and strategies will help you influence the outcome.

Chapter 21 is "The Rules of Adverse Assumptions." We describe the assumptions you must make and how preparing for conflict helps you avoid conflict. You will learn about proof and evidence and how to present your case.

In Chapter 22, you learn about documentation. You will learn how to use logs, calendars, and journals to create paper trails. When you train yourself to write things down, you are taking steps to protect your child's interests.

Chapter 23 is about writing letters to the school. We describe the five purposes of letters and strategies you can use to ensure that your letters accomplish their purpose. You will learn editing and presentation techniques to enhance the effectiveness of your letters. This chapter includes frequently asked questions and the "nuts and bolts" of writing business letters. At the end of the chapter are sample letters that you can tailor to your circumstances.

In Chapter 24, you will learn about writing the "Letter to the Stranger." In this chapter, you will discover the identity of the mysterious Stranger and what you want to accomplish when you write to him or her. You will learn about the blame approach and the story-telling approach, angry letters and the sympathy factor, persuasion, and the importance of making a good impression. At the end of this chapter are a series of letters that show you how a parent can write persuasive letters.

Chapter 25 is "Preparing for Meetings: Taking Control." In this chapter, you will learn how preparing for meetings enables you to control the process. You will learn how to use meeting worksheets and parent agendas to clarify issues, make requests, describe problems, and offer solutions.

Chapter 26 is "Meeting Strategies: Maintaining Control." In this chapter, we teach you how to use a simple problem resolution worksheet to keep track of issues and requests. You will learn how to use 5 Ws + H + E questions to discover hidden agendas, plans, and fears. You will learn to use the post-meeting thank you note to document issues and problems.

Tactics and strategies will help you secure services for your child and resolve problems in other areas of your life. Let's learn about the Rules of Adverse Assumptions.

21 | The Rules of Adverse Assumptions

"It's not the will to win, but the will to prepare to win that makes the difference."
— Bear Bryant, University of Alabama football coach

If you are like most parents, you want the school to provide your child with quality special education services and supports–and you want to avoid a due process hearing. When you think about requesting a due process hearing, you feel anxious so you push these thoughts out of your mind. You will hope for the best.

Assume you ask the school to provide services for your child. The school refuses. You try to resolve your dispute informally and through IEP meetings. Nothing changes. What will you do? Give in? Press on?

Assume you request services for your child. Assume the school responded by requesting a special education due process hearing against you. That is what happened to Lisa:

> *I just had a due process hearing for my son. I do not have a lawyer. I am doing this on my own and I am being killed. The school asked for the due process hearing against me. The school psychologist lied about things I said. The district's attorney trashed me personally. The experience has been awful.*

When the school district requested a due process hearing against Lisa, she was not prepared.

You need to prepare for a "worst case scenario." If you work for a company that recently merged with another company, you may prepare for a layoff. If your spouse becomes distant, begins to stay out all night, you may prepare for a separation.

If you live in earthquake country, you will prepare for an earthquake. If you live in hurricane-prone areas, you should prepare for a hurricane. When you prepare for a disaster, you are more likely to survive a disaster.

If you prepare for a due process hearing, you are more likely to prevail if a hearing is necessary. If you prepare for a due process hearing while maintaining good relationships with school personnel, your child is likely to receive good services and you will probably not have to request a due process hearing.

In this chapter, we will describe the six assumptions you must make when you advocate for your child. You will learn about proof and evidence and how to use the school's evidence to prove your case. You will learn why your testimony is not sufficient and how to use letters, documents and independent witnesses to prove your case. You will learn about simple themes and the dangers of presenting a laundry list of complaints against the school.

The Rules of Adverse Assumptions

The Rules of Adverse Assumptions are the keys to your success or failure. If you have a dispute with the school, you must make several negative assumptions.

- Assume that a due process hearing will be held to resolve your dispute.
- Assume you will request the hearing.
- Assume the school personnel on whom you relied for help will testify against you.
- Assume the school personnel that violated your child's rights will not tell the truth.
- Assume the Hearing Officer or Administrative Law Judge is biased against parents of children with disabilities.
- Assume that you cannot testify.

"What?" you ask. "I don't understand."

A due process hearing will be held. All school employees will testify against you. The Judge is biased against you. You cannot testify.

A wave of dizziness hits. Your chest feels tight. Good! Fear is a great motivator. Fear will force you to prepare.

"Wait a minute," you say. "No one would go through a due process hearing if the cards were stacked against them!"

Let's examine these assumptions, one by one.

Assumption 1: There will be a due process hearing.

You must assume that a hearing will be necessary to resolve your dispute. Why? Assume the school draws a line in the sand and refuses to provide your child with the help he or she needs. What will you do? You resolve special education disputes by due process hearings.

Never assume that a hearing will not happen. If you assume that a hearing will not happen, you are assuming that you will back down, or the school district will back down. Never assume that the other side will back down.

If you assume the school district will back down, you will not see the train coming until it is too late. You will get complacent. You will not prepare. In the end, you will lose. This is what happened to Lisa.

In the Wrightslaw model of special education advocacy, you prepare for a "worst case scenario." You assume you will have a disagreement and that a hearing will be necessary to resolve your dispute. After you take this mental step, you will focus on the steps you must take to enhance your chance of a good outcome. When you change your thinking, you will begin to prepare.

Assumption 2: You will initiate the due process hearing.

"You're crazy," you say. "Why would I request a hearing?"

I ask, "What position do you prefer? Do you want to take the offense and define the issues of the case, or do you want to be on the defense like Lisa?"

From a psychological and a legal perspective, it is better to take the offense. When you take the offense, you gain control of the process.

When you initiate the hearing, you define the theme of the case, the issues to be resolved, when the hearing will be held, and the relief you seek. You set the stage, arrange the props, audition the cast, hold rehearsals, practice, and schedule the play.

Assumption 3: All school personnel will testify against you.

School personnel may empathize with you, or agree with your concerns and complaints. Perhaps they want you to feel better. Perhaps they agree with you. Does this mean that school staff will be your allies in a legal dispute against their employer?

Do you think the teacher who said, "This program is damaging your child" will testify to this? Is it fair to call this teacher as your witness? Think about it.

The teacher will feel that you betrayed her and are now trying to use her. What happens when people feel betrayed? Betrayed people want revenge!

If the teacher feels you betrayed her, will she be a good witness for you? A witness who feels betrayed and wants revenge will damage your case more than all the other witnesses combined.

Assumption 4: The school personnel you thought could be forced to make damaging admissions will not do so.

By the time your due process hearing rolls around, the school personnel will have reviewed the facts of your case many times. As they review your case, they will become even more convinced that their position and actions were correct. This is how you should expect them to testify:

The regular education teacher will testify:

I did not follow the IEP to the letter because Mom told me she wanted other areas to be given more emphasis. That's what I did.

The special education teacher will testify:

We were just following the parents' wishes when we made changes to the child's program. We've worked so hard to help this child. We certainly didn't think the parents would sue us!

The special education director will testify:

Apparently, Mom and Dad thought they heard me say "resource program." What I said was "remediation program." I was trying to say that a resource program would not be appropriate, but I lost my composure. Please bear with me. Let me explain.

I've worked in this field for more than twenty years and I don't think I've ever been in a more difficult meeting . . . Dad was standing up. You can see that he is a big man. He raised his voice at me . . . well, to be completely honest, he yelled at me. I know they were upset and they want what they think is best for their child.

I was flustered. I may have used the word "resource" by mistake. I cannot remember. I should have written a follow up letter to clarify my statement. But I never dreamed that they would take this statement literally. I am so sorry. This is my fault. I should have known they did not understand what I was saying.

Assumption 5: Your Hearing Officer or Administrative Law Judge is biased against parents of children with disabilities.

Assume that your Hearing Officer views his or her role as the gatekeeper and protector of taxpayer dollars. Assume that your Hearing Officer's spouse works for a neighboring school district.

If the hearing officer is biased against you, how will you present your case? You must prepare your case for the skeptic. Educate the skeptic. Develop a visual picture of the decision-maker in your mind's eye. Persuade the skeptical decision-maker to rule in your favor.

Assumption 6: You cannot testify at your due process hearing.

"What? I can't testify? Why not?"

"Because you are emotional, biased, and want what's best for your child," I reply.

Your testimony will have less weight than the testimony of other witnesses. As a parent, you are biased in favor of your child. You have less credibility than public school employees and private sector professionals. Yes, you can testify at your child's hearing. But when you prepare your case, you must assume that you cannot testify.

"If I can't testify, how can I prevail? How can I prevail if the Hearing Officer is biased and all the school witnesses will testify against me," you ask.

To Avoid Conflict, Prepare for Conflict

Change the facts. Assume you were a passenger in a cab. The cab driver ran into a light pole. You were injured. Over the next several months, you had operations and physical therapy. You are partially disabled and cannot return to your job.

The cab driver's insurance company refuses to pay your medical bills. The insurance company claims that you distracted the driver so the accident was not the driver's fault. The insurance company claims you are not disabled and can return to work. What will you do?

You will consult with an attorney who specializes in personal injury cases. The attorney will get your records, including your medical and employee records. The attorney will arrange for you to be evaluated by medical specialists. When you go to court, these specialists will testify about the extent and impact of your injuries and will offer opinions about the scope of your disability.

The insurance company will hire medical specialists who will testify about your injuries and offer their opinions that you can return to work immediately.

You would not go to court without witnesses. You would not assume that your testimony alone would be sufficient to prove your case.

You know that a judge or jury would not rule in your favor based solely on your testimony about the accident, the extent of your injuries, degree of disability, lost income, and long-term prospects. This is normal in civil litigation.

A due process hearing is civil litigation. To prevail in a due process hearing or a personal injury case, you need proof and evidence.

Proof and Evidence

When you prepare for a due process hearing, you must have independent evidence to prove you case. Can you testify at your due process hearing? Of course, you can. Your testimony will not be powerful because you are biased in favor of your child. Your testimony will not be powerful because the hearing officer or judge knows you are biased in favor of your child.

Your Evidence

How will you prove that your child needs a specific service or support? How will you prove that your child needs a different educational program or placement? You cannot testify. The school staff is adverse. Where is the evidence that proves your case?

Your evidence includes the letters you wrote after meetings, notes from meetings, test scores and errors in test scores. Your evidence includes your journal and your contact log of telephone calls. Your evidence includes notes and transcripts of meetings you attended.

Your evidence includes reports, evaluations, IEPs, and observations of your child. Your evidence may include research reports, newspaper articles, school guidelines, handbooks, publications, and audits of your school system.

Your evidence includes new evaluations of your child by independent experts from the private sector–evaluations that you arranged when you realized that your dispute may not be resolved.

Their Evidence

Because you cannot testify, your evidence will come from external sources. Begin with the school district's documents. The best evidence often comes from two surprising sources: the child's school file and reports of conversations and meetings held during the crisis.

Are you still worried that you will not be able to tell your side of the story? If you write polite letters to the school that document your concerns and your efforts to resolve problems, your letters will tell your side of the story.

Your Witnesses

Who will testify for you? You must have independent experts who will testify on your behalf. Your experts will base their testimony on the facts of the case, school evaluations, and their observations and evaluations.

Simple Themes Win Cases

You will make your case to a hearing officer or Administrative Law Judge. The decision-maker will be a stranger who does not know you or your child.

Do not expect the decision-maker to keep an open mind until after all the facts are in. Decision-makers are influenced by first impressions and gather data to support their first impressions. If you make a good impression on the decision-maker, you will make it easier for the decision-maker to rule in your favor.

If you are like most parents, you have a long list of complaints. Do not present a laundry list of complaints and violations. If you present a long list of complaints, you will not elicit sympathy and compassion for your child or a desire to help. The decision-maker is more likely to view you as a whiny, demanding, unrealistic parent. The decision-maker will have difficulty believing that the school committed so many terrible violations, so will minimize all of your complaints.

Simple themes win cases. Reduce your case to one or two issues. Use a simple, emotionally compelling theme to bind your issues into a neat package. You want to make it easy for the decision-maker to rule in your favor.

In Summation

In this chapter, you learned about the Rules of Adverse Assumptions. You learned that special education disputes are like other types of civil litigation and that you must have external evidence to prove your case. You learned that documentation and paper trails are good sources of external evidence. We will move on to Chapter 22 where you will learn about documentation and paper trails.

Your Notes Here

22 Creating Paper Trails

"If it was not written down, it was not said. If it was not written down, it did not happen."

—Pete Wright

In the last chapter, you learned that if you have a dispute with the school, you must have independent evidence that supports your position. In this chapter, you will learn how to use logs, calendars, and journals to create your paper trail. When you write things down when they happen, you are taking steps to protect your child's interests. In this chapter, we show you how to document problems and handle telephone calls.

Why Document?

Good records are essential to effective advocacy. When you deal with a bureaucracy like the Internal Revenue Service or your state tax office, you understand that you need to keep detailed records. Many parents do not realize that their school districts are bureaucracies.

Keep a log of your contacts with the school. In addition to meetings, your log should include telephone calls and messages, conversations, and correspondence between you and the school. (You will learn how to write effective letters in Chapter 23).

☑ **Keep copies of all letters, reports, and consent forms.**

Train yourself to write things down! If you have a dispute with the school, your contact log is independent evidence that supports your memory.

Documentation that supports your position is a key to resolving disputes. Your tools are simple:

- Logs
- Calendars
- Journals

Documents Support Testimony

If you have a dispute with the school, assume that you will testify about your recollections. Memories are unreliable and influenced by emotions. If your problem boils down to your word against the word of a school employee, you are not likely to prevail without proper documentation.

However, if your recollections are supported by a journal, contact log, or calendar that describes the problem or event, you will be in a stronger position. To be admissible as evidence, your journal or log must be contemporaneous (i.e., written when the events or incidents occurred). If you can also produce a letter that describes what the school agreed to do or refused to do, your position will be stronger.

☑ **If the school asks you to sign a consent or permission form, get a copy for your records. Your copy establishes what you agreed to.**

Documents Answer Questions

Documents provide answers to "Who, What, Why, When, Where, How and Explain" questions.

- What services or supports did the school agree to provide?
- What services or supports did the school refuse to provide?
- What reasons did the school give for their refusal?
- Who attended the meeting when these decisions were made?
- Why was the parent not advised about this meeting?
- When was this meeting held?
- When did the parent receive the IEP in the mail?
- When did the school inform the parent about this change in program and placement?
- Explain how the new IEP was implemented.

Logs, Journals and Calendars

Your Contact Log

Use a log to document all contacts between you and the school. Your log should include telephone calls, messages, meetings, letters, and notes between you and the school staff. (For sample contact log entries, see Table 22-1, Table 22-2, Table 22-3, and Table 22-4.)

You can use a bound notebook as your log. If you use an electronic log, be sure to back up your files on more than one computer. Print the log often.

Table 22-1	Contact Log: Telephone Contact Information
Who	Person's name, title, phone number
When	Date, time, place of contact
What you wanted	A few words about the purpose of the call
What you were told	A short description of what you were told
Notes	Other information that is important or useful

Table 22-2	Contact Log Entry: Telephone call from parent to school
Who	Emily Jones, Guidance counselor. 555-1212
When	11/30/05 at 9:15 am
What you wanted	Information about accommodations Mark will receive when he takes the state achievement test next week.
What you were told	Mrs. Jones will put this information in an envelope. I will pick it up at the school after 4 pm tomorrow.
Notes	

Table 22-3	Contact Log Entry: Telephone call from school to parent
Who	Dr. Matthews, assistant principal. 444-0101
When	11/15/05, 10:15 am.
What person wanted	Left message on my office voicemail to advise that he suspended Chris from school again.
What you were told	Did not speak to him. I called him at school 3 times today (see other entries) but he did not return my calls.
Notes	This is 3rd suspension in 2 weeks

Table 22-4	Contact Log Entry: Meeting with child's teacher
Who	Meeting with Mrs. Smith, social studies teacher, about Joey's grades and need for accommodations.
When	4/12/06, 3:30 pm.
What I wanted	Want teacher to provide the accommodations in Joey's IEP.
What you were told	She is stressed out because has 15 special ed kids and no help. She doesn't believe in accommodations, says they are unfair to other kids. (See my journal for more info)
Notes	Joey failed social studies in last grading period.

Your log is a memory aid and will help you remember what happened and why. Your log is a record of:

- Whom you met or talked with
- When the contact occurred
- What you wanted
- What you were told

Your Journal

Your journal may be important evidence in your child's case. Your journal is like a diary and should be clear and legible.

If you request a due process hearing, your writings, journals, logs, calendars, letters and other items may be subpoenaed by the school district. You must assume that school personnel and the school attorney will read your papers. Do not use the journal to report your feelings and frustrations.

When you write in your journal, write to the Stranger who has the power to fix problems. When the Stranger reads your journal, the Stranger will understand your perspective and want to fix your problems. In the next two chapters, you will learn how to write good evidence letters and powerful, persuasive "Letters to the Stranger."

Your Calendar

Many parents like to record their appointments in a monthly calendar. Calendars can provide good evidence about meeting dates and times. If you document meeting dates and times in a calendar, write a description of what happened at the meeting in your journal or log.

Do not throw your calendar away at the end of the year!

How to Use a Problem Report

If you have chronic problems with the school (i.e., your child is bullied, suspended or expelled), you should document these problems. You can use this Problem Report (Table 22-5) to document most school problems (i.e., frequent suspensions; child is bullied, homework problems).

Table 22-5	*Problem Report*

Date: _____/_____/_____
      Month   Date   Year

Problem: _____

_____

People involved: _____

_____

Facts (5 Ws + H + E)

What happened? _____

When did it happen? _____

Who was involved? _____

Where did it happen? _____

Why did it happen? _____

Who witnessed? _____

What action did school take? _____

What action did you take? _____

Other facts: _____

_____

Handling Telephone Calls

Prepare before you make a telephone call. Why are you calling? What do you want? Write your questions down before you place your call. When you call, be sure you have paper and pencil handy so you can make notes about the call and the answers you receive.

If the person cannot answer your question, ask who can help. Log this information into your contact log. Playing phone tag is frustrating. If you leave a message, include the reason for your call, you phone numbers, your email address, and when you will be available

If you are polite and treat the person with whom you speak respect and kindness, you are more likely to receive the information you want.

☑ **You have a right to a copy of your child's evaluations and IEPs.**

In Summation

In this chapter, you learned why you should document events. We described how to use low-tech tools including logs, journals, and calendars. You learned to think about the powerful decision-making Stranger when you write descriptions of events, concerns and problems. You learned how to use a problem report to document negative events and how to prepare for telephone calls.

In the next chapter, you will learn how to write effective letters to the school.

23 | How to Write Good Evidence Letters

"There are no secrets to success. It is the result of preparation, hard work, and learning from failure."
— Colin Powell, soldier and statesman

In the next two chapters, you will learn how to write effective letters to the school. In this chapter, you will learn about the five purposes of letters and how to use the letter's purpose to guide you. You will learn strategies to ensure that your letters accomplish their purpose. We provide advice about how to write business letters and letter-writing tips. At the end of these chapters, you will find several sample letters that you can adapt to your own circumstances.

Why You Write Letters

You write letters to:

- Request information
- Request action
- Provide information or describe an event
- Decline a request
- Express appreciation

You also use letters to build relationships, identify and solve problems, clarify decisions that are made or not made, and motivate people to take action.

When you write a letter, be guided by your purpose. What is your purpose? What do you want your letter to accomplish?

Focus on one issue or two issues at most. Do not use one letter to accomplish several purposes. Long letters about several issues are confusing. If the reader is confused, your letter will not accomplish its purpose. Let's look at the five purposes for writing letters.

To Request Information

You write letters to request information. Most requests for information are straightforward. Read the sample letter to request information (letter #1) at the end of this chapter. You may:

- Request a copy of your child's confidential and cumulative files
- Request evaluation results before an IEP meeting
- Request test scores as standard scores and percentile ranks

To Request Action

You are likely to write letters to request action. For example, you may write to:

- Request that your child be evaluated for special education
- Request an IEP meeting because you have concerns about your child's educational program or placement
- Request a meeting with a teacher to discuss your child's progress
- Request a re-evaluation of your child's progress

When you write a letter to request action, you may anticipate that your reader will be resistant. If you expect resistance, provide information that supports your request.

To learn how to request action and provide information that supports your request, read the sample letter to request a meeting at the end of this chapter (letter #2)

To Provide Information or Document a Problem

If you have concerns about your child's progress or special education program, you must express these concerns in writing. If you do not express your concerns in writing, then for practical and legal purposes you have never expressed any concerns.

You should also provide the school with important information about your child. For example, you should advise the school about new evaluations of your child, new medical conditions, and changes in medication.

Get into the habit of writing letters after meetings, conversations and events. After meetings, write follow-up letters to document what you requested, the school's response (what the school agreed to provide or refused to provide), and what you were told about these decisions.

You should write letters to document negative incidents and events. For example, if your child is suspended or inappropriately disciplined, you should write a letter to document this event.

To learn how to document a problem, read the sample letter from the parent who asks the school administrator to reconsider his decision to suspend her child (letter #3). In this letter, the parent describes the child's educational history and requests a face-to-face meeting with the administrator. Despite her belief that the punishment is inappropriate, she does not discuss feelings in the letter. This letter will elicit sympathy from the Stranger. If the school continues to discipline her child for minor infractions, she can use this letter as evidence.

Problem letters are difficult to write. Your emotions may interfere with your ability to present information logically. For help writing problem letters, read the sample problem letters at the end of this chapter (letters #3 and 5) and the letters at the end of Chapter 24. You can adapt these letters to your situation.

To Decline a Request

On occasion, you may have to write a letter to decline a request or convey bad news. When you must decline a request or convey bad news, you should make an effort to maintain a good relationship with the reader. The tone of your letter should be polite not defensive.

To learn how to decline a request, read the sample letter from the parent who is writing to reschedule an IEP meeting (letter #6) at the end of this chapter.

To Express Appreciation

Everyone has an invisible sign hanging from his or her neck saying, "Make me feel important." Never forget this when you deal with people.
—Mary Kay, business owner

After meetings, you should write thank-you letters that also document what you were told. Read the sample letter to express appreciation at the end of this chapter to see how the parent graciously thanks the teachers for meeting with her, while also weaving important information into the letter (letter #5)

If a teacher or staff members is especially helpful, write a short note to express your appreciation. When you write thank you letters and offer positive feedback, you are more likely to get help when you ask for it. If you complain and demand, do not be surprised when you run into resistance. (See letter #6 at the end of Chapter 24)

Strategies: Writing Good Letters

When you write a letter, you want someone to read it. If you follow these steps, you increase the odds that someone will read and respond to your letter. Your letter will accomplish your purpose.

Easy Reading

You write letters to communicate. Use clear, everyday language. Avoid vague words, educational jargon, and rambling sentences. Use short sentences (10 to 20 words) and short paragraphs (generally no more than six to eight lines). Short paragraphs are easier to read.

When you use short sentences, short paragraphs, and simple language, your message is easier to understand. You create a favorable first impression.

Get to the Point

If you are writing to request that your reader take action, get to the point. Tell the reader what you want in the first paragraph. Your readers are busy people. They are unlikely to finish your letter if you do not get to the point and tell them what you want them to do.

Think about your reaction to letters. If you begin to read a letter and do not know what the letter wants you to do within the first few sentences, you are likely to put the letter down.

Should you always get to the point immediately?

There are two exceptions to this rule: when you are writing to convey bad news or to persuade the reader to take action that he or she may not want to take. If you anticipate that getting to the point immediately may upset, anger, or alienate your reader, follow the advice in "To Decline a Request (above). You will learn how to write persuasive letters in the next chapter.

Speak to the Recipient

You write letters to communicate. What do you want your reader to get from this letter? Consider your reader's perspective. You can add empathy to your letters by using the words "you," "we," and "our."

Be Courteous

When you write a letter to request information, request action, or provide information, treat your reader with courtesy and kindness.

Do not demand that the reader take action. If you make demands, you ensure that your reader will try not to comply with your request. (You will learn about demanding letters in Chapter 24.). If you need to provide the reader with suggestions or guidance, direct the reader with courtesy. Be sure to say "please" and "thank you."

Make It Easy to Follow

Each paragraph of a letter should convey one idea that is expressed within the first sentence or two. Supporting information should follow the main idea. Do not make your reader slog through the paragraph to discover the main idea.

Prompt the Reader to Act

At the beginning of a letter, explain why you are writing and what you want the reader to do. Your reader is more likely to remember the first and last thing he or she reads. In the last line of your letter, restate the action you want the reader to take.

End with Courtesy

Your reader will remember the final impression of your letter. Make sure you end your letter with courtesy. The decision to help is in the reader's hands. Convey your request as a request, not as a demand.

For example, you should write: " I would appreciate a prompt response" not "I demand a response within ten days."

You should write: "Please let me know when I can pick up this information" not "I expect you to comply with my request immediately."

Give Contact Information

Make it easy for the reader to respond to your letter. Include a telephone number, fax number, or email address at the end of your letters. If the reader has questions, you make it easy to contact you immediately for answers.

You may write, "If you have questions about my request for a meeting, please call me at work (877-555-1212) or at home (877-555-1313) weekdays after 6 p.m."

☑ **Try to end the letter with a benefit for the reader. For example:**

To save us both time during this hectic season, please send the evaluation results to me at least five days before the IEP meeting scheduled for May 25. Please advise by phone if you would prefer that I come by the school on May 18 to pick up this information.

Letter Writing Pitfalls

If you are like most parents, you are more likely to write a letter if you have a problem or complaint. Perhaps you want to protect your child or right a wrong. Perhaps you experienced a series of negative incidents with the school. Do not send that angry letter! Before you send an angry letter, think about these statements.

- **After you send a letter, you cannot change it.** Your letter will live on, forever.
- **Strangers will read your letter.** School administrators are Strangers who have power and will not feel intimidated by you. Strangers who do not know you, your child, or the history behind your letter may have the power to resolve your problem.
- **People do not read long letters.** You must capture the reader's interest and attention within the first few sentences. If you do not get the reader's interest quickly, the reader will skim the first paragraph or two and then put your letter aside.
- **People do not like angry letter-writers.** Your letter is a personal statement about you and your situation. If you write an angry, threatening, or

demanding letter, what are impression will you make? What are you saying about yourself? Decision-making Strangers do not know or care about your pain, suffering, or frustration.

Think about the impression you want to make. Your letters are opportunities to make a good impression and tell your side of the story.

Think about the Stranger who has the power to fix the problem. Do you want the Stranger to view you as an angry hothead? Do you want the Stranger to conclude that you are a complainer? Do you want the Stranger to understand that you are a thoughtful person who expresses concerns calmly and rationally?

Read *Letter Writing Tips* (Table 23-1).

Before you write a letter, think about your purpose. Jot down your thoughts. Do not worry about sentence structure or prioritizing. Get your thoughts on paper. In a few minutes, you will have the important issues written down. You should be able to answer these questions:

- Why are you writing this letter?
- What is your purpose?
- What are you trying to accomplish?
- What do you want?

Using Strategies in Letters

If you are writing a letter to describe a problem or negative event, you need to use tactics and strategies.

Remember the Rules of Adverse Assumptions

Assume your problem will not be resolved. Your problem will escalate into a serious dispute. Do you remember the Rules of Adverse Assumptions? You must assume that a due process hearing will be held and that you will not be able to testify.

These assumptions are the keys to successful letter writing. Assume that the problem will get worse. Assume that a successful outcome depends on how well you describe the events that caused you to write this letter.

The letter you write today will be placed in your child's file. If you have a dispute later, your well-written letters are powerful evidence in your favor. Similarly, angry, irrational letters will work against you. If you are still tempted to write an angry letter, read about the "Sympathy Factor" in the next chapter.

| Table 23-1 | *Letter Writing Tips* |

Image & Presentation
- First impressions are lasting impressions
- Use businesslike letters to create a good impression.
- Type letters or print from your computer.
- Use quality paper. Do not use cute stationery with flowers or little animals.
- Include contact information – phone number, fax number, and/or email.

Set the Right Tone
- Do not demand. Do not apologize. Do not threaten to sue.
- End your letter with courtesy.

Write to the Right Person
- Who can resolve your problem? Write your letter to this person.
- Address your letter to a real person. Use the person's name and job title. No one likes to receive letters addressed "To Whom It May Concern."

Delivery Options
- Deliver important letters by hand. Log in the time and date, identity of the person who received the letter, what the person told you, what they were wearing, what was happening at the time.
- Do not send certified or registered letters to the school.
- Do not mark letters "personal" or "confidential."

How Long?
- In general, keep your letters short, no more than one page.
- Get to the point in the first paragraph.

What To Include
- Tell the reader why you are writing the letter and what you want the reader to do.
- Cite facts that support your position or request. Be sure your facts are correct.

Deadlines
- Set a time limit for a reply. Two weeks is fair. (Do not make demands!)
- Write, call, write. Write a letter. Wait ten days, then call.

What to Do If They Do Not Respond
- If you do not receive a response, write a second letter, and include a copy of your first letter.
- If you get no response, set a short deadline before going higher. Ten days is reasonable.
- If you receive no response to the second letter, go higher in the chain of command.

Visualize the Stranger

When you write a letter about problems or concerns, you are writing a "Letter to the Stranger." Assume that someone outside of the school or school district will decide the issue. This decision-making Stranger has no personal interest in you or your child. The Stranger does not care that your child is enrolled in a One-Size-Fits-All (OSFA) program. If you go to court, the Stranger who controls outcome may be the Judge's young law clerk.

Assume that before you mail your letter, your letter slips out of your notebook and falls into the street. Later, a Stranger sees your letter and picks it up. The Stranger puts the letter in his pocket and takes it home to read. What impression will your letter make on this Stranger?

Who is the Stranger? How does he think? Visualize the Stranger in your mind's eye. The Stranger is an older person who is conservative, fair, and open-minded. He dresses casually. When he sits down to read your letter, he sips a cup of tea and lights a pipe.

☞ **Read the original "Letter to the Stranger" at the Wrightslaw site: www.wrightslaw.com**

The Stranger does not know you, your child, or your situation. Your letter is your opportunity to sell the Stranger on the justice of your cause. Describe your problem. Tell the Stranger what should be done to make things right. Hearing Officers and Judges are Strangers. Most judges do not know about children with disabilities or special education. When you write letters, you want to educate and inform the Stranger.

☑ **When you write letters, do not use acronyms. Do not expect a Stranger to understand the alphabet soup of special education acronyms. Write out the full names of programs and teams.**

Make Your Problem Unique

Once dispelled, ignorance is difficult to re-establish. —Laurence J. Peter

Assume you are writing about a problem. Try to make your problem unique. You want the reader to believe your problem is different and think, "We've never had this problem before!"

You want to avoid these responses:

- We always handle this situation this way
- We have always handled this situation this way
- We will always handle this situation this way
- We never make exceptions
- We cannot make an exception for you

Schools are bureaucracies. Bureaucracies run by rules. If you can make your problem unique, your problem is less likely to be listed in the *Bureaucrat's Big Book of Rules and Procedures.* If your situation is unique, people who work in the system may view your situation differently. If they see things differently, they may handle your situation differently.

Edit and Revise

The first letter you write is always a draft. After you write the first draft, put your letter away. Allow yourself a cooling-off period of at least 24 to 48 hours before you edit the letter.

After the cooling-off period, you will be able to view your letter more objectively. When you edit a letter, you want to clarify, condense and strengthen your message.

Ask at least one cool-headed person to edit your letter. Choose a person who will tell you the truth and respect your confidentiality. Ask your editor to answer these questions:

- What is the purpose of my letter?
- What is my point?
- What do I want?
- Should I shorten the letter?
- Should I tone the letter down?

If your editor cannot answer the first three questions easily and quickly without more explanations or prompting from you, your letter is not clear. You need to do more editing.

☑ **When you edit, read your letter aloud. When you proofread and edit, read your letter backwards. These strategies will help you spot spelling and grammar errors.**

Make a Good First Impression

Write your letter on a computer. After your write the first draft, double-space the letter and change your font to Courier 14 points. When you print your letter, typographical errors, poor sentence structure, and rambling sentences will be easier to spot. Edit the letter again. **Remove every unnecessary word.** To find spelling errors, read the letter aloud.

If you have access to a computer, you can use the spell check and grammar check programs to flag some spelling errors. You cannot rely on spell check programs to catch all spelling errors (for example, if you write "it" instead of "if).

For more advice about letters, read *Nuts and Bolts of Letter Writing* (Table 23-2) and *Frequently Asked Questions about Letters* (Table 23-3) at the end of this chapter.

Table 23-2	*Nuts and Bolts of Letter Writing*

Your letters to the school are business letters. The parts of business letters are standard.

Parts of a Letter

Heading or Letterhead. Your heading or letterhead will include your name, address, and telephone number.

Date. The month, day and year you write the letter.

Inside address. The recipient's full name, title, school, and address.

Reference line. Your child's full name, grade and school.

Salutation. Greeting that begins with the word "Dear." Examples: Dear Mr. Clark, Dear Dr. Jones.

Body of the Letter. The body of your letter should be single-spaced with two spaces between paragraphs. The first line of each paragraph may or may not be indented. Be consistent.

Closing. Appropriate closings include:

- Sincerely
- Sincerely Yours
- Respectfully
- Regards

Signature. You should sign all letters. Type your full name beneath your signature.

Additional Notations. Use notations at the end of your letter to indicate that:

- something is enclosed with the letter
- something is attached to the letter
- something else has been sent
- other individuals will receive copies of the letter

Table 23-3	*Frequently Asked Questions About Business Letters*

Question: Should I type letters?

Answer: Letters carry more weight if they are typed, especially if the topic is serious. If you are writing a note to your child's teacher about a routine matter, you may write your letter by hand. If the topic of your letter is important, you should type the letter, sign it, and keep a signed copy for your records. Use Times New Roman font. Never use a script or cursive type font.

Question: What kind of paper should I use?

Answer: Your letters to the school are business letters and should be written on 8½ x 11-inch paper. Paper can be white, off-white, ivory, or pale gray.

Question: How should I format the second page of a letter?

Answer: If your letter goes to a second page, try to condense it into one page. Many people will set two-page letters aside, believing they will get to them later.

If you cannot avoid a second page, follow these guidelines:

- Keep your page margins the same as page one
- Do not write "Continued," or "over" on page one
- Write the recipient's name as it appeared on the inside address, the date, and page number on the top of page two.

The left margin of your second page should look like this.

Louise Jones
January 21, 2006
Page 2

Question: How wide should my margins be?

Answer: Consistent symmetrical margins will make your letter easy to read. In a short letter, use wider margins. In a long letter, use narrower margins (but no less than one inch). The text should appear centered or slightly higher on the page.

Question: How should I address the envelope?

Answer: Send letters in # 10 envelopes (4 ½ x 9 ½ inches). Type the address with no punctuation. Use two letter state abbreviations and zip codes. Include the additional four digits if you can.

Speak to the Reader

You are writing to a person who has the power to resolve the problem. You are not writing to the person at a meeting who blamed you for your child's problems. Imagine you are talking to the Stranger about your problem. Use words like "you," "we," and "our" to make your letter more personal. When people read your letter, they will feel that your message is directed at them.

In Summation

In this chapter, you learned that you write letters to request information, request action, provide information, describe a problem or event, decline a request, and express appreciation. You learned about the qualities of good letters that will accomplish their purpose.

You learned strategies that will help you make a good impression. In the next chapter, you will learn about persuasive letters and how to write a "Letter to the Stranger."

#1. Sample Letter to Request Information

Mary Parent
500 Oak Street
Centerville, IN 60010
(899) 555-1234

September 22, 2005

Dr. Ruth Boss, Superintendent
Independent School District #1
1000 Central Avenue
Centerville, IN 60010

Reference: Jennifer Parent
               DOB: 01/01/94
               School: Stonewall Middle School

Dear Dr. Boss:

Please send me a complete copy of my child's cumulative and confidential educational records, including medical records, special education records, formal and informal correspondence, discipline records, tests, evaluations, and teacher-to teacher notes. If there is a cost and policy about photocopies, please let me know immediately.

If you have questions about my request, please call me at work (555-9876) or at home (555-1234) after 6 p.m. I appreciate your help and quick response.

Sincerely,

Mary Parent

#2. Sample Letter to Request a Meeting

Mary Parent
500 Oak Street
Centerville, IN 60010
(899) 555-1234

November 8, 2005

Eleanor Randolph
Stonewall Middle School
1000 Central Avenue
Centerville, IN 60010

Reference: Jennifer Parent
               DOB: 01/03/94
               School: Stonewall Middle School

Dear Mrs. Randolph:

I am writing to request an appointment with you on November 15 at 3:30 p.m. I would like to talk with you about Jennifer's behavior problems. As you know, Jennifer is having difficulty with the transition from elementary school to middle school. Two weeks ago, she was suspended again for "inappropriate behavior."

Please call me at work (555-9876) or home (555-1234) after 6:00 p.m. to confirm this date and time or to suggest an alternative date and time. If I am not available, please leave a message on my answering machine.

I appreciate your taking the time to meet with me.

Sincerely,

Mary Parent

#3. Sample Letter to Document a Problem

Mary Parent
500 Oak Street
Centerville, IN 60010
(899) 555-1234

November 15, 2005

John Belcher
Stonewall Middle School
1000 Central Avenue
Centerville, IN 60010

Reference: Jennifer Parent
DOB: 01/01/94
School: Stonewall Middle School

Dear Mr. Belcher:

I am writing to ask you to reconsider your decision to suspend Jennifer from school for three days. I do not believe that talking to a classmate during a quiz is an offense that warrants such serious disciplinary action.

As you know, Jennifer has autism. Four years ago, she was unable to communicate with other children. Her social skills deficits were severe. Jennifer has made remarkable progress in these areas. Despite this, her behavior is not always appropriate. The transition from elementary school to middle school has been difficult for her. Suspending Jennifer from school does not teach her how to behave more appropriately.

I am also concerned that this is the third time Jennifer has been suspended for behavior problems this year.

I am requesting a meeting with you to discuss your decision to suspend Jennifer and her needs as a child with autism. Please call me at work (555-9876) or at home (555-1234) after 6:00 p.m. to schedule a meeting. I look forward to your call.

Sincerely,

Mary Parent

#4. Sample Letter to Express Appreciation and Document Problems

Mary Parent
500 Oak Street
Centerville, IN 60010
(899) 555-1234

November 27, 2005

Lee Green Special Education Teacher
Eleanor Randolph, Math Teacher
Stonewall Middle School
1000 Central Avenue
Centerville, IN 60010

Reference: Jennifer Parent
               DOB: 01/01/94
               School: Stonewall Middle School

Dear Ms. Randolph and Ms. Smart:

I am writing to thank you for meeting with me on November 25 to discuss Jennifer's progress and grades. As a parent, I sometimes find report cards confusing.

Ms. Randolph, I appreciate your explanation of Jennifer's progress. For example, you explained that her grade of A in math was based on the second grade math book that she has used for two years. I was not aware that her grades were raised because of good attendance.

Ms. Green advised me that Jennifer continues to need an aide 100% of the time. I appreciate the school's attempts to help Jennifer by providing an aide. However, I have serious concerns about this aide. She has received no training about autism and is not being supervised. Instead, of teaching Jennifer to communicate, Ms. Jones speaks for Jennifer. Recently, I learned that Ms. Jones has been doing Jennifer's homework.

If you are interested in learning about Jennifer's type of autism, I have lots of information and will be happy to share this information with you. Thank you again for the meeting and your time. I am glad you enjoyed the cake I brought.

Sincerely,

Mary Parent

#5. Sample Letter to Document an IEP Problem

Mary Parent
500 Oak Street
Centerville, IN 60010
(899) 555-1234
January 2, 2006

Lee Green, Special Education Teacher
Stonewall Middle School
1000 Central Avenue
Centerville, IN 60010

Reference: Jennifer Parent
               Sixth Grade
               School: Stonewall Middle School

Dear Ms. Green:

I am writing to thank you for your telephone call about Jennifer's problems in Mr. Small's class. I appreciate your offer to intervene with Mr. Small on Jennifer's behalf.

I am concerned that Mr. Small is not implementing Jennifer's IEP. As you know, the IEP provides for Jennifer to have a quiet place to go when she is overwhelmed. You assured me that Mr. Small has been advised to follow the IEP. You also advised me that the school would provide a quiet place near Mr. Small's class.

Why does Mr. Small refuse to allow Jennifer to go the quiet place when she is overwhelmed? If she cannot get away when she is overwhelmed, she has behavior problems. She has already been suspended three times this year for behavior problems.

I am confused. The elementary school teachers worked with Jennifer. They taught her communication and social skills. Because of their efforts, she made wonderful progress. We will always feel grateful to these teachers.

The middle school teachers seem to have a "sink or swim" attitude about Jennifer. The IEP team spent hours writing an IEP that would provide Jennifer with an appropriate education. How can a teacher refuse to implement the IEP? Why does Mr. Belcher think he can teach Jennifer to behave appropriately by suspending her?

Please schedule an IEP meeting to address these issues. You can contact me at work (555-9876) or at home (555-1234) after 6:00 p.m. I look forward to meeting with the IEP team.

Sincerely,
Mary Parent

#6. Sample Letter to Decline a Request

Mary Parent
500 Oak Street
Centerville, IN 60010
(899) 555-1234

April 4, 2006

Dr. Alan Brown
Independent School District #1
1000 Central Avenue
Centerville, IN 60010

Reference: Jennifer Parent
                DOB: 01/01/94
                School: Stonewall Middle School

Dear Dr. Brown:

On Thursday evening, April 3, I received a letter from you advising me that an IEP meeting had been scheduled for Monday, April 7, at 2:15 p.m.

I regret that I must ask that this meeting be rescheduled. Unfortunately, I cannot cancel my work obligations on such short notice. I hope this request does not inconvenience the team members. As I advised your secretary, I am available on April 9, 10, and 11.

If you have any questions, please call me at work (555-9876) or at home (555-1234) after 6:00 p.m. I look forward to meeting with the team on one of these dates.

Sincerely,

Mary Parent

24 | Writing the "Letter to the Stranger"

> "If you would persuade, you must appeal to interest rather than intellect."
>
> — Benjamin Franklin, inventor

In this chapter, you will learn about two approaches to letter writing – the Blame Approach and the Story-Telling Approach. You will learn about the Sympathy Factor and why you must not write angry letters to the school. Your goal is to use the Story-Telling Approach to write persuasive letters.

At the end of this chapter, you will read a series of letters that tell the story of a parent's attempts to get services for her child. As events unfold, she becomes increasingly aware that a "Stranger" may have to resolve her dispute with the school.

The Blame Approach

A father wrote this letter after an IEP meeting. This father is a businessman who writes letters in his work. This letter was a trial exhibit and an issue in his child's case. When you read his letter, pay attention to your reactions.

Dear Dr. Smith:

You asked that I advise you about my objections to the IEP that your staff of "professional educators" wrote for my daughter. Despite my own lack of training, I can say that the IEP developed by your staff was preposterous. Let me share a few observations with you.

Your staff FAILED to include anyone on the IEP team who thoroughly understands my daughter's background.

Your staff FAILED to perform an observation on my daughter before they developed the IEP.

Your staff FAILED to include information from the most recent testing by the private evaluator and relied on out-dated testing that is nearly two years old.

Your staff FAILED to target her specific needs and unique abilities.

Your staff FAILED to include any objective criteria to measure her progress or lack of progress.

Your staff FAILED to include any evaluation procedures to measure progress, as related to annual goals and objectives.

(This list continued for two pages . . .)

Given their years of training and experience I would expect your staff to be capable of writing a simple IEP. Although I have no training in IEPs or special education, I can see how inadequate this document is.

I must conclude that your staff is incompetent and inept. This IEP is evidence that your staff is incapable of teaching my daughter, who is smarter than your entire team.

Sincerely,

Bob Bombastic

What is your reaction to this letter? Do you understand why Bob wrote the letter? Do you know what Bob wants from the school? What solution did he suggest? Do you understand his position? Do you agree with him? Alternatively, did you have a different response?

A few weeks before Bob wrote this letter, the special education director accused him of not advising the school about his objections to their IEP. Bob was not going to let this happen again! He included a laundry list of complaints in his letter. Bob believed he had to give detailed notice about his objections to the proposed IEP. He felt angry and defensive.

Impact of Angry Letters

Unfortunately, when the decision-making Stranger read Bob's letter, he did not know the history behind the letter because Bob neglected to include this information. Bob's letter is worded so strongly that it created sympathy for the people who received it.

Have you seen couples arguing or parents disciplining their children in public? What was your reaction?

If you are like most people, you felt uncomfortable. Perhaps you had a stronger emotional reaction. You did not like it! You felt sympathy for the person who was being humiliated. People have the same reaction when they read angry letters.

If you are tempted to write an angry and demanding letter, think about Bob.

The Story-Telling Approach

Let's look at another letter written by a father after an IEP meeting. This father's letter was an exhibit in a case too.

Dear Dr. Smith;

First, let me thank you for allowing me to participate in the development of Carrie's IEP. I appreciate your willingness to meet with me.

As you know, Carrie has received special education services for two years. You may remember that Dr. Smith completed a comprehensive evaluation on her on [date]. I provided you with a copy of this evaluation and expressed concerns that Carrie has made no progress in the two years she has received special education services.

At last week's IEP meeting, your staff kindly answered my questions. I appreciated their kindness since I had not met most of the people at the IEP meeting before. I was sorry that neither of Carrie's teachers could attend the meeting. I understand that her regular education teacher was on a field trip and that her special education teacher had to leave for a doctor's appointment.

Unfortunately, we did not have enough time to develop an IEP for Carrie. Although the team allotted twenty-five minutes for the meeting, the meeting began late. I understand that several IEP meetings ran late that day. I know that things are very rushed at the end of the school year.

The team did not have the new, most recent evaluation of Carrie. The psychologist thought the new evaluation might have been misfiled. Perhaps this is why the team leader gave me an IEP to sign that placed Carrie in the same program. You will recall that I expressed reservations about last year's IEP because it did not include current information from tests in the present levels of academic achievement and functional performance. I also expressed concerns about the vague goals and lack of any objective evaluation procedures.

I am sure you understand why I could not sign the IEP presented to me. Given the confusion and rushed atmosphere, I thought we should schedule another meeting later, when we have enough time to discuss these issues.

I asked the IEP team to review the new evaluation results before we get together to write the IEP. I am including another copy of the new [date] evaluation with this letter.

Please check with your staff and send me times that are convenient for them. I look forward to a productive meeting. If you have any questions, please call me at work (888-555-1212) or at home (888-444-1110). You can also contact me by email at mike@mikemanners.com.

Sincerely,

Mike Manners

What is your reaction to Mike Manners' letter? Do you know why Mike wrote this letter? Do you know what he wants? Do you understand his position? When you read Mike's letter did you realize what he was dealing with the same factual issues as Bob? Read Bob's letter again.

Each letter describes an IEP meeting for a child. Each letter refers to procedural violations by the school in developing the child's IEP. In each case, the parent was presented with an IEP that pre-determined the child's program and placement. Neither parent had any input into the child's IEP. The IEP teams did not include the results of new testing in the children's IEPs. The teachers did not attend the IEP meetings.

Use Persuasive Strategies in Letters

You want to write persuasive "Mike Manners" letters. List your concerns in a pleasant business-like way. How you lay out the facts in a letter is important. Mike lays out his facts without blaming or name-calling. If Mike needs to go to a mediator, hearing officer, or judge, his letters will make a good impression.

When Bob took his case to a decision maker, he was in trouble. Bob's letters included angry blaming statements. He did not include information that would help the Stranger understand the background of his case. The tone of his letters was harsh. His angry letters alienated neutral decision-makers.

Avoid the "Sympathy Factor"

If you write an angry, demanding letter, you are likely to trigger the "Sympathy Factor." This sympathy will not be for you or for your child. When people read angry, demanding letters, they feel sympathy for the person who received the letter. This is what happened in Bob's case.

At some point in our lives, most of us have received angry letters. You may have received angry letters from a jilted lover, jealous ex-spouse, angry relative, or a demanding creditor. When you read an angry letter, you felt threatened, defensive, ashamed, or angry. You filed these reactions in your emotional memory bank.

When you read an angry letter, the letter may evoke sympathy for the recipient. Based on your personal experiences, you may decide that the recipient did not deserve the attack. You may think, "Maybe the person did make a mistake. Everyone makes mistakes. No one is perfect." From the Stranger's perspective, the fact that a person makes a mistake does not give you an excuse to attack.

Make a Good Impression

When you write letters to the school, you must expect that people who do not know you will read your letters. In many cases, teachers, guidance counselors, and assistant principals do not have the authority to make important decisions. If you write a letter to the school, you should assume you are writing to a Stranger who has the power to make decisions.

In your letter, you are introducing yourself to the decision-making Stranger. While reading your letter, the Stranger will form an impression of you. First impressions are powerful. If you make a negative first impression, the Stranger will have difficulty accepting positive information about you. This happened to Bob.

After Bob fired off his letter, the school went into a defensive mode. From their perspective, if they gave Bob anything he wanted, they would admit that he was right and that they FAILED to educate his child. Of course, the school had a different perspective. They disagreed with Bob. They did not believe they failed to provide his daughter with an appropriate education. What happened next?

The school responded to Bob with a non-committal business letter. The tone of their letter was pleasant. They explained that they disagreed with him but were willing to meet with him to resolve their differences. They offered several meeting times. Bob did not respond. He believed he made his point and provided them with the required "Notice." The school filed his letter away. Nothing changed.

A few months later, Bob requested a due process hearing. The school board attorney submitted this letter and other similar letters from him as exhibits in their case.

The school wanted the hearing officer to see Bob from their perspective and conclude that he was a jerk. They wanted the hearing officer to understand that, while Bob was a "difficult parent," they were prepared to meet with him. Although Bob was difficult, the school could provide his unfortunate daughter with an excellent education.

What are the lessons you can learn from this story? If you create a negative first impression, you increase the odds that you will lose the battle and the war. Strangers who read your negative letters will write you off as a loose cannon and may feel sorry for your child.

That poor kid. No wonder he has so many problems. Can you imagine what it must be like to live with such an irrational self-centered parent?

You do not want this reaction!

Writing "Letters to the Stranger"

In the last chapter, you learned that one purpose of letters is to persuade someone to take action. If you want to persuade the school to take an action or provide a service and you expect them to resist, write your letter to the decision-making Stranger.

Hearing Officers and Judges are Strangers. Most judges are not knowledgeable about special education or children with disabilities. When you write your letter, your goals are to educate, inform, and persuade the Stranger.

To Negotiate

As a parent, you negotiate with the school district for special education services. Whether you negotiate with the school about services or you negotiate with a salesman about a new car, the principles are the same.

You do not begin negotiations by telling the other side your bottom line. Many parents assume they must share everything with the school immediately. They hope the school will reward them by providing the help their child needs. In most cases, this does not happen.

You should share the results of an evaluation or other information about your child when you receive it. However, when you negotiate, you do not share your wish list or your bottom line. You will learn more about negotiating in Chapters 25 and 26 about meetings.

To Persuade

When you write a persuasive Letter to the Stranger, you will present your case. The Stranger will not understand the background or history of your problem unless you include this information in your letter. You can provide background naturally and easily by going back to the beginning and telling your story chronologically.

For example: "On September 1, our son entered your special education program because . . ."

You can move the clock back: "We realized that our daughter's problems were serious when she was not talking by her third birthday."

Where should you begin? Begin where you want to begin. In your mind, you know when things began. Continue with your story: "When she entered school . . ."

Use facts to tell your story. Select your facts carefully. Keep your opinions to a minimum. When you tell your story, you want to plant seeds in the mind of the Stranger who will read your letter. Let the Stranger's imagination water the seeds.

Write your letter chronologically. If you jump from one issue to another, the Stranger will get confused, then frustrated. If the Stranger is frustrated, he will quit reading and will blame you for this frustration. You will create a negative first impression. You do not want this to happen!

When you write a persuasive letter, speak directly to the reader. Use the same words and figures of speech you use in normal conversation. Visualize the Stranger. Imagine that you are talking to him about your problems. Re-read the advice about editing in Chapter 23. Revise your letter so it makes a good impression and persuades the Stranger.

Do Not Send Certified Letters

If you are like many parents, you think you should send important letters by certified mail. If you send a letter to the school by certified mail, you put the recipient on notice that you want proof of delivery, probably for legal and evidence purposes. The recipient will feel defensive and mistrustful. If you send a certified letter, this will have a negative impact on your relationship with school personnel.

When you deal with the school, your goal is to secure a good educational program for your child. If you take actions that cause school personnel to feel defensive, you are less likely to accomplish your goal.

How can you establish that the school received your letter? Hand-deliver your letter to the recipient.

Strategies: Hand-Deliver Letters

When you go to the school, take your original letter and one signed copy. When you enter the office, note the time. Observe the office layout. Do you recognize anyone? When you hand your letter to the secretary or office manager, pay attention to the person. Note the person's age, dress, hair color and style, and other distinctive characteristics. Ask the person to give your letter to Dr. Kate Gardner, principal. Do not ask the person to sign a receipt.

If you do not know the person's name, you can get the person's name by introducing yourself, "Hi. I'm Debra Harrison, Gillian Harrison's mom. I have a letter for Dr. Gardner. Would you mind giving it to her? I don't think we've met before. Your name is…"

After you leave, write the date, time, name, and description of the person who received your letter on the back of your copy of the letter. Write what you said and what you were told.

If a week passes and you do not receive a response, write a short follow-up letter. Attach a copy of your original letter to the follow-up letter. (See sample letters at the end of Chapters 23 and 24)

When you go to the office, you may have a chance to refresh the secretary's memory, "Hi, I'm Debra Harrison, Gillian Harrison's mom. We met last week. You are Karen Brannen, Dr. Gardner's assistant. You may remember that I gave you a letter for Dr. Gardner last week. I have not heard from her yet. Do you know if she got the letter? I have another copy of the letter, in case the other one got lost."

The secretary will probably say, "Oh, I remember. Yes, she got it. I gave it to her right away. I don't know what happened. She has been very busy. I'll check on it." Thank the secretary and leave. Because you remembered her name, she will not forget you. She will not deny that you delivered the letters to her. When you leave, write the details of what happened on the back of your follow-up letter.

You have proof of receipt. Your proof includes your testimony and your contemporaneous notes that you wrote when you delivered the letters. You did not create hostility and mistrust. You did not polarize the relationship with the school. You may have made a new friend in Karen.

In Summation

In this chapter, you learned about persuasive letters. You learned about the Blame Approach and the Story-Telling Approach, first impressions, and why you must not write angry letters to the school. You learned strategies that allow you to prove that the school received your letter without polarizing your relationships with school staff.

In the next chapter, you will learn how to prepare for meetings.

You will learn how preparation and presentation can help you control meeting outcomes.

#1. Letter to Principal to Request Child's Records

Jane Smith
500 Oak Lane
Centerville, IL 60010
(899) 555-1234

September 18, 2005

George Williams, Principal
Grove Middle School
1000 Main Street
Middleburg, IL 60010

Reference: Michael K. Smith
               DOB: 01/02/94
               School: Grove Middle School

Dear Mr. Williams:

On September 17, I received a letter advising me that a meeting with Michael's teachers has been scheduled for October 2. At this meeting, we will discuss Michaels' educational problems and how we may help him. So that I may be better prepared for the meeting, please send me a complete copy of my son's entire cumulative and confidential records. Please be sure to include copies of all evaluations and actual test scores. If there is a cost and policy about photocopies, please let me know immediately.

I will need time to review Michael's educational records before this important meeting.

If you have questions about my request, please call me at work (555-9876) or at home (555-1234), after 6:00 pm.

Thank you for your assistance and quick response.

Sincerely,

Jane Smith

☑ If you send one letter to the principal and one letter to the superintendent, it is less likely that one person will assume the other person acted on your request.

☑ Do not send letters by certified mail. Hand-deliver important letters to the principal's office. Provide the guidance counselor with copies of important letters.

#2. Letter to Superintendent to Request Child's Records

Jane Smith
500 Oak Lane
Centerville, IL 60010
(899) 555-1234

September 18, 2005

Ruth Meadows, Superintendent
Independent School District #1
10 Main Street
Middleburg, IL 60010

Reference: Michael K. Smith
DOB: 01/02/94
School: Grove Middle School

Dear Dr. Meadows:

On September 17, I received a letter advising me that a meeting with Michael's teachers has been scheduled for October 2. At this meeting, we will discuss Michaels' educational problems and how we may help him. So that I may be better prepared for the meeting, please send me a complete copy of my son's entire cumulative and confidential records. Please be sure to include copies of all evaluations and actual test scores.

I will need time to review Michael's educational records before this important meeting.

If you have questions about my request, please call me at work (555-9876) or at home (555-1234), after 6:00 pm.

Thank you for your assistance and quick response.

Sincerely,

Jane Smith

#3. Second Request for Records

Jane Smith
500 Oak Lane
Centerville, IL 60010
(899) 555-1234

October 4, 2005

George Williams, Principal
Grove Middle School
1000 Main Street
Middleburg, IL 60010

Reference: Michael K. Smith
                DOB: 01/02/94
                School: Grove Middle School

Dear Mr. Williams:

I am concerned that I have not received a copy of my son's educational records. I requested these records on September 18, 2005 (copy of letter enclosed). When I did not receive the records or any response, I called your office on September 25, September 28, and October 1, 2005.

As I mentioned in my earlier letter, a meeting with my son's teachers was scheduled for October 2. I needed to review Michael's educational records before this meeting. Because I did not receive the records, the meeting had to be cancelled. Michael is still not receiving any help from the school.

I would appreciate your prompt attention to resolve what I view as the beginning of a serious problem. I can come to the school to help photocopy these records. If you need to discuss my request, please call me at work (555-9876) or home (555-1234). Thank you for taking the time to resolve this problem.

Sincerely,

Jane Smith

Enc: September 18 letter requesting records

#4. Letter to Request a Meeting with a Teacher, Includes Educational History

Jane Smith
500 Oak Lane
Centerville, IL 60010
(899) 555-1234

October 15, 2005

Robert Underwood, Teacher
Grove Middle School
1000 Central Avenue
Middleburg, IL 60010

Reference: Michael K. Smith
DOB: 01/02/94
School: Grove Middle School

Dear Mr. Underwood:

I am very concerned about Michael's school problems. I would like to meet with you and get your ideas about his problems and how we can help him.

School has been always been difficult for Michael. He repeated first grade. At that time, I asked for special help for Michael. This was denied. In fourth grade, I again asked that he receive special help. The special education staff found him eligible and provided special education services, but felt that he was not far enough behind in reading to receive reading remediation. I told them that he could not read.

In September, 2004, I arranged for Michael to receive private tutoring at our expense. He received tutoring until Christmas when the tutor moved away. Michael was showing improvement, but he needs more help. In the first and second grades, he was happy and energetic. Now he seems sad, depressed, and tells us that children make fun of him because he cannot read. He does not want to go to school.

I understand that you meet with parents on Mondays, Tuesdays, and Thursdays, from 3:15 p.m. to 4:30 p.m. I would like to schedule a meeting with you on Tuesday, October 22 at 3:30 p.m. Please call to confirm this date or suggest an alternative date and time. You can call me at work (555-9876) or home (555-1234) after 6:00 p.m. If I am not available, please leave a message on my answering machine. My job requires me to attend meetings every Monday until 5:00 p.m.

I appreciate your taking time to meet with me. I look forward to your advice about how we can help Michael learn how to read.

Sincerely,

Jane Smith

#5. Letter to Request a Review of Educational Records

Jane Smith

500 Oak Lane, Centerville, IL 60010

(899) 555-1234

November 12, 2005

George Williams, Principal
Grove Middle School
1000 Main Street, Middleburg, IL 60010

Reference: Michael K. Smith
DOB: 01/02/94
School: Grove Middle School

Dear Mr. Williams:

On September 18, I requested a complete copy of my son's educational records. When I did not receive these records, I hand-delivered a second letter to your office on October 4. (Enclosed are copies of the letters.) I did not receive copies of Michael's records until November 8. I immediately began organizing his file. I found that the records I received from the school appear to be incomplete. He was tested several years ago. That information is missing.

Because Michael's parents and teachers need to have access to the same information, I am requesting that all my son's educational records be brought together in one place for my review. I understand that I may examine all personally identifiable records regarding Michael. This includes medical records, special education records, formal and informal correspondence, discipline records, tests, evaluations, and teacher-to teacher notes.

I appreciate your having a staff member present at this review to certify that these records represent all records held regarding Michael. My friend, Louisa Johnson, will help me to log in records as we review them.

Please call so we can schedule a convenient time to review Michael's educational records. Since Thanksgiving is just around the corner, I would like to finish this task within the next five days. You can reach me at work (555-9876) or at home (555-1234) in the evening. I appreciate your help in this matter.

Sincerely,

Jane Smith

Enc: Letters dated September 18 and October 4, 2005

#6. Letter to Express Appreciation for Help

Jane Smith
500 Oak Lane
Centerville, IL 60010
(899) 555-1234

November 15, 2005

Nathan Weiss, Director of Special Education
School District #10
1001 Main Street
Middleburg, IL 60010

Reference: Michael K. Smith
                  DOB: 01/02/94
                  School: Grove Middle School

Dear Dr. Weiss:

I greatly appreciate the help your office manager, Debra Pratt, provided during the recent review of my son's educational records.

With Ms. Pratt's help, we were able to locate several records that had been misfiled. Because of Ms. Pratt's suggestions and assistance, we were able to complete the records review more quickly.

You are fortunate to have such a capable office manager.

Sincerely,

Jane Smith

#7. Letter to Request an Evaluation for Special Education Services

Jane Smith
500 Oak Lane
Centerville, IL 60010
(899) 555-1234

November 20, 2005

George Williams, Principal
Grove Middle School
1000 Main Street
Middleburg, IL 60010

Reference: Michael K. Smith
DOB: 01/02/94
School: Grove Middle School

Dear Mr. Williams,

I am writing to ask that my son, Michael Smith, be considered for special education services so he can learn to read. He is in the sixth grade at Grove Middle School.

A brief summary of Michael's educational history follows: Michael was retained in first grade because the teacher felt his problems with reading would improve when he got older. When I asked for special help for Michael, this was denied.

In fourth grade, Michael could not read the labels on cans and boxes at the grocery store. I asked that he receive special education services. He was found eligible and received some services. Although I told your staff that Michael could not read, they said he did not qualify for reading remediation. The special education staff decided to wait to see if his problems improved by the end of the school year. His problems did not improve. I arranged for private tutoring. Michael is now in sixth grade and cannot read labels at the grocery store.

When I met with his teacher last week, Mr. Underwood told me that because Michael's reading skills are so deficient, he will not be able to pass the state proficiency tests. He said Michael is reading at the 2nd to 3rd grade level. He is aware of the severity of Michael's reading problems and is doing all that he can. He suggested that I contact you.

When I first wrote to Mr. Underwood, I told him that in the first and second grades, Michael was happy and energetic. Now he is sad and depressed. He is having nightmares. He says other children make fun of him because he cannot read. He does not want to go to school.

I am afraid that I am losing my child.

Michael needs our help. If you need more information about my request for reading remediation, please call me at home (555-1234) or at work (555-9876). I appreciate your prompt attention to this problem.

Sincerely,

Jane Smith

#8. Letter to Request Test Scores as Standard Scores and Percentile Ranks

Jane Smith
500 Oak Lane
Centerville, IL 60010
(899) 555-1234

February 21, 2005

Nathan Weiss, Director of Special Education
School District #10
1001 Main Street
Middleburg, IL 60010

Reference: Michael K. Smith
              DOB: 01/02/94
              School: Grove Middle School

Dear Dr. Weiss:

I attended a special education meeting for my son on February 20. When I reviewed Mike's test results, I was distressed to find that his scores were reported as "ranges" (i.e. below average, average), not as percentile ranks and/or as standard scores. Because I did not receive his test scores, it was impossible to know where Michael is functioning.

Please send all of Michael's test scores as standard scores and percentile ranks.

The eligibility team will meet again on **March 20**. To prepare for this meeting, I need the test scores no later than **March 13**. If I do not have this information, the team will have to cancel another meeting and waste more valuable time. I understand that your staff is busy. I will pick the information up at the school. If I can do anything to expedite this request or provide any help, please let me know immediately.

Enclose please find a copy of a comprehensive psych-evaluation of Michael by John Black, Ph.D, NASP, certified school psychologist, that was completed on February 12, 2006. I received this evaluation by mail yesterday, while we were at the eligibility meeting.

If you have questions about my request, please let me know. You may call me at work (555-9876) or at home (555-1234). I look forward to receiving these test results no later than **March 13**. Thank you for your assistance.

Sincerely,

Jane Smith

#9. Follow-up Letter after IEP Meeting to Document Unresolved Problems

Jane Smith
500 Oak Lane
Centerville, IL 60010
(899) 555-1234
April 9, 2006

Nathan Weiss, Director of Special Education
School District #10
1001 Main Street, Middleburg, IL 60010

Reference: Michael K. Smith
               DOB: 01/02/94
               School: Grove Middle School

Dear Dr. Weiss:

On April 3, I met with you and your staff to develop an appropriate educational program for my son. I provided you with the comprehensive psych-educational evaluation of Michael by Dr. John Black, certified school psychologist. According to this evaluation, after two years of special education, Michael made no progress learning to read. His self-concept has been damaged.

On April 3, Dr. Black attended a meeting at Grove Middle School to discuss the test results and his recommendations with you and the IEP team. He explained the legal requirements for research based reading programs. He advised you that Michael needs a research-based reading program that is based on a multi-sensory, sequential approach. Michael has dyslexia that was not identified until Dr. Black evaluated him. Dr. Black explained that it is not too late to teach Michael to read, but that he requires intensive services and specialized remediation. I asked the district to provide remediation. You said Michael could attend summer school but advised that the district does not provide reading remediation in summer school.

I am losing confidence in the district's ability to teach Michael how to read. The district has not provided any remediation. The gap between Michael's ability and achievement grows larger and larger. Other children make fun of him because he cannot read. He has nightmares. His self-concept has been damaged.

How can Michael become independent, hold a job, and get further education if the school will not teach him to read?

I appreciate your taking the time to attend the April 3 meeting. If you can help, please let me know. We are running out of time. You may call me at work (555-9876) or at home (555-1234) after 6:00 p.m.

Sincerely,

Jane Smith

cc: Dr. Black

#10. Ten-day Notice Letter to Withdraw Child from Public School

Jane Smith
500 Oak Lane
Centerville, IL 60010
(899) 555-1234

May 25, 2006

Nathan Weiss, Director of Special Education
School District #10
1001 Main Street
Middleburg, IL 60010

Reference: Michael K. Smith
               DOB: 01/02/94
               School: Grove Middle School

Dear Dr. Weiss:

As you know, my son Michael attends Grove Middle School. Michael has dyslexia. Although he was placed in support classes for two years, he did not learn to read.

Michael has been evaluated by the school psychologist and a private sector school psychologist. Last week, he was evaluated by Dr. Kay, a neuro-psychologist. The enclosed findings are clear and not disputed. Michael has not learned to read. According to all these evaluations, he has fallen further behind. The school personnel blame Michael for his lack of progress.

I advised the team that I may place Michael in private school if the school district will not provide an intensive program of reading remediation. I was told that Michael received the services that were available and that nothing else could be done. The school psychologist said I should not expect Michael to learn to read. Dr. Black tested Michael in February. He says Michael will learn to read if he is taught with a research based instructional method by a teacher who is highly skilled in using this method. Dr. Kay concurs with Dr. Black.

Michael has a right to an appropriate education. I have spent two frustrating years in meetings, trying to educate the district and myself. What can I do? If you were Michael's parent, would you think it is unreasonable to expect the school to teach your child to read?

I plan to remove Michael from Independent School District #10 and place him in the Dewey

School, a private school that specializes in teaching children like Michael to read. If Michael makes progress in the private program, I will ask the district to reimburse me for the cost of his education.

If you have any questions, you may call me at work (555-9876) or at home (555-1234).

Sincerely,

Jane Smith

cc: Dr. Black
       Dr. Kay

25 | Preparing for Meetings: Taking Control

"If you're sure you can't, you won't. If you think you can, you might. If you know
you can, you will."   — Fable

If you are like most parents, you feel confused, frustrated and intimidated at school meetings. How can you get the school to answer your questions? How can you get the school to respond to your requests? How can you get the school to provide the services and supports your child needs? What is your role?

As a parent, you negotiate with the school for services on your child's behalf. In this chapter, you will learn about negotiating and problem solving. You will learn about organizing the file, knowing what you want, anticipating obstacles, and presenting your requests.

The pre-meeting worksheet will help you identify needs, clarify concerns, anticipate problems, and make requests. (You will learn how to use the IEP worksheet in the next chapter.) You will learn how to use a parent agenda to express concerns, describe problems, and make requests. If your relationship with the school is strained or damaged, these steps will help you mend fences and build healthy working relationships with school personnel.

You are a Negotiator

If you are like many parents, you did not realize that you negotiate with the school for special education services and supports. When you attend meetings about your child's special education program, you are representing your child's interests.

When you understand that you are negotiating, the process begins to make sense. Think about other situations where you negotiate. You may have more experience as a negotiator than you realize.

You negotiate with co-workers about work schedules. You negotiate with your employer about your salary. You negotiate with family members about housework and the budget. When you purchase a car or house, you negotiate with strangers. When you negotiate with the school, you have an advantage–you can prepare.

Here are five rules for successful problem solving . Keep these rules in mind when you prepare for meetings.

Five Rules for Successful Problem Solving

"If we or our argument is perceived as a threat, we will never be heard."

   – Gerry Spence, trial lawyer and writer

Rule 1: Know what you want.

"When I told the team that I was dissatisfied with Jeremy's progress, the chairman said, 'What do you want us to do?' Several people laughed. I was so embarrassed! Don't they know what to do? They were trying to make me feel stupid." - Marie at a parent training session.

Did the team intend to make Marie feel stupid? We do not know. Was the school's request unreasonable? No.

If you have a problem, you need to think about possible solutions to the problem. Prepare solutions that may resolve the problem. If the school ignores or belittles your solutions, you should document this in your polite follow-up letter.

If you are like many parents, you think you must use educational jargon to make requests and express concerns. Not so! You will not gain credibility with educators by speaking their jargon. Make your requests in clear simple language. You want the decision-making Stranger to understand the problem and your proposed solutions. Prepare to answer these questions:

- What do you want?
- What action do you want the school to take?
- What facts support your request?

Rule 2. Do not blame or criticize.

When you report problems or express concerns to a school team, stick to the facts. Do not blame or criticize. If a team member reacts defensively, be careful!

Assume you take off work to attend an IEP meeting. The special education supervisor does not show up. After 30 minutes, the team cancels the meeting. When you leave the building and walk toward your car, you pass the supervisor in the parking lot. You say, "I have to go back to work."

The supervisor says, "I have five hundred kids." What happened? Because the supervisor felt defensive about missing the meeting, she reacted to your statement as personal criticism.

Look at your statement again. You made a simple statement, not a criticism. Because she assumed your comment was criticism, she feels angry and overwhelmed.

You may be able to use this information to create a different relationship with the supervisor – and gain services for your child. When you meet again, she expects you to criticize her. This expectation will keep her guilt feelings alive. The next time you see her, make a friendly comment about her workload. Express your understanding that she cannot be in two places at one time. Do not mention any problems caused by her failure to show up.

What do you think will happen? It is likely that her defensiveness toward you will dissipate. She may feel grateful that you did not criticize her. By taking this approach, you may increase the odds that she will give you what your child needs.

When you negotiate, you are dealing with people. When people feel defensive, anxious or angry, their ability to solve problems drops. If you stick to facts, you make it more likely that the team will develop creative solutions to problems.

Rule 3. Protect the parent-school relationship.

In parent-school negotiations, personal relations are entangled with problems. Separate your relationships with people from the problems. If you view the people and the problem as the same, you will feel angry, bitter, and mistrustful.

When you negotiate, you have two interests:

- To solve problems
- To protect relationships

You will negotiate again!

Rule 4. Seek win-win solutions to problems.

When you use traditional win-lose bargaining, you are playing hardball. People who play hardball believe that if they give in, they lose. When parents and school play hardball, the relationship and the issue are at risk.

Do not play hardball to resolve parent-school problems. When teams develop win-win solutions to problems, the members are committed to the success of their solutions. If the school loses, expect them to undermine and sabotage the solution.

Rule 5. Understand the school district's position.

You need to be able to step into the shoes of the the people on the other side of the table. You need to be able to answer questions like these:

- What are their perceptions? How does the school see the problem?
- What are their interests? What does the school want?
- What are their fears? What are they afraid will happen if they give you what you want?

When you answer these questions, it will be easier to develop solutions that allow you and the school district to get your needs and wants met.

Discovering the School's Position

How do you find out what the school wants and what they fear? Do not expect them to tell you. It is possible that they do not know what they want and fear. You will discover the answers to these questions by asking 5 Ws + H + E questions and listening carefully to the answers.

Perceptions

How does your school district perceive parents? How does the school perceive parents of children with disabilities? How does your child's school perceive you? Does the school think you are demanding? Are you a complainer? Do they believe you are passive and uninvolved?

Interests

What is important to your school district? What do they want? What is their mission?

Fears

What does your school district fear? If the school gives you what you want, have they failed? Will school personnel have to admit that they were wrong? Will school personnel have to do things they do not want to do?

If the district gives you what you want, are they afraid the floodgates will open? Is the district afraid they will lose power? Will the district lose face?

Preparing for School Meetings

The keys to successful IEP meetings are organizing, preparing, and knowing how to present your requests. When you learn that a meeting is scheduled, follow this process to prepare.

Use the Pre-Meeting Worksheet

Make several copies of the pre-meeting worksheet (Table 25-1). Fill in the information about the meeting time and date, location, purpose, and who requested the meeting. As you prepare, you will be able to answer more of the questions in the pre-meeting worksheet.

| **Table 25-1** | *Pre-Meeting Worksheet* |

Location:_____

Date:_____

What is purpose of the meeting?_____

Who requested the meeting?_____

Who will attend the meeting (e.g., teachers, administrators, parent, child)?

_____

_____

What do you want? _____

_____

What do they want? _____

_____

What action do you want them to take? _____

_____

How motivated are they to give you what you want?_____

_____

What will prevent them from giving you what you want?_____

_____

How can you alleviate their concerns?_____

_____

Organize and Review the File

Review your child's file. File all loose documents. Do you have all recent test data? Review all test results, including all state and district testing on your child.

If your child has an IEP, review the IEP goals. Compare the current test data to the earlier test data. Is your child making progress? Is your child's progress acceptable? Do you have concerns about your child's program or progress?

Review your notes from prior meetings. Review your contact log. What issues are unresolved? Are there problems you want to bring up at the meeting?

Brainstorm

When you review your child's file, your contact logs, and your notes, think about issues you want the team to address. Open your notebook and write 5 Ws + H + E at the top of the page. List your questions and concerns.

How do you view your child's problems? How does the school view your child's problems? How is the school likely to respond to your concerns? Your success in devising solutions to problems will depend on knowing what they want. If you know the perceptions of your school district, it will easier to answer these questions.

Write the answers to these questions in the pre-meeting worksheet:

- What do you want?
- What does the school want?
- What action do you want the school to take?
- How motivated are they to give you what you want?
- What will prevent them from giving you what you want?
- How can you address their concerns and fears?

Use a Parent Agenda

The parent agenda is a valuable tool. You can use a parent agenda to:

- Prepare for meetings
- Identify concerns and list problems
- Propose solutions to problems
- Identify issues and problems that are not resolved
- Improve parent-school relationships

To learn how to use a parent agenda, read the agenda written by AJ's parents (Table 25-2). AJ is in middle school. He is failing several subjects. He is embarrassed about having to go to the nurse's office to get his medication. His disability makes it difficult for him to produce written work. His teacher makes negative comments about AJ to other students and their parents.

Table 25-2	*Sample Parent Agenda*

The Good News

AJ is a bright, energetic, sensitive, thoughtful child. He grasps complex concepts easily. He has good memory for facts and details. He loves to read. He is patient with his six-year-old sister Suzy who has Down Syndrome.

Our Frustrations (Parents and Teachers)

AJ is easily distracted and has difficulty focusing on tasks. His organizational skills are immature. He is "consistently inconsistent."

AJ is sometimes driven to tears over his inability to get organized, find homework assignments, notes, and papers. He completes assignments, misplaces them, completes them again, and forgets to turn them in. AJ is described by teachers as "lazy, careless, uncooperative, and choosing not to complete assignments."

AJ's Frustrations

I DON'T WANT to have ADD. I want to be normal. I don't want to take medication that changes my appetite and emotions. It is embarrassing to go to the nurse's office for medication. It is obvious that I'm not normal. I've been on different medications and I've been failing school since the 4th grade.

I have three or four hours of homework a night. I don't think the teachers talk to each other because they all give long projects on the same day. When I don't understand an assignment, they get mad at me.

What AJ Needs

1. **Please understand that ADD is a MEDICAL condition**.
2. **A drastic reduction in written work and homework**. An average child may spend 20 minutes on an assignment that takes AJ several hours to complete. Homework is a nightmare. Teachers add to the stress by sending class work home. If AJ cannot complete the work during the school day, it is unlikely that he will complete it in the evening.
3. **Prioritize and modify AJ's assignments**. These homework problems are preventing AJ from being a child. We arranged for him to take Aikido because it is a healthy outlet and good therapy. He must miss Aikido to do homework.
4. **Avoid ridicule.** AJ's self-esteem is fragile. He perceives himself as a failure. Negative comments sent home or made to parents in front of him are inappropriate and ineffective. We have received one positive note and dozens of negative notes from the school. Would you want to be AJ?
5. **Teach AJ organizational skills.** AJ needs your help to keep track of homework and assignments.
6. **AJ is distractible**. He needs to sit in front of the class.
7. **Value AJ's strengths**. Provide him with chances to do well in front of his peers. Catch him doing something right. *"AJ, I'm very proud of your perfect attendance. Even when school is frustrating, you don't give up. Good for you!"*
8. **Believe in him**. Don't give up when Plans A and B fail. Try Plans C and D.
9. **Accept our support**. We understand and appreciate your efforts. We are here to help you in any way we can.

This parent agenda begins with "Good News." Because the agenda does not begin with complaints, you continue to read. Good News is followed by "Our Frustrations (parents and teachers)." By framing AJ's problems as "Our Frustrations," his parents emphasize their belief that parents and educators share responsibility for developing solutions to AJ's problems.

When the parents use AJ's words to describe his perception of school, you step into his shoes. As a Stranger, you feel sympathy for him. After you read his frustrations, the parents express their concerns and make their requests.

AJ's parents used this parent agenda to identify problems and offer solutions without blaming school personnel or making them feel defensive. The parents understood the importance of presentation.

In the final section of the agenda, "What AJ Needs," the parents describe problems and offer solutions. The parents use facts to support each request. You learn that AJ has Attention Deficit Disorder (ADD) and that ADD is a medical condition.

When AJ's parents ask the teachers to reduce homework, they support their request by describing the toll homework is taking on AJ. As the Stranger, you find yourself agreeing that several hours of homework are unreasonable.

The parents bring up more difficult issues when they ask the teacher to avoid ridicule, value AJ's strengths, and "believe in him."

This agenda ends with the parents' offer of support and appreciation for efforts made on behalf of their son. Wisely, the parents placed these statements at the end. They know that what is read last is most likely to be remembered.

Writing a parent agenda is hard work. As these parents told their son's story, you stepped into AJ's shoes and saw the world through his eyes. The parents did not overtly blame or criticize the school.

AJ's parents were surprised at the success of this strategy. The special education director and school psychologist recommended that AJ be transferred to a new school with a low student-teacher ratio.

Instead of failing grades, AJ is getting A's. His medication has been reduced. His attitude has turned around. He is so bright and capable. A few months ago, we thought he was lost.

Handouts and Charts

If you plan to use handouts, visual aids or graphs, prepare them ahead of time. If you use handouts, bring several extra copies to the meeting. If you are concerned about your child's lack of progress, use test data to support your position.

If you use a parent agenda, you may want to send your agenda to team members before the meeting. Do not assume that the team members will read your agenda ahead of time. Most people will not read the agenda until they get into the meeting. Bring extra copies for people who misplaced or lost their copies.

Practice!

When you make requests, practice. When you practice, you prepare. Practice will reduce your anxiety. You need to state your problems or concerns clearly and offer suggestions about how you want the problem to be resolved. If you belong to a support group, role-play or rehearse what you plan to say before your group. Ask the group for help in polishing your presentation.

Image and Presentation

Your goal is to develop a good working relationship with school personnel. When you dress neatly and conservatively for school meetings, you convey a businesslike image. When you organize your child's file and bring the file to meetings, you send a message that you expect to work with the school as a partner.

Arrive early for meetings. When you arrive early, you will have time to relax and focus on what you want to accomplish. You may also discover who attended the "pre-meeting" that was held before the real meeting with you.

A Secret Weapon: Food

Most parent-school communication is by letters, telephone calls, and face-to-face meetings. If you have a problem, it is likely to be resolved in a meeting.

If you anticipate a long meeting, bring food. For an early morning meeting, bring donuts or sweet rolls. If you have a lunch meeting, bring a sandwich tray. For a late afternoon meeting, bring energy food (i.e., fruit, cookies, brownies). Always bring more food than the group will consume. Never take leftovers when you leave.

Sharing food and drink helps to build productive working relationships. This is especially true if relationships are strained and tense. When school personnel consume food you bring to a meeting, it is difficult for them to feel angry or antagonistic toward you.

After you leave, other school personnel will share your offerings. A positive buzz will begin in the teacher's lounge. "Who brought this food?" "Gillian's mom. We have some battles with her but she's a great Mom!"

In Summation

In this chapter, you learned that you negotiate with the school for services. The keys to successful meetings are preparing, organizing information, and knowing how to present your requests. You learned how to use the pre-meeting worksheet to prepare for meetings and the parent agenda to describe problems, offer solutions, and make requests. You discovered that you have a secret weapon – food!

Let's move on to the next chapter and learn about strategies for successful meetings.

Your Notes Here

26 | Meeting Strategies: Maintaining Control

"Winning is getting what we want, which also means helping others get what they want."
— Gerry Spence, Trial Lawyer and Author

You have learned that preparation and planning are the keys to successful advocacy. In the last chapter, you learned how to use the pre-meeting worksheet to clarify issues and identify problems and the parent agenda to present problems, offer solutions and make requests. In this chapter, you will learn strategies to control the outcome of meetings, including the problem resolution worksheet and the post-meeting thank you note.

School Meeting Anxiety

This is how one father, a successful salesman, describes school meetings:

I always feel anxious when I go to the school for a meeting. I start to feel anxious before I get there. By the time I drive into the parking lot, my stomach is in knots. I feel intimidated. When they ask me what I think, I do not know what to say.

If you have a child in special education, you know about school meeting anxiety. Many factors contribute to school meeting anxiety, including your life experiences, fears about your child, uncertainty about your role, and your interpersonal style.

Your personal experiences will affect your feelings about school meetings. When you walk into your child's school, you are transported back to your own earlier years in school. For many parents, memories of school are painful and unpleasant. If you had school problems, school meetings may bring back old feelings of guilt, shame, and anxiety.

Your reaction to school meetings is also influenced by your interpersonal style. If you are a conflict-avoider, your motto is "peace at any price." You may keep your concerns about your child's education to yourself until you cannot avoid conflict any longer. If you are eager to please, your desire to be liked may cause you to agree to anything the school proposes. If you are a controller, you may feel out of control at school meetings.

Meeting Strategies

The right word may be effective, but no word was ever as effective as a rightly timed pause. —Mark Twain

Both Parents Attend Meetings

If possible, both parents should attend school meetings. When parents go to meetings together, they present a strong, unified front. If one parent has more business experience, that parent may be more comfortable in the role of negotiator.

Fathers should take an active role in educational decisions and planning. **Mothers who attend meetings alone do not operate from a position of strength.** School personnel tend to view mothers as more emotional and less objective about their children.

Discuss what you want to accomplish ahead of time. Decide what your child needs. Do not air your personal problems during school meetings.

Do Not Go Alone

If the other parent cannot attend, ask a friend or family member to accompany you. You may also ask your minister, priest, rabbi, or religious leader to attend the meeting with you. If you go alone, you are more likely to feel intimidated and to make decisions that you will regret later. When you have a friend or family member with you, you will feel less vulnerable. This person can provide support and help you analyze the meeting afterwards.

Tape Recording Meetings

If you have problems or you anticipate a dispute about your child's IEP, it is a good idea to tape record IEP meetings. Some parents routinely record all meetings, even when parent-school relationships are good. There are several advantages to recording meetings.

If you are like most parents, IEP meetings are confusing and overwhelming. You want to take an active role in the IEP process but you cannot ask questions, discuss issues, make decisions, and take notes at the same time. When you tape record meetings, you can ask questions, express concerns, offer solutions, and make decisions without also having to take notes.

Perhaps you asked an important question. After the meeting, you cannot remember how or if your question was answered. If you recorded the meeting, you can listen to the tape and find the answer to your question.

Table 26-1	*Tips for Recording Meetings*

> Practice using the recorder several times before the meeting.
> Put fresh batteries in the recorder before the meeting
> Mark tapes as #1, #2, and #3 before the meeting.
> Bring several blank tapes to the meeting.
> For a clear recording, place the recorder on a book on the table.
> Use an external, battery-powered microphone like those used by newscasters.
> To make the microphone omni-directional, clip the microphone to an object a few feet away from the recorder.
> Make sure the microphone battery is turned on.

After the tapes are transcribed, you have a transcript of what was proposed, considered, and rejected during the meeting. If you request a hearing to resolve a dispute, transcripts of meetings may be evidence that supports your position.

Assume that you successfully recorded a meeting. The meeting is ending. Do not turn off your recorder until after you leave the building. School personnel often make important statements when your hand is on the doorknob.

Within a day or two, listen to the tapes. When you listen to the tapes, you may realize that important questions were not answered. You may discover that issues you thought were resolved are still on the table.

At school meetings where several people are talking at once, there is often confusion about who agreed to deal with an issue. You may believe that Ms. Jones agreed to examine the issue, while Ms. Jones believes that Mr. Smith agreed to look into the issue. When meetings are recorded, these problems are easier to resolve.

Tape-recording: What Does the Law Say?

The IDEA statute does not mention tape-recording meetings. The federal statutes do not authorize or prohibit parents or school officials from recording IEP meetings. Many states have language in their special education regulations about their policy on audio- and videotaping. Read your state's regulation about recording before you broach the subject to the school.

If your school district adopts a rule about taping, the school must apply this rule uniformly. Schools cannot record meetings while prohibiting parents from recording. If the school records a meeting, the tapes become part of your child's educational record. You are entitled to copies of your child's educational records, including tapes of meetings.

If the school claims they have a policy that prohibits parents from taping, write a polite letter to request a copy of this policy. Ask if the taping policy was adopted by the school administration, school board, or other entity. If the school district has a policy that prohibits taping, the district must make exceptions if this policy interferes with your ability to participate in the IEP process.

- If the policy prevents you from participating in an IEP meeting
- If your spouse is unable to attend the meeting
- Other factors that interfere with your parental rights

More Meeting Strategies

Taping Issues

Put the recorder on a book in the middle of the table, turn it on, and identify the meeting. If a school employee says you cannot record, pick up the microphone and ask the person to state his or her name and that the school district is forbidding you to record the meeting. In most cases, the person will back down. If the person does not back down, you have this on tape.

Meeting Dynamics

When you enter the meeting room, make a pleasant comment to break the ice. Shake hands. Make eye contact with each team member.

Pay attention to non-verbal behavior. Watch body language. Who sits at the head of the table? Who takes notes? Who is the most powerful person in the room?

☑ If you sit next to the most powerful person, you make it more difficult for this person to minimize you and your concerns.

Common Meeting Problems

"We Can't Do That"

School personnel often tell parents that "the law" does not allow the school to provide a service. Do not accept legal advice from your child's special education team. Read the law and regulations for yourself. You may need to consult with a qualified special education attorney so you have a clear sense of what the law says.

Ask questions. When you ask 5 Ws + H + E questions, frame your sentences so they begin with one of these words: What, Why, When, Who, Where, How, and Explain.

"Where does it say you can't provide one-on-one speech therapy?" "Where does it say that my child's IEP cannot have more than four goals?"

You will not change minds by arguing with people. When you ask questions, you often raise questions. When you ask questions, you will learn how the school views your child's problem and what the school plans to do to help your child. This information will help you anticipate problems and develop solutions that may resolve the problem and allow both sides to win. You will discover the answers to questions like these:

- How does the school view my child's problems?
- What does the school think my child needs?
- What does the school think they should do about my child's problem?
- Does the school have a plan to educate my child?
- What are the components of this plan?
- What does the school propose to do now?
- How will I know if the plan is working?
- What does the school propose to do if their plan does not work?

"The Law Does Not Allow Us to Do That"

If the school says, "The law does not allow us to do that," take out your copy of *Wrightslaw: Special Education Law, 2nd edition* (to be published in Spring 2006) and ask the team to help you find this in the law. Ask for help. You must be sincere. "When I read the law, I did not find this."

If you cannot find the issue, the usual fallback position is, "It's in the regulations." If the team cannot find the answer, you can say, "I haven't found this in the state regulations either." Make sure you have done your legal research and are on firm ground!

If you cannot find an answer to the question in the regulations, the school may claim that the issue is in their school district policies and guidelines. Ask for these documents. Be polite. In most cases, the school policies and guidelines will not deal with the issue.

Dealing with the "Draft IEP"

Many parents complain that when they go to an IEP meeting, they are handed a completed IEP to sign. If this happens to you, do not panic and do not get mad.

You have a right to participate in the development of your child's IEP. The fact that the school presents you with a draft IEP does not mean that you must accept the IEP. View the draft IEP as a "draft" and as information about what the school wants to provide. The draft IEP gives you information about the resources the school is willing to commit. The draft IEP is their first offer in the negotiation process.

You can say, "Thank you for drafting your ideas as a starting point for our discussion." Then pass out copies of your parent agenda or problem resolution worksheet!

When the Meeting Ends Without Resolution

Do not be surprised if the meeting ends before you finish the IEP. Do not be surprised if the school asks you to sign the incomplete IEP. Do not sign! Write that you attended the meeting but have not agreed to the services or program.

If you are being rushed to sign the IEP, you can say:

> *"This is an important document. I have not read it or had time to go over it so I cannot sign it. I would like to take a copy home with me. After I have reviewed it, I will send you a written consent or I will contact you to discuss any problems that I have with it."*

☑ **You have a right to a copy of the IEP and any evaluations of your child. When you sign an IEP, get a copy for your records. If you are advised that the IEP will be cleaned up and typed, get a "dirty" copy before you leave. Your copy establishes what the team agreed to.**

Strategies to Use in Disputes

If you have a dispute or disagreement, expect the school to put their defenses in place. They are preparing for battle. Will you request a due process hearing? The fear of the unknown will make everyone anxious.

Try to discover the basis of their refusal. How can you get school personnel to tell you their perceptions, interests and fears when they feel defensive and anxious?

Ask 5 Ws + H + E questions. Listen to the answers. Do not argue. You may be surprised at the useful information you discover!

Use the IEP Meeting Worksheet

In the last chapter, you learned how to use the pre-meeting worksheet to prepare for meetings. You learned how to use a parent agenda to describe problems and propose solutions.

If you anticipate problems, fill out the problem resolution worksheet before you go to the meeting (Table 26-2). The problem resolution worksheet is a simple strategy that will help you keep track of the issues you want to resolve.

Make a table with five columns. Write "Child's need/ Parent's request" above the first column, "School's response" above the second column, "Resolved?" above the third column, "Start Date" above the fourth column, and "Responsible Person" above the fifth column. (See the IEP Meeting Worksheet in Table 26-2)

In the first column, list the services and supports you think your child needs. For example, "My child needs one-on-one reading help" or "My child needs an aide." See Table 26-3 for the IEP Meeting Worksheet that has the parent's requests filled in.

At the beginning of the meeting, provide the team members with your IEP Meeting Worksheet. Advise the team that these are the issues you want to resolve. This strategy will help the team focus on these important issues.

If the team does not respond to a request or question, you can say, "Shall I write that one down as 'no response'?"

Table 26-2 | *IEP Meeting Worksheet*

Child's Name:

Date:

School:

Child's Need/ Parent Request	School's Response	Resolved	Start Date	Responsible Person

Table 26-3 | *IEP Meeting Worksheet*

Name: Joseph Doe

Date: December 2, 2005, 3:30 pm

School: Park Valley Middle School

Child's Need/ Parent Request	School's Response	Resolved	Start Date	Responsible Person
1. Reading skills 2 years behind. Needs 1:1 remediation.				
2. Teacher trained in Wilson Reading Method.				
3. Reduced homework (no more than 1 hour a night)				
4. Preferential Seating (front row, close to teacher)				

Do not argue. Ask questions and take notes. Before the meeting ends, tell the team that you want to review your notes. Read what you have written. If the team does not agree with your notes, ask them to tell you what they do not agree with. Note this on your worksheet.

At the end of the meeting, you have a document that is a concise list of your requests, the school's response to your requests, and a list of the issues that were resolved and not resolved. Your worksheet is a written record created during the meeting. If you need to request a hearing later, this document is powerful evidence. To see how the IEP Meeting Worksheet may look at the end of the meeting, see Table 26-4.

Post-meeting Strategies

Your most important post-meeting strategies are your written recollections and your thank-you letter.

Table 26-4	IEP Meeting Worksheet at End of Meeting

IEP Meeting Worksheet (includes your notes)

Name: Joseph Doe

Date: December 2, 2005, 3:30 pm

School: Park Valley Middle School

Child's Need/ Parent Request	School's Response	Resolved	Start Date	Responsible Person
1. Reading skills 2 years behind. Needs 1:1 remediation.	We don't do that	No		
2. Teacher trained in Wilson Reading Method.	We have never done that	No		
3. Reduced homework (no more than 1 hour a night)	We can't write that into the IEP, it's up to the teachers	No		
4. Preferential Seating (front row, close to teacher)	We will try it in Ms. Jones' class	Yes	12/3/05	Mrs. Jones

Your Recollections

After the meeting, write or dictate your recollections about what happened. Do this immediately. Do not wait. Memories fade. What issues were resolved? What issues are still on the table? We recommend that you use a small tape recorder to dictate your recollections.

When you write or dictate your recollections, you may realize that the meeting was more successful than you thought. Perhaps you resolved some of your problems. Perhaps the school agreed to provide some of the services you requested. What do you think? Did you make some progress?

Your Thank-You Letter

After the meeting, write a thank-you letter. In your letter, briefly describe the meeting, your understanding of what the school agreed to, and any issues that are unresolved. Your letter should be polite. Frame issues and problems as "ours." Offer to meet again to resolve the remaining issues.

Review Chapter 23 about writing letters to the school.

Make a copy of your IEP Meeting Worksheet or parent agenda and attach this document to your thank-you letter. Send your thank-you letter and supporting documents to the IEP team leader.

Keep a copy of your signed letter and documents for your records.

When you use these strategies, you will resolve many problems with the school. You created contemporaneous documentation during the meeting. After the meeting, you documented what you requested, what you were told, what was agreed to, and what was not resolved.

In Summation

In this chapter, you learned strategies for successful school meetings. You learned about common meeting problems and strategies you can use to deal with these problems. You learned how to use the problem resolution worksheet and the post-meeting thank-you letter to create a contemporaneous record of meetings.

When you prepare for meetings, write agendas, use problem resolution worksheets, and write polite thank-you letters that document what happened during meetings, you can prevent problems and get the services your child needs. Now, it's time to take stock of what you have learned. If you turn the page, we will offer our thoughts and ideas.

Your Notes Here

27 | In Summation

> "Revenge is the bastard child of justice.
> If we or our argument are perceived as a threat, we will never be heard."
> – Gerry Spence, trial lawyer and writer

In this final chapter of *Wrightslaw: From Emotions to Advocacy*, we will offer advice and issue a warning about pitfalls to avoid. First, we will summarize the components of effective advocacy.

Learn about your child's unique needs. Think about the skills your child must learn to be an independent, self-sufficient member of society: communication skills, social skills, and reading, writing, and mathematics skills. Ensure that your child acquires these skills.

Learn about research based instructional methods and "proven methods of teaching and learning for children with disabilities. (20 U.S.C. § 1400(c)(4)). Learn about assistive technology and how technology can help your child master essential skills.

Learn how to find answers to your questions in the laws, regulations and legal decisions. Do not learn the law so you can threaten or browbeat school personnel.

Get your state special education regulations and *Wrightslaw: Special Education Law, 2nd edition* (to be published in Spring 2006). When you cross-reference these publications, you will understand the relationships between the rules of procedure (as discussed in Section 1415) and substantive issues (as discussed in Sections 1412 and 1414). Because you are familiar with the Individuals with Disabilities Education Act (IDEA 2004), you will know that the statutes about IEPs are in Section 1414(d).

But learning the law is less important than learning about evaluations and test results. You cannot be an effective advocate until you know how to use test scores to measure progress or lack of progress. You learned about standard scores, percentile ranks, standard deviations, and subtest scores. When you look at your child's test scores, you will know if your child is acquiring skills or is falling further behind.

The IEP drives your child's educational program. You have learned about SMART IEPs that are Specific, Measurable, use Action words, are Realistic and Time Specific. Work with school personnel to develop SMART IEPs that relate to the purposes of the IDEA.

Your child's IEP should be designed to meet your child's unique needs and prepare your child for further education, employment, and independent living. (Section 1400(d)(1)(A)). This is your mission. Do not allow yourself to be distracted from this long-term goal: to prepare your child for further education, employment and independent living."

Learn about evidence and presentation. Organize your child's file. Secure evaluations of your child from evaluators in the private sector. Apply the Rules of Adverse Assumptions. Use 5 Ws + H + E questions to discover hidden agendas. Document events. Use negotiation skills. Write polite, persuasive letters. These are the keys to successful advocacy.

How can you master these skills if you are feeling frustrated, angry, and frightened about the future? Accept your emotions as normal. Understand that if you do not control your emotions, you may damage or destroy your child. Use your emotions to motivate you to learn new information and skills. Remember – your journey is from emotions to advocacy.

From Emotions to Advocacy

Prepare. Prepare. Prepare. And win. — Gerry Spence

Do not blame or find fault. If you want to force your district to admit that they are wrong, you will lose the battle and the war. If you want your district to change their policies and practices, you need to educate and persuade the decision-makers.

This chapter opened with statements by Gerry Spence, famous trial attorney and writer. Pete's style of litigation is similar that of Gerry Spence, and relies on tactics and strategies. Read *How to Argue and Win Every Time* by Gerry Spence (see bibliography). *How to Argue* will teach you about persuasion. If you can see issues through the eyes of others, you can help others see through your eyes. They are more likely to use their power to give you what you want.

The strategies in this book are not unique to special education advocacy. You can use these strategies to resolve problems and disputes in other areas of your life. If you have a dispute with an insurance company, a bureaucrat, your boss, or your neighbor, think about the Rules of Adverse Assumptions. Document your problem, create paper trails, and write polite, persuasive Letters to the Stranger.

As your child's advocate, your goal is not to litigate. Your goal is to use tactics and strategies to secure quality services for your child. When you negotiate with school personnel, you market win-win solutions to problems. In the end, you and school personnel should be able to sit down together and break bread. When you can do this, you have successfully completed your journey from emotions to advocacy.

I am only one. But still I am one.

I cannot do everything. And because I cannot do everything,

I will not refuse to do the something that I can do.

–Helen Keller, advocate for people with disabilities

APPENDIX A

Glossary of Special Education and Legal Terms

A

Accommodations. Changes in how test is administered that do not substantially alter what the test measures; includes changes in presentation format, response format, test setting or test timing. Appropriate accommodations are made to level the playing field, i.e., to provide equal opportunity to demonstrate knowledge.

Achievement test. Test that measures competency in a particular area of knowledge or skill; measures mastery or acquisition of skills.

Adequate Yearly Progress (AYP). Refers to annual improvement that states, school districts and schools must make each year, as measured by academic assessments, so that all public elementary and secondary schools have the same high academic standards.

Americans with Disabilities Act of 1990 (ADA). Legislation enacted to prohibit discrimination based on disability.

Attention Deficit Disorder/Attention Deficit Hyperactivity Disorder (ADD/ADHD). Child with ADD or ADHD may be eligible for special education under other health impairment, specific learning disability, and/or emotional disturbance categories if ADD/ADHD condition adversely affects educational performance.

Adversarial system. The system of trial practice in which each of the opposing parties has an opportunity to present and establish opposing contentions before the court.

Alternative dispute resolution. See mediation.

Appeal. Procedure in which a party seeks to reverse or modify a judgment or final order of a lower court or administrative agency, usually on grounds that lower court misinterpreted or misapplied the law, rather than on the grounds that it made an incorrect finding of fact.

Assessment. Systematic method of obtaining information from tests or other sources; procedures used to determine child's eligibility, identify the child's strengths and needs, and services child needs to meet these needs. See also evaluations.

Assistive technology device. Equipment used to maintain or improve the capabilities of a child with a disability.

Audiology. Related service; includes identification, determination of hearing loss, and referral for habilitation of hearing.

Autism. Developmental disability that affects communication and social interaction, adversely affects educational performance, is generally evident before age 3. Children with autism often engage in repetitive activities and stereotyped movements, resist environmental change or change in daily routines, and have unusual responses to sensory experiences.

B

Basic skills. Skills in subjects like reading, writing, spelling, and mathematics.

Behavior disorder (BD). See emotional disturbance.

Behavior intervention plan. A plan of positive behavioral interventions in the IEP of a child whose behaviors interfere with his/her learning or that of others.

Brief. Written argument that supports a case; usually contains a statement of facts and a discussion of law.

Burden of proof. Duty of a party to substantiate its claim against the other party; in civil actions, the weight of this proof is usually described as a preponderance of the evidence.

Business day. Means Monday through Friday, except for federal and state holidays.

C

Calendar day. (See "day").

Case law. Decisions issued by a court.

Child find. Requirement that all children with disabilities are identified, located and evaluated, and determine which children are receiving special education and related services.

C.F.R. Code of Federal Regulations.

Child with a Disability. A child with mental retardation, hearing impairments (including deafness), speech or language impairments, visual impairments (including blindness), emotional disturbance, orthopedic impairments, autism, traumatic brain injury, other health impairments, or specific learning disabilities; and who needs special education and related services.

Class action. A civil action filed in a court on behalf of a named plaintiff and on behalf of other individuals similarly situated.

Classroom-Based Instructional Reading Assessment. A reading assessment that relies on teacher observations.

Complaint. Legal document that outlines plaintiff's claim against a defendant.

Confidential file. File maintained by the school that contains evaluations conducted to determine whether child is handicapped, other information related to special education placement; parents have a right to inspect the file and have copies of any information contained in it.

Consent. Requirement that the parent be fully informed of all information that relates to any action that school wants to take about the child, that parent understands that consent is voluntary and may be revoked at any time. See also Procedural safeguards notice and prior written notice.

Controlled substance. Means a drug or other substance identified under schedules I, II, III, IV, or V of the Controlled Substances Act; does not include a substance that is legally possessed or used under the supervision of a licensed health care provider.

Core Academic Subjects. English, reading or language arts, mathematics, science, foreign languages, civics and government, economics, arts, history, and geography.

Counseling services. Related service; includes services provided by social workers, psychologists, guidance counselors, or other qualified personnel.

Cumulative file. General file maintained by the school; parent has right to inspect the file and have copies of any information contained in it.

D

Damages. Monetary compensation that may be recovered by a person who has suffered loss, detriment or injury to his person, property or rights, through the unlawful act or negligence of another; damages are not generally available under the IDEA.

Day. Means calendar day unless otherwise indicated as school day or business day.

Deaf-blindness. IDEA disability category; includes hearing and visual impairments that cause severe communication, developmental and educational problems that adversely affects educational performance.

Deafness. IDEA disability category; impairment in processing information through hearing that adversely affects educational performance.

Diagnostic Reading Assessment. A valid, reliable assessment based on scientifically based reading research that is used to identify a child's areas of strengths and weaknesses. A diagnostic reading assessment identifies difficulties a child has in learning to read, the cause of these difficulties, and possible reading intervention strategies and related special needs.

Disability. In Section 504 and ADA, defined as impairment that substantially affects one or more major life activities; an individual who has a record of having such impairment, or is regarded as having such an impairment.

Discovery. Term for methods of obtaining evidence in advance of trial; includes interrogatories, depositions and inspection of documents.

Due process hearing (impartial due process hearing). Procedure to resolve disputes between parents and schools; administrative hearing before an impartial hearing officer or administrative law judge.

E

Early intervention (EI). Special education and related services provided to children under age of 5.

Education records. All records about the student that are maintained by an educational agency or institution; includes instructional materials, teacher's manuals, films, tapes, test materials and protocols.

Educational consultant/diagnostician. An individual who may be familiar with school curriculum and requirements at various grade levels; may or may not have a background in learning disabilities; may conduct educational evaluations.

Emotional disturbance (ED). Disability category under IDEA; includes depression, fears, schizophrenia; adversely affects educational performance.

EMR. Educable mentally retarded.

ESY. Extended school year services.

Essential Components of Reading Instruction. Explicit and systematic instruction in phonemic awareness, phonics, vocabulary development, reading fluency, oral reading skills, and reading comprehension strategies.

Exhibit. Anything tangible that is produced and admitted in evidence during a trial.

F

FAPE. Free appropriate public education; special education and related services provided in conformity with an IEP; are without charge; and meets standards of the SEA.

FERPA. Family Educational Rights and Privacy Act; statute about confidentiality and access to education records.

Fluency. The capacity to read text accurately and quickly.

G

General curriculum. Curriculum adopted by LEA or SEA for all children from preschool through high school.

Gifted and Talented. Students who are capable of high achievement in intellectual, creative, artistic, or leadership areas or academic fields and who need services or activities to develop these capabilities.

Guardian ad litem. Person appointed by the court to represent the rights of minors.

H

Hearing impairment. Disability category under IDEA; permanent or fluctuating impairment in hearing that adversely affects educational performance.

Highly Qualified Teacher. New teachers and teachers in Title 1 programs who are certified by the state or pass the state teacher examination, demonstrate competence in the subject(s) they teach, and hold a license to teach. Teachers who are working under license or certification waivers are not highly qualified.

Highly Qualified Paraprofessional. A paraprofessional who has a high school diploma or equivalent, completes two years of study at a college or university, has an associate's degree (minimum), or takea a rigorous skills test.

Homeless Children and Youth. Children and youth who do not have a fixed, regular, nighttime residence. Includes children who live in motels, hotels, trailer parks, or campgrounds; children who live in emergency shelters; children who are abandoned or are waiting for foster care placement; children who live in cars, parks, public spaces, abandoned buildings, substandard housing, bus or train stations; and migratory children who are homeless.

I

IDEIA. The Individuals with Disabilities Education Improvement Act of 2004.

IDELR. Individuals with Disabilities Law Reporter.

IEE. Independent educational evaluation.

IEP. Individualized Educational Plan.

IFSP. Individualized family service plan.

Illegal drug. A controlled substance; does not include substances that are legally possessed or used under the supervision of a licensed health-care professional.

Impartial due process hearing. See due process hearing.

Inclusion. Practice of educating children with special needs in regular education classrooms in neighborhood schools. See also mainstreaming and least restrictive environment.

Interrogatories. Written questions served on a party that must be answered under oath before trial; method of discovery.

ITP. Individual Transition Plan.

J

Judgment. Order by a court.

L

Learning disability. See specific learning disability (SLD).

Local Educational Agency (LEA). A board of education or public authority that has administrative control or direction of public schools and is recognized as an administrative agency for public schools.

LRE. Least restrictive environment; requirement to educate special needs children with children who are not disabled to the maximum extent possible.

Limited English Proficient. A child who was not born in the United States or whose native language is not English, or a migratory child whose native language is not English.

M

Mainstreaming. Practice of placing special needs children in regular classrooms for at least a part of the children's educational program. See also least restrictive environment and inclusion.

Manifestation determination review. If child with disability engages in behavior or breaks a rule or code of conduct that applies to nondisabled children and the school proposes to remove the child, the school must hold a hearing to determine if the child's behavior was caused by the disability.

Mediation. Procedural safeguard to resolve disputes between parents and schools; must be voluntary, cannot be used to deny or delay right to a due process hearing; must be conducted by a qualified and impartial mediator who is trained in effective mediation techniques.

Medical services. Related service; includes services provided by a licensed physician to determine a child's medically related disability that results in the child's need for special education and related services.

Mental retardation. Disability category under IDEA; refers to significantly sub-average general intellectual functioning with deficits in adaptive behavior that adversely affects educational performance.

Modifications. Substantial changes in what the student is expected to demonstrate; includes changes in instructional level, content, and performance criteria, may include changes in test form or format; includes alternate assessments.

Multiple disabilities. Disability category under IDEA; concomitant impairments (such as mental retardation-blindness, mental retardation-orthopedic impairment, etc.) that cause such severe educational problems that problems cannot be accommodated in special education programs solely for one of the impairments; does not include deaf-blindness.

N

Native language. Language normally used by the child's parents.

Norm-referenced test. (See standardized test)

O

OCR. Office of Civil Rights.

Occupational therapy. Related service; includes therapy to remediate fine motor skills.

Opinion. Formal written decision by judge or court; contains the legal principles and reasons upon which the decision was based.

Orientation and mobility services. Related service; includes services to visually impaired students that enable students to move safely at home, school, and community.

Orthopedic impairment. Disability category under IDEA; orthopedic impairment that adversely affects child's educational performance.

OSERS. Office of Special Education and Rehabilitative Services.

OSEP. Office of Special Education Programs.

Other health impairment. Disability category under IDEA; refers to limited strength, vitality or alertness due to chronic or acute health problems that adversely affects educational performance.

P

Paraprofessional. An individual employed in a public school who is supervised by a certified or licensed teacher; includes individuals who work in language instruction educational programs, special education, and migrant education.

Parent. A legal guardian or other person standing in loco parentis, a grandparent or stepparent with whom the child lives, or a person who is legally responsible for the welfare of the child.

Phonemic Awareness. The ability to hear and identify individual sounds, or phonemes.

Phonics. The relationship between the letters of written language and the sounds of spoken language.

Physical therapy. Related service; includes therapy to remediate gross motor skills.

Precedent. A court decision that will influence similar cases in the future.

Proficient. Solid academic performance for the grade, demonstrates competence in subject matter.

Prior written notice. Required written notice to parents when school proposes to initiate or change, or refuses to initiate or change, the identification, evaluation, or educational placement of the child.

Pro se. Representing oneself without assistance of legal counsel.

Procedural safeguards notice. Requirement that schools provide full easily understood explanation of procedural safeguards that describe parent's right to an independent educational evaluation, to examine records, to request mediation and due process.

Psychological services. Related service; includes administering psychological and educational tests, interpreting test results, interpreting child behavior related to learning.

Public Law (P.L.) 94-142. The Education for All Handicapped Children Act; enacted into law in 1975.

Pupil Services Personnel. School counselors, school social workers, school psychologists, and other qualified professional personnel who provide assessment, diagnosis, counseling, educational, therapeutic, and other necessary services, including related services, as part of a comprehensive program to meet student needs.

R

Reading. A complex system of deriving meaning from print that requires all of the following:
- The skills and knowledge to understand how phonemes, or speech sounds, are connected to print.
- The ability to decode unfamiliar words.
- The ability to read fluently.
- Sufficient background information and vocabulary to foster reading comprehension.
- The development of appropriate active strategies to construct meaning from print.
- The development and maintenance of a motivation to read.

Reasonable accommodation. Adoption of a facility or program that can be accomplished without undue administrative or financial burden.

Recreation. Related service; includes therapeutic recreation services, recreation programs, and leisure education.

Rehabilitation Act of 1973. Civil rights statute designed to protect individuals with disabilities from discrimination; purposes are to maximize employment, economic self-sufficiency, independence, inclusion and integration into society.

Rehabilitation counseling services. Includes career development, preparation for employment, and vocational rehabilitation services.

Related services. Services that are necessary for child to benefit from special education; includes speech-language pathology and audiology services, psychological services, physical and occupational therapy, recreation, counseling, orientation and mobility services, school health services, social work services, parent counseling and training.

Remediation. Process by which an individual receives instruction and practice in skills that are weak or nonexistent in an effort to develop/strengthen these skills.

S

Scientifically Based Research. Research that applies rigorous, systematic, and objective procedures to obtain reliable, valid knowledge about education activities and programs.

School day. A day when children attend school for instructional purposes.

School health services. Related service; services provided by a qualified school nurse or other qualified person.

Screening Reading Assessment. A brief assessment based on scientifically based reading research that is designed to identify children who may be at risk for reading problems or academic failure.

Section 504. Section 504 of the Rehabilitation Act protects individuals with disabilities from discrimination due to disability by recipients of federal financial assistance.

Settlement. Conclusion of a legal matter by agreement of opposing parties in a civil suit before judgment is made.

Special education. Specially designed instruction, at no cost to the parents, to meet the unique needs of a child with a disability.

Specific learning disability (SLD). Disability category under IDEA; includes disorders that affect the ability to understand or use spoken or written language; may include difficulties with listening, thinking, speaking, reading, writing, spelling, and doing mathematical calculations.

Speech or language impairment. Disability category under IDEA; includes communication disorders, language impairments, voice impairments that adversely educational performance.

Statutory rights. Rights protected by statute, as opposed to constitutional rights that are protected by the Constitution.

Statute of limitations. Time within which a legal action must be commenced.

Standardized test. Norm-referenced test that compares child's performance with the performance of a large group of similar children (usually children who are the same age).

State education agency (SEA). State departments of education.

Statutory law. Written law enacted by legislative bodies.

Supplementary aids and services. Aids, services, and supports provided in regular education classes so children with disabilities can be educated with nondisabled children.

T

Testimony. Evidence given by a person as distinguished from evidence from writings and other sources.

Transcript. Official record taken during a trial or hearing by an authorized stenographer.

Transition services. IEP requirement; designed to facilitate movement from school to the workplace or to higher education.

Transportation. Related service about travel; includes specialized equipment (i.e., special or adapted buses, lifts, and ramps) if required to provide special transportation for a child with a disability.

Traumatic brain injury. Disability category under IDEA; includes acquired injury caused by external physical force and open or closed head injuries that result in impairments; does not include congenital or degenerative brain injuries or brain injuries caused by birth trauma. **Travel training.** See orientation and mobility services.

U

U.S.C. United States Code.

V

Visual impairment including blindness. Impaired vision that adversely affects educational performance.

Vocabulary. Words that students must know to read effectively.

W

Weapon. Means a "dangerous weapon" as defined in the United States Code.

Z

APPENDIX B

Glossary of Assessment Terms

A

Ability. A characteristic that is indicative of competence in a field. (See also aptitude.)

Ability Testing. Use of standardized tests to evaluate an individual's performance in a specific area (i.e., cognitive, psychomotor, or physical functioning).

Achievement tests. Standardized tests that measure knowledge and skills in academic subject areas (i.e., math, spelling, and reading).

Accommodations. Describe changes in format, response, setting, timing, or scheduling that do not alter in any significant way what the test measures or the comparability of scores. Accommodations are designed to ensure that an assessment measures the intended construct, not the child's disability. Accommodations affect three areas of testing: 1) the administration of tests, 2) how students are allowed to respond to the items, and 3) the presentation of the tests (how the items are presented to the students on the test instrument). Accommodations may include Braille forms of a test for blind students or tests in native languages for students whose primary language is other than English.

Age Equivalent. The chronological age in a population for which a score is the median (middle) score. If children who are 10 years and 6 months old have a median score of 17 on a test, the score 17 has an age equivalent of 10-6.

Alternative assessment. Usually means an alternative to a paper and pencil test; refers to non-conventional methods of assessing achievement (e.g., work samples and portfolios).

Alternate Forms. Two or more versions of a test that are considered interchangeable, in that they measure the same constructs in the same ways, are intended for the same purposes, and are administered using the same directions.

Aptitude. An individual's ability to learn or to develop proficiency in an area if provided with appropriate education or training. Aptitude tests include tests of general academic (scholastic) ability; tests of special abilities (i.e., verbal, numerical, mechanical); tests that assess "readiness" for learning; and tests that measure ability and previous learning that are used to predict future performance.

Aptitude tests. Tests that measure an individual's collective knowledge; often used to predict learning potential. See also ability test.

Assessment. The process of testing and measuring skills and abilities. Assessments include aptitude tests, achievement tests, and screening tests.

B

Battery. A group or series of tests or subtests administered; the most common test batteries are achievement tests that include subtests in different areas.

Bell curve. See normal distribution curve.

Benchmark. Levels of academic performance used as checkpoints to monitor progress toward performance goals and/or academic standards.

C

Ceiling. The highest level of performance or score that a test can reliably measure.

Classroom Assessment. An assessment developed, administered, and scored by a teacher to evaluate individual or classroom student performance.

Competency tests. Tests that measure proficiency in subject areas like math and English. Some states require that students pass competency tests before graduating.

Composite score. The practice of combining two or more subtest scores to create an average or composite score. For example, a reading performance score may be an average of vocabulary and reading comprehension subtest scores.

Content area. An academic subject such as math, reading, or English.

Content Standards. Expectations about what the child should know and be able to do in different subjects and grade levels; defines expected student skills and knowledge and what schools should teach.

Conversion table. A chart used to translate test scores into different measures of performance (e.g., grade equivalents and percentile ranks).

Core curriculum. Fundamental knowledge that all students are required to learn in school.

Criteria. Guidelines or rules that are used to judge performance.

Criterion-Referenced Tests. The individual's performance is compared to an objective or performance standard, not to the performance of other students. Tests determine if skills have been mastered; do not compare a child's performance to that of other children.

Curriculum. Instructional plan of skills, lessons, and objectives on a particular subject; may be authored by a state, textbook publisher. A teacher typically executes this plan.

D

Derived Score. A score to which raw scores are converted by numerical transformation (e.g., conversion of raw scores to percentile ranks or standard scores).

Diagnostic Test. A test used to diagnose, analyze or identify specific areas of weakness and strength; to determine the nature of weaknesses or deficiencies; diagnostic achievement tests are used to measure skills.

E

Equivalent Forms. See alternate forms.

Expected Growth. The average change in test scores that occurs over a specific time for individuals at age or grade levels.

F

Floor. The lowest score that a test can reliably measure.

Frequency distribution. A method of displaying test scores.

G

Grade equivalents. Test scores that equate a score to a particular grade level. Example: if a child scores at the average of all fifth graders tested, the child would receive a grade equivalent score of 5.0. Use with caution.

I

Intelligence tests. Tests that measure aptitude or intellectual capacities (Examples: Wechsler Intelligence Scale for Children (WISC-III-R) and Stanford-Binet (SB:IV).

Intelligence quotient (IQ). Score achieved on an intelligence test that identifies learning potential.

Item. A question or exercise in a test or assessment.

M

Mastery Level. The cutoff score on a criterion-referenced or mastery test; people who score at or above the cutoff score are considered to have mastered the material; mastery may be an arbitrary judgment.

Mastery Test. A test that determines whether an individual has mastered a unit of instruction or skill; a test that provides information about what an individual knows, not how his or her performance compares to the norm group.

Mean. Average score; sum of individual scores divided by the total number of scores.

Median. The middle score in a distribution or set of ranked scores; the point (score) that divides a group into two equal parts; the 50th percentile. Half the scores are below the median, and half are above it.

Mode: The score or value that occurs most often in a distribution.

Modifications. Changes in the content, format, and/or administration of a test to accommodate test takers who are unable to take the test under standard test conditions. Modifications alter what the test is designed to measure or the comparability of scores.

N

National percentile rank. Indicates the relative standing of one child when compared with others in the same grade; percentile ranks range from a low score of 1 to a high score of 99.

Normal distribution curve. A distribution of scores used to scale a test. Normal distribution curve is a bell-shaped curve with most scores in the middle and a small number of scores at the low and high ends.

Norm-referenced tests. Standardized tests designed to compare the scores of children to scores achieved by children the same age who have taken the same test. Most standardized achievement tests are norm-referenced.

O

Objectives: Stated, desirable outcomes of education.

Out-of-Level Testing. Means assessing students in one grade level using versions of tests that were designed for students in other (usually lower) grade levels; may not assess the same content standards at the same levels as are assessed in the grade-level assessment.

P

Percentiles (percentile ranks). Percentage of scores that fall below a point on a score distribution; for example, a score at the 75th percentile indicates that 75% of students obtained that score or lower.

Performance Standards. Definitions of what a child must do to demonstrate proficiency at specific levels in content standards.

Portfolio. A collection of work that shows progress and learning; can be designed to assess progress, learning, effort, and/or achievement.

Power Test. Measures performance unaffected by speed of response; time not critical; items usually arranged in order of increasing difficulty.

Profile. A graphic representation of an individual's scores on several tests or subtests; allows for easy identification of strengths or weaknesses across different tests or subtests.

R

Raw score. A raw score is the number of questions answered correctly on a test or subtest. For example, if a test has 59 items and the student gets 23 items correct, the raw score would be 23. Raw scores are converted to percentile ranks, standard scores, grade equivalent and age equivalent scores.

Reliability. The consistency with which a test measures the area being tested; describes the extent to which a test is dependable, stable, and consistent when administered to the same individuals on different occasions.

S

Scaled score. Scaled scores represent approximately equal units on a continuous scale; can convert to other types of scores; can use to examine change in performance over time.

Score. A specific number that results from the assessment of an individual.
Speed Test. A test in which performance is measured by the number of tasks performed in a given time. Examples are tests of typing speed and reading speed.

Standard score. Score on norm-referenced tests that are based on the bell curve and its equal distribution of scores from the average of the distribution. Standard scores are especially useful because they allow for comparison between students and comparisons of one student over time.

Standard deviation (S.D.) A measure of the variability of a distribution of scores. The more the scores cluster around the mean, the smaller the standard deviation. In a normal distribution,

68% of the scores fall within one standard deviation above and one standard deviation below the mean.

Standardization. A consistent set of procedures for designing, administering, and scoring an assessment. The purpose of standardization is to ensure that all individuals are assessed under the same conditions and are not influenced by different conditions.

Standardized tests. Tests that are uniformly developed, administered, and scored.

Standards. Statements that describe what students are expected to know and do in each grade and subject area; include content standards, performance standards, and benchmarks.

Stanine. A standard score between 1 to 9, with a mean of 5 and a standard deviation of 2. The first stanine is the lowest scoring group and the 9th stanine is the highest scoring group.

Subtest. A group of test items that measure a specific area (i.e., math calculation and reading comprehension). Several subtests make up a test.

T

T-Score. A standard score with a mean of 50 and a standard deviation of 10. A T-score of 60 represents a score that is 1 standard deviation above the mean.

Test. A collection of questions that may be divided into subtests that measure abilities in an area or in several areas.

Test bias. The difference in test scores that is attributable to demographic variables (e.g., gender, ethnicity, and age).

V

Validity. The extent to which a test measures the skills it sets out to measure and the extent to which inferences and actions made on the basis of test scores are appropriate and accurate.

Z

z-Score. A standard score with a mean of 0 (zero) and a standard deviation of 1.

Sources: Center for Research on Evaluation, Standards, and Student Testing (CRESST), Graduate School of Education & Information Studies, UCLA; American Guidance Service; Harcourt, Inc.; Office of Special Education and Rehabilitative Services, U. S. Department of Education.

Bibliography

The authors acknowledge the following references used in this book.

Alessi, Galen. (1988) "Diagnosis Diagnosed: A Systemic Reaction," *Professional School Psychology 3*: 145-151.

Allington, Richard L., Anne McGill-Franzel, Ruth Schick. (1997) "How Administrators Understand Learning Difficulties," *Remedial and Special Education 18*: 223-232.

Bateman, Barbara and Cynthia Herr. (2003) *Writing Measurable IEP Goals and Objectives.* Attainment Company, 2003.

Bramson, Robert M. (1981) *Coping with Difficult People.* New York: Dell Publishing.

Carrow-Woolfolk, E. (1999) *Comprehensive Assessment of Spoken Language.* Circle Pines, MN: American Guidance Service, Inc.

Carrow-Woolfolk, E. (1995). *Oral and Written Language Scales.* Circle Pines, MN: American Guidance Service, Inc.

Conners, C.K. (1997). *Conners' Rating Scales.* North Tonewanda, NY: Multi-Health Systems, Inc.

Connolly, A.J. (1998). *KeyMath Revised: A Diagnostic Inventory of Essential Mathematics.* Circle Pines, MN: American Guidance Service, Inc.

Council for Exceptional Children. (1998) "Assessments Fail to Give Teachers Relevant Information," *CEC Today 5.*

Dunn, L.M., & Dunn, L.M. (1997). *The Peabody Picture Vocabulary Test (3rd ed.).* Circle Pines, MN: American Guidance Service, Inc.

Elliot, C.D. (1990). *The Differential Ability Scales*. San Antonio, TX: The Psychological Corporation.

Fisher, Roger and William Ury. (1991) *Getting to Yes: Negotiating Agreement without Giving In*. New York: Penguin Books.

Fisher, Roger and Alan Sharp. (1998) *Getting It Done: How to Lead When You're Not in Charge*. New York: Harper Business.

Hall, Susan and Louisa Moats. (2002) *Parenting a Struggling Reader*. Broadway.

Hammill, D.D., & Larsen, S. (1996) *Test of Written Language- Third Edition*. Austin, TX: PRO-ED.

Hammill, D.D., & Newcomer, P.L. *Test of Language Development: Intermediate, 3rd Ed.* Austin, TX: PRO-ED.

Heath, Suzanne. (2003) *A Parent's Guide to No Child Left Behind*. Available at www.wrightslaw.com/info/nclb.parent.guide.heath.htm

Heath, Suzanne. (2003) *No Child Left Behind: What Teachers, Principals and Administrators Need to Know*. Available at www.wrightslaw.com/info/nclb.teachers.admins.htm

Hettleman, Kalman R. (2004) *The Road to Nowhere: The Illusion and Broken Promises of Special Education in the Baltimore City and Other Public School Systems*. Available at www.abell.org/publications/detail.asp?ID=92

Hresko. W.P., Schlieve, P.L., Herron, S.R., Swain, C., & Sherbenou, R.J. (2003) *Comprehensive Mathematical Abilities Test*. Austin, TX: PRO-ED.

Kaufman, A.S., & Kaufman, N.L. (2004) *Kaufman Test of Educational Achievement, Second Edition*. Circle Pines, MN: American Guidance Service, Inc.

Lake, Jeannie and Bonnie Billingsley. (2000) "An Analysis of Factors That Contribute to Parent-School Conflict in Special Education" *Remedial and Special Education* 21: 240-151.

Levine, Mel. (2003) *A Mind at a Time*. New York: Simon & Schuster.

Mager, Robert F. (1997) *Goal Analysis*. Atlanta: Center for Effective Performance.

Mager, Robert F. (1997) *Making Instruction Work*. Atlanta: Center for Effective Performance.

Mager, Robert F. (1997) *Measuring Instructional Results*. Atlanta: Center for Effective Performance.

Mager, Robert F. (1997) *Preparing Instructional Objectives*. Atlanta: Center for Effective Performance.

Markwardt, Frederick C. (1998). *Peabody Individual Achievement Test – Revised: Normative Update*. Circle Pines, MN: American Guidance Service, Inc.

Mayerson, Gary. (2004) *How To Compromise With Your School District Without Compromising Your Child*. New York: DRL Books.

National Research Council. (2005) *Scientific Research in Education*. National Academy Press.

National Research Council. (2002) *Minority Students in Special and Gifted Education*. Washington, DC: National Academy Press.

National Research Council. (1998) *Preventing Reading Difficulties in Young Children*. Washington, DC: National Academy Press.

Psychological Corporation (2001). *Wechsler Individual Achievement Test, 2nd Ed*. San Antonio: Author.

Roid, G.H. & Miller, L.J. (1997). *Leiter International Performance Scale – Revised*. Wood Dale, IL: Stoelting.

Sattler, Jerome M. (2001) *Assessment of Children: Cognitive Applications*. San Diego: Jerome M. Sattler, Publisher, Inc.

Sattler, J.W., & Dumont, R. (2004). *Assessment of Children: WISC-IV and WPPSI-III Supplement*. San Diego, CA: Jerome M. Sattler, Publisher, Inc.

Shaywitz, Sally. (2003) *Overcoming Dyslexia: A New and Complete Science-Based Program for Reading Problems at Any Level*. New York: Knopf, 2003.

Smith, Tom and James R. Patton. (1998) Section 504 and Public Schools: A Practical Guide for Determining Eligibility, Developing Accommodation Plans, and Documenting Compliance. Pro-Ed.

Spence, Gerry. (1995) *How to Argue and Win Every Time*. New York: St Martin's Press.

Stanovich, K.E. (1986). Matthew effects in reading: Some consequences of individual differences in the acquisition of literacy. *Reading Research Quarterly, 21*, 360-407.

Wagner, R.K., Torgesen, J.K., Rashotte, C.A. (1999). *Comprehensive Test of Phonological Processing*. Austin, TX: PRO-ED.

Weber, Mark. (2002) *Special Education Law and Litigation Treatise, 2nd ed.* Horsham, PA: LRP Publications.

Wechsler, D. (2003) *Wechsler Intelligence Scale for Children - Fourth Edition.* San Antonio, TX: The Psychological Corporation.

Wechsler, D. (2003) *WISC-IV Administration and Scoring Manual.* San Antonio, TX: The Psychological Corporation.

Wechsler, D. (2003) *WISC-IV Technical and Interpretive Manual.* San Antonio, TX: The Psychological Corporation.

Wechsler, D. (1997) *Wechsler Adult Intelligence Scale (3rd Ed.).* San Antonio, TX: The Psychological Corporation.

Wechsler, D. (2002) *Wechsler Preschool and Primary Scale of Intelligence – III.* San Antonio, TX: The Psychological Corporation.

Wiederholt, J.L., & Bryant, B.R. (2001) *Gray Oral Reading Tests, Fourth Edition.* Austin, TX: PRO-ED.

Wilkinson, G.S. (1993) *The Wide Range Achievement Test (3rd Ed.).* Wilmington, DE: Wide Range, Inc.

Williams, K.T. (1997) *Expressive Vocabulary Test.* Circle Pines, MN: American Guidance Service, Inc.

Woodcock, R.W. (1998) *Woodcock Reading Mastery Tests – Revised.* Circle Pines, MN: American Guidance Service, Inc.

Woodcock, R.W., McGrew, K.S., Mather, N. (2001) *Woodcock-Johnson III.* Itasca, IL: Riverside Publishing.

Wright, Peter W. D., Pamela Darr Wright. (2005) *Wrightslaw: IDEA 2004.* Hartfield, VA: Harbor House Law Press,.

Wright, Peter W. D., Pamela Wright, Suzanne Heath. (2003) *Wrightslaw: No Child Left Behind.* Hartfield, VA: Harbor House Law Press, Inc.

Index

Columbo Strategy, 127
Communication
    as basic skill, 120
    mediator's role, 190
    needs must be considered in IEP, 165
Complainers, dealing with, 39
Composite Scores, 87-88, 90-91
Comprehensive Achievement Tests, 106
Conflict
    beliefs, perceptions, interests, 42
    expense and control, 43
Conflict Avoiders, dealing with, 37
Congressional Findings, 135-137
Contact Log, 218-220
Continuum of Alternative Placements, 135
Controlled Substance
    defined, 187
Conversion Table
    standard scores and percentile ranks, 96
Crisis Management, 54
Criterion-referenced tests, 92
Cumulative File, 68
Current Educational Placement, see Stay Put

D

Data
    objective, 110
    use to compare individual to group, 80
Deaf or Hard of Hearing,
    IEP issues, 162
Definitions
    child find, 146-47
    child with a disability, 139, 142
    controlled substance, 187
    dangerous weapon, 188, 193
    free appropriate public education, 140, 142
    highly qualified teacher, 142, 202-203
    illegal drug, 187, 193
    individualized education program, 161-162
    least restrictive environment, 132
    parent, 140, 143
    related services, 140
    serious bodily harm, 188, 193
    specific learning disability, 141, 143
    special education, 141, 143
    supplementary aids and services, 141
    transition services, 141, 143
    weapon, 170
Difficult People, dealing with, 34-39
Discipline, 184-188, 198

Discrepancy Formulas, 159, 168
Discrimination, 196
Dispute Resolution. *See* Mediation
Document Management, 67-72
Drugs, illegal, 187, 193
Due Process Hearing, 179-181, 190
    appeal, 181
    due process complaint notice, 175, 189
    resolution session, 179
    rulings, 191
    safeguards, 181, 191
    statute of limitations, 175, 180, 191
    under Section 504, 198
Dyslexia, 141

E

*Education for All Handicapped Children Act of
    1975*, 133-34
Educational Achievement Tests, 76-78, 102-109
Electronic Mail, 188
Eligibility, 159
    and educational need, 159
    lack of appropriate instruction, 159
    for specific learning disability, 159
    present levels of academic achievement and
        developmental needs, 169
    under Section 504, 196
ESY. *See* Extended School Year
Evaluations
    comprehensive, 61, 78
    eligibility and educational need, 159, 168-169
    functional, developmental, academic informa-
        tion for IEP, 158
    independent educational evaluation (IEE), 177,
        189
    initial, 156, 167
    non-discriminatory, 159
    parental consent for, 156, 167
    parental request for, 169
    procedures, 158, 167
    reevaluations, 157-158, 167
    requirements for, 160
Exhibits, 191
Experts, dealing with, 36
Extended School Year (ESY), 145

F

Fair Hearing. *See* Due Process Hearing